Ainu Archaeology as Ethnohistory

Iron technology among the Saru Ainu of
Hokkaido, Japan, in the 17th century

Yuriko Fukasawa
深澤 百合子

BAR International Series 744
1998

Published in 2019 by
BAR Publishing, Oxford

BAR International Series 744

Ainu Archaeology as Ethnohistory

© Yuriko Fukasawa and the Publisher 1998

ISBN 9780860549772 paperback
ISBN 9781407350660 e-book

DOI https://doi.org/10.30861/9780860549772

A catalogue record for this book is available from the British Library

BAR Publishing is the trading name of British Archaeological Reports (Oxford) Ltd.
British Archaeological Reports was first incorporated in 1974 to publish the BAR
Series, International and British. In 1992 Hadrian Books Ltd became part of the BAR
group. This volume was originally published by John and Erica Hedges Ltd. in
conjunction with British Archaeological Reports (Oxford) Ltd / Hadrian Books Ltd,
the Series principal publisher, in 1998. This present volume is published by BAR
Publishing, 2019.

BAR
PUBLISHING

BAR titles are available from:

BAR Publishing
122 Banbury Rd, Oxford, OX2 7BP, UK
EMAIL   info@barpublishing.com
PHONE   +44 (0)1865 310431
FAX   +44 (0)1865 316916
www.barpublishing.com

Contents

Please note that additional material is available to download from www.barpublishing.com/additional-downloads.html.
The original foldout has been reduced in size to match the A4 format of this book, the image is therefore not as clear as the original foldout. Please refer to the original foldout via the download for the original content.

Preface

This book describes a course of research undertaken at the Department of Archaeology, University of Cambridge for a dissertation entitled **Ainu archaeology as ethnohistory,** which was submitted for the Degree of Doctor of Philosophy at the University of Cambridge in February 1995, and accepted in June 1995. Since this is a Cambridge dissertation, it is limited to 80,000 words.

1. The present Ainu identity

The Ainu in Hokkaido, the northernmost island of Japan, are not treated politically as a distinct ethnic group in Japan today, although they are commonly thought to be an aboriginal people in Hokkaido. The Ainu share the way of life and living standards of contemporary Japanese society. They speak Japanese in daily communication and their education is the same as the Japanese. They have ostensibly been almost totally integrated into the civilisation of modern Japan.

However, the Ainu have established a nation-wide association called the Utari Association in order to maintain their traditional culture and to retain a sense of Ainu solidarity through the holding of occasional ceremonies and encouragement of practices expressing their cultural identity. The Utari Association defines an Ainu as a person who has Ainu blood, is recognised as an Ainu by other people and who would like to express herself/himself as an Ainu. They believe that they are the Ainu. The Ainu language is now taught at local Ainu language schools both by Japanese linguists and by Ainu who remember the language.

I recognise the Ainu as the ethnic group of people who still have a consciousness of their ethnicity and attempt to carry on their cultural tradition. Therefore, I perceive that Ainu culture is not extinct, but has been and is still changing continuously.

2. Iron and the emergence of Ainu identity

The present understanding of Ainu culture is based on Ainu studies in the past. The image of Ainu culture has been created by previous researchers.

What I would like to present in this book is an *archaeological* challenge to explain the ethnohistory of the Ainu and to reappraise the Ainu culture. The challenge is posed by the existence of iron-working hearths in excavated Ainu villages dated before 1667. Owing to a lack of records concerning Ainu smithing in Japanese historical documents, it had been thought that the Hokkaido Ainu did not practise iron technology. This view persisted until iron-working hearths in the Saru River area in Hokkaido were excavated by the author, indicating that iron-working technology had existed among the Hokkaido Ainu. The excavations took place at the Iruekashi site in 1988 and at the Pipaushi site in 1990 under the name of Biratori-cho Iseki Chosakai in Biratori-cho, Hokkaido. Both sites clearly indicate Ainu settlements and include post holes of dwellings associated with materials and organic remains such as cultivated seeds,

burials, and iron-working hearths. It is archaeologically significant in that one of the hearths is identified by tephrochronological studies as dating from between 1663 and 1667. Thus, this hearth itself has considerable archaeological value as an absolute date within the chronological order of the Ainu material culture.

There are several reasons for focusing on iron working technology in the context of Ainu culture in this book. First, the Ainu culture has hitherto been thought of as largely a hunting, fishing and gathering society. Ethnographic analogies have employed the Ainu in studies of hunter-gatherer adaptive processes and subsistence economies (Watanabe 1972).

The archaeological evidence, however, suggests something more complex than a hunter-gatherer society, and leads to the hypothesis that this labelling of the Ainu may be a consequence of historical, academic and political distortion (cf. Wilmsen 1989). For example, the use of the Ainu in analogical models of hunter-gatherers appears to have been applied with no consideration of the sequence of social change over time among the Ainu (Watanabe 1972, 1990). The chronological sequence of Ainu culture needs to be established, employing both historical and archaeological evidence. It is necessary to apply archaeological methods to Ainu material culture in order to reconstruct its chronology and social change and set it in a historical context (cf. Trigger 1980).

The reason why iron-working technology was chosen as the subject for this book is that it is possible to discuss technology as a form of social expression (cf. Lemonier 1983) as well as a techno-complex. The importance of iron in the history of humankind is due to its superior qualities and consequent impact on the cultural context as a whole. It is, therefore, necessary to understand the meaning of iron and the role of iron within societies from a cultural as well as a material point of view (cf. Hodder 1987).

Taking account of the attempts mentioned above, this book will try to provide a more detailed understanding of both the emergence of Ainu cultural identity and of social change among the Ainu by examining cultural contact and interaction between the Ainu and outsiders in the past.

Although the Ainu do not have a written language, their oral tradition, including epic forms, is a rich information source for understanding Ainu society. Yukara, an epic form of oral tradition, have been recorded using various methods, including tapes and transcription into both *kana* (the Japanese syllabary) and the roman alphabet. However, the use of yukara as a source of information with regard to social meaning has not yet been attempted by linguists. I shall examine this aspect of yukara for understanding Ainu society based on the anatomy of yukara. This can be done by extracting the expression of society as much as possible among yukara. This approach is essential for an understanding of the Ainu cultural context, and to find out their way of thinking as well as their material culture.

3. The structure of the book

Chapter 1 discusses the way in which the image of the Ainu has been created. Chapter 2 builds models for Ainu archaeology. Chapter 3 considers a methodological approach to the data relating to Ainu archaeology. Chapter 4 and Chapter 5 discuss the technological aspects of Ainu iron working. Chapter 6 and Chapter 7 discuss words and the epic type of oral tradition as a means of understanding the social context. Chapter 8 considers Ainu archaeology as ethnohistory. The contents of the chapters are summarised below.

Chapter 1, How an image of the Ainu was created

The current outsider's image of the Ainu was created as a result of preconceptions based on interaction between socio-political and academic manipulation. It is important to recognise the role of Hokkaido, where the Ainu live, under the Westernisation of Japan in the 19th century. Throughout this period, information and knowledge about the Ainu which had accumulated in the previous period were not smoothly transmitted to the new era. For example, documents about the Ainu which were written in the 18th century have still not been fully evaluated in Ainu studies. This is one of the reasons for the present image of the Ainu. Japanese modern history needs to be taken into account in order to understand the existing image of the Ainu.

Chapter 2, Model-building for Ainu archaeology

It can be said that Ainu studies were also affected by preconceptions of ethnic differences from the Japanese point of view to manipulate theory, thereby setting up an inappropriate model. Labelling which is the result of 'scientific academic work' needs to be filtered out within a current theoretical framework, and account needs to be taken of the socio-political framework of modern Japanese history. A criticism of the present model is presented, and two new models, a 'cultivation-prohibition model' and an 'iron-prohibition model', are built for Ainu archaeology.

Chapter 3, Chronology and cultural contact between Hokkaido and Tohoku

Tephrochronology is a vital tool in Japanese archaeology for locating material cultures in time. The archaeological remains of the Ainu culture fall within the Japanese historical period. Eruptions of volcanoes are therefore recorded and their precise data is generally known. Ainu archaeology within the Hokkaido sequence and the material culture in the Tohoku sequence are described. Cultural contact between the two areas may be predicated from the archaeological evidence which is described. A methodological approach to Ainu archaeology is discussed.

Chapter 4, Iron technology in the Hokkaido and Tohoku districts: Ainu iron technology in context

The way in which archaeologists recognise and evaluate iron technology from material evidence is discussed. The analytical results of material from the sites, based on archaeometallurgical analyses (essential to the recognition of the processes used in iron technology), are discussed. The relationship between Hokkaido and Tohoku as indicated by the results is also outlined. In particular, consideration is given to technological differences which may imply diffusion of iron technology to the Ainu, and also to differences in distribution networks which draw attention to technological differences between the two areas.

Chapter 5, The steel-production technology of the Saru Ainu in the 17th century

The major archaeological evidence relating to the Ainu used in this book was obtained from Nibutani village in the Saru River area of Hokkaido (see Map 5-1 in Chapter 5). This area is central to the discussion and includes the Ainu sites which have yielded iron-technological evidence. The ways in which the Ainu obtained iron and the level of technology employed in each process are discussed. The technological process can be traced back to the previous culture, the Satsumon, in terms of the existence of a refining process. The stage reached by the Saru Ainu, who found it difficult to obtain steel, offers interesting parallels with the situation of Japanese traditional sword smiths at the present time. The evidence, however, also indicates the possibility that the Saru Ainu could have developed methods of producing iron as material source for themselves.

Chapter 6, An examination of words for materials and other things in order to understand the Ainu cultural context

In an examination of the material culture of a society, it is instructive to consider the relationship between the things and the names by which they are called, since this leads to an understanding of the meaning of the things within a society. Bearing this in mind, the words which relate to iron and iron technology in Ainu society are examined in order to determine their meaning and hence understand the role of iron in the context of Ainu society.

Chapter 7, The anatomy of Yukara

An epic type of oral tradition in Ainu society, yukara, are analysed. In particular, the yukara of the Saru River area are identified as a valuable source for reconstructing the character of Saru Ainu society. The significance of yukara for the study of material culture is discussed, since this is a subject which they illuminate in many ways. Loan words from Japanese are also examined in order to highlight the relationships between the two cultures at a material level. Further, the social meaning of iron and iron technology in Saru Ainu society can be inferred from passages in yukara.

Chapter 8, Conclusion: Ainu archaeology as ethnohistory

Different modes of data which are expressions of history are used in this book. Each reveals different facets of ethnohistory. An ethnohistory of the Ainu can be drawn by using their own expressions — such as Ainu archaeology approached through contextual archaeology, and yukara. This can be called the archaeology of "Ainupuri", the "Ainu way".

4 Acknowledgements

I am most grateful to all the people and institutions who gave me help and advice during the course of the research presented in this book, especially to my supervisor and adviser, Dr Gina Barnes and Dr Ian Hodder, Department of Archaeology, University of Cambridge.

I am especially grateful to Mr Kaoru Ito, laboratory of metallurgy, Nippon Steel Company for the analysis of my iron material and slag samples.

I wish to thank, in particular, those who allowed me to examine iron, slag and other materials in their collections and I also thank those who gave me permission to use photographs and to use data from forthcoming publications.

Thanks are due to :

Akita-ken Maizobunkazai Centre
Aomori-ken Maizobunkazai Centre
Hokkaido Maizobunkazai Centre
Iwate-ken Maizobunkazai Centre
Biratori-cho Iseki Chosakai
The Museum of Archaeology and Anthropology Cambridge
The Needham Research Institute Cambridge
The Museum of Mankind: British Museum
Hokkaido Kaitaku Kinenkan

Mr Shigeki Akino (The Ainu Museum Shiraoi)
Dr Hideo Akanuma (Iwate Kenritsu Hakubutsukan)
Dr Morio Akamatsu (Hokkaido Kaitaku Kinenkan)
Mr Tetsuya Amano (Hokkaido University)
Mr Yun-sik Choo (Department of Archaeology)
Mr Koji Deriha (Hokkaido Kaitaku Kinenkan)
Dr Brian Durrans (British Museum)
Mr Kazumi Fujishima (Esashi-cho Kyoiku-iinkai)
Mr Noboru Fujita (Mori-cho Kyoiku-iinkai)
Ms Katsuyo Honda (Researcher in archaeology and history)
Ms Aoi Hosoya (Department of Archaeology)
Mr Shinya Isogawa (Kyoto University)
Professor Martin Jones (Department of Archaeology)
Mr Simon Kaner (Department of Archaeology)
Mr Motoi Kawauchi (Biratori-cho Iseki Chosakai)
Mr Henry Kenny (Department of Archaeology)
Mr Jon-il Kim (Seoul National University)
Mr Toshihiro Kohara (then of Shizunai-cho Kyoiku-iinkai)
Mr Kenichiro Koshida (Hokkaido Maizobunkazai Centre)
Mr Yasushi Kubo (Matsumae-cho Kyoiku-iinkai)
Mr Mizuho Matsuzaki (Katsuyamadate Iseki Chosakai)
Mr Norio Mino (Hokkaido Kaitaku Kinenkan)
Mr Keisuke Miura (Aomori-ken Maizobunkazai Centre)
Mr Hiroshi Miya (Yoichi-cho Kyoiku-iinkai)
Dr Martin Morris (Tokyo University)
Mr Hiroshi Nakagawa (Chiba National University)
Professor Taryo Obayashi (Tokyo Joshi University)
Mr Osami Okuda (Sapporo Gakuin University)
Professor Otsuka Kazuyoshi (Nat. Ethnological Museum)
Dr David Phillipson (Museum of Arch. & Anth.)

Mr Takayuki Sato (Esashi-cho Kyoiku-iinkai)
Dr Nathan Schlanger (Department of Archaeology)
Dr Colin Shell (Department of Archaeology)
Dr Laurence Smith (Department of Archaeology)
Professor Anthony Snodgrass (Faculty of Classics)
Mr Toshihiro Tamura (Chitose-shi Kyoiku-iinkai)
Mr Kaoru Tezuka (Hokkaido Kaitaku Kinenkan)
Dr Diura Thoden van Velzen (Department of Archaeology)
Ms Yumi Tokui (deceased)(Ochanomizu University)
Mr Teruji Toyohara (Researcher in archaeology)
Ms Yasuyo Tsubakizaka (Hokkaido University)
Mr Toshiaki Tsurumaru (Sapporo Gakuin University)
Dr Donald Wagner (Needham Research Institute)
Dr Todd Whitelaw (Department of Archaeology)
Ms Jane Wilkinson (Royal Museum of Scotland)
Mr Takeshi Yabunaka (The Ainu Museum Shiraoi)
Mr Goro Yamada (Hokkaido Kaitaku Kinenkan)
Professor Ichiro Yamanaka (Kyoto University)
Professor Masakazu Yoshizaki (Hokkaido University)

Finally, I wish to thank my parents, Shuhei Fukasawa and Tokuko Fukasawa, for all their support during the course of my research.

Style Note

Romanisation

Romanisation of foreign words employs the Pinyin system for Chinese, the MaCune-Reischauer system for Korean, and a modified Hepburn system for Japanese and Ainu. It was not, however, possible to include diacritic marks over Japanese and Ainu words. There is tremendous variation in writing Ainu in romanised forms of Ainu due to the fact that Ainu words are based on syllables. As I am an archaeologist, not a linguist, I have used the spelling used by the reference concerned.

Names

In the text, Japanese personal names are given according to the Western system; given name first, followed by family name.

The Administrative division of place names are followed by the Japanese system: ken = prefecture, gun or kori = county, shi = city, cho or machi = township, mura = village.

Vocabulary

Japanese and Ainu vocabulary are given in italics.

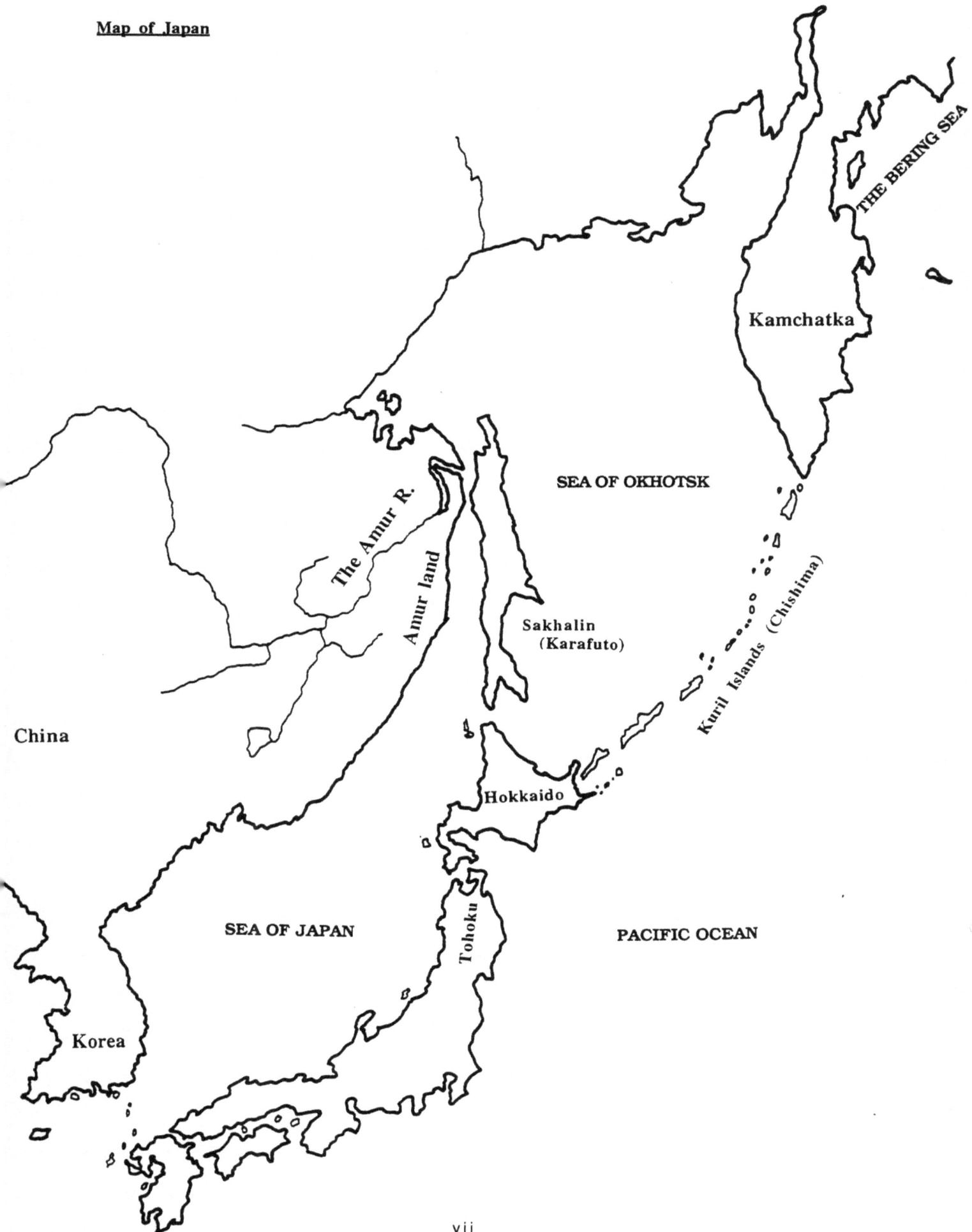

Map of Japan

THE BERING SEA

Kamchatka

SEA OF OKHOTSK

The Amur R.

Amur land

Sakhalin
(Karafuto)

Kuril Islands (Chishima)

China

Hokkaido

Korea

Tohoku

SEA OF JAPAN

PACIFIC OCEAN

Chapter 1

How the image of the Ainu was created

1-1 Introduction

It is very important to consider the political framework of Japanese history both during throughout the existence of Ainu culture and that during which studies of it have been undertaken. Without this background, the Ainu culture cannot be fully understood. The purpose of this chapter is to show how socio-political factors have affected the history of the Ainu and studies of them across a range of different disciplines.

Although the Ainu have been studied for over a hundred years by a range of experts in disciplines including ethnology, anthropology, linguistics, archaeology, history, and sociology, the concept of the Ainu can shift depending on the time at which the Ainu were considered to be the Ainu as known at present. Studies of the Ainu need to state clearly what criteria they are using to identify the Ainu. There needs to be a clear definition in those studies of what scale they use in time and space, in other words, what they consider to be the concept of the Ainu. Thus, in this chapter I discuss how the image of the Ainu has emerged within the history of the Ainu studies.

1-2 Hokkaido, under the Western-modernisation of Japan and foreign influences

The year 1868 constitutes a watershed which is important not only in the history of the Ainu culture and Ainu studies but also in the history of Japan as a whole. In 1868 the Meiji-Ishin (Restoration) occurred, which ended the Tokugawa Shogunal government and established the Meiji government. This great change in the Japanese political framework cannot be ignored. One of the greatest changes was that foreigners were able to visit the land of Japan again. Japan had been a closed country for 229 years, since 1639, when it was closed in order to avoid the influence of Christianity. This is called 'sakoku', the policy of closed country — one of the distinctive policies of the Tokugawa Shogunal government. It stipulated that foreigners who landed in Japan were to be killed, with the exception of the Dutch, who were permitted only on the island of Dejima in Nagasaki, where they had a trading depot. Japanese were also not allowed to leave their country. If they went abroad, they were forbidden to re-enter the country.

Although it is not my intention to assess the role of the Meiji government here, I would like to emphasise that it is important to know what happened during that period in Hokkaido, where the Ainu lived. It has been pointed out that the relationship between the Japanese and the Ainu has historical parallels with that of the European colonisers of North America and the American Indian (Fawcett 1986:43, Stuart 1991:27). The question is whether or not Hokkaido was a Japanese colony. It is also necessary to consider the nature of the Japanese assimilation of the Ainu under the Meiji government.

The Meiji government was mainly dominated by individuals from two of the domains under the Shogunal government: the Satsuma-Han and the Choshu-Han. It was a government that ruled in the name of the *Tenno* (Emperor), to whom the last Tokugawa shogun had ceded the right to govern upon his abdication.

When the *Kaitakushi* (administrative headquarters) in Hokkaido was set up under the Meiji government in 1869, Kiyotaka Kuroda after some factional struggles took up the post of Governor of Hokkaido. He was a native of the Satsuma-Han which was located in Kyushu at the southern-most end of Japan, and therefore he did not know much about the natural features and culture of Hokkaido. Kuroda invited Horace Capron from the United States to come and to make a master plan for Hokkaido in 1871. Horace Capron was the second governor of the Department of Agriculture of the United States, a pioneer who carried out operations in "the frontier spirit". He came to Japan with 76 members of the Hokkaido Master Plan Project, most of whom were Americans (Uemura 1990:249).

According to Uemura (1990), there was a problem in deciding an appropriate plan for developing Hokkaido. Antisel, one of the project members, who was British, proposed a plan based on British colonisation theory, in opposition to Capron, who had already proposed a plan based on American frontier colonisation theory. The debate hinged upon whether to use Hokkaido on the one hand as a defence zone against Russia, leaving Hokkaido as a free economic land in accordance with the principles of *laissez faire* economics, but with links to the mainland (the British view), or, on the other hand, to develop this island as a land of food production and independent exploitation with a view to self-sufficiency in food resources (the American view). Ultimately, it was Capron who presented reports and official letters to the *Kaitakushi* and made blueprint plans, after Antisel was sacked in 1875. The self-sufficient type of exploitation, based on American frontier theory, was adopted for the Hokkaido master plan (ibid. :252).

It is clear therefore that exploitation proceeded in Hokkaido along the lines suggested by the Americans, and many Japanese immigrants who wanted to have their own land were sent to deforest Hokkaido. Among them were *shizoku* (*samurai* or *bushi*)[1], who belonged to the warrior class and had formerly been employed by each domain (*Han*) under the previous Shogunal government. They had lost their jobs under the new government due to the breakdown of the old system. It was vital for the new government to find jobs for them. One solution was to open up Hokkaido and encourage

---

[1] They were the highest class in a caste system which consisted of four classes: the samurai or bushi, the farmers, the craftspeople, and the merchants, under the Shogunal government.

ex-samurai to become pioneer farmers there, under the Meiji government (Kuroda 1942).

In this sense, Hokkaido might be seen as a colony from the Western point of view, and the relationship between the Japanese and the Ainu can be seen as parallel with that between frontier Europeans and American Indians.

However, the word 'colony' did not exist, as there was no concept for it either in Japanese or in Chinese, according to Nitobe (Nitobe 1911). The word 'colony' was introduced by a book entitled "The theory of isolation policy" written by Kaempfer, and translated by Tadao Shizuku in 1741. In this book the word 'volkplanting' was translated into Japanese as '*shoku-min*' ("planted people" or "people planting"). In the first Dutch-Japanese dictionary in Japan, "Edo Haruma", published in 1796, the word 'colony' was translated as '*kai-koku*' (literally 'open country': i.e. a country that was being opened up), and 'volkplanting' was translated as '*shoku-min*'. Later, by the time of the English-Japanese dictionary published by Hori in 1862, and 1867, the word 'colony' was translated as '*shoku-min*' (Kuroda 1942). Thus, the word is now '*shoku-min*' in Japanese. What needs to be examined is the set of conditions under which the concept of a modern nation state filtered into the consciousness of the traditional Japanese. Without consideration of such concepts, which are used in a different historical context, it is misleading to draw an analogy between the Japanese and the Ainu and the European colonisers and the American Indian.

There are more complex social structures to interrelate with the three different concepts in terms of the West, Japan, and the Ainu in the Meiji period. This was expressed as:

> . . . eastern savagery and western civilisation met in this hut, savagery giving and civilisation receiving, the yellow skinned Ito the connecting link between the two, and the representative of a civilisation to which our own is but an "infant of days" (Bird 1880).

Isabella Bird, a British woman explorer, expressed this feeling when she was in an Ainu's hut in an Ainu village. She went to Hokkaido accompanied only by one Japanese interpreter, Ito, in 1878. This was only 10 years after Japan had opened the country to foreigners.

The notion of Western civilisation as superior to Japanese was commonly accepted and indeed implicit in the Meiji government's determination to absorb Western material culture and technology. In this regard, the analogy of the Ainu vis-a-vis the Japanese and the American Indians vis-a-vis the Europeans is not precise, since Western influence had affected the Meiji government. The following evidence also indicates the importance of considering the political relationship between the West and Japan under the policy of the Meiji government.

According to Uemura (Uemura 1990), it was suggested (in the reports and official letters submitted to the *Kaitakushi* by Capron) that the traditional lifestyle of the Japanese needed to be changed in the case of those who immigrated to Hokkaido because Japanese wet rice - cultivation was not appropriate under the climatic conditions prevailing there. Capron

criticised Japanese wet rice - cultivation methods on the grounds that there had been no progress for several hundred years, and because there was no rotation of crops. It was considered an inefficient cultivation method because it produced less nutritious grain despite high production costs. He, therefore, urged that Japanese immigrants should eat wheat and potatoes rather than rice. Moreover, he advocated a change in other areas of the traditional Japanese lifestyle, suggesting that Japanese immigrants to Hokkaido needed to live in stone houses, use tables and chairs, and so on. Uemura has highlighted the fact that an extreme policy of Westernisation was implemented not only in Tokyo but also in Hokkaido at that time. As the result of Capron's suggestion, seeds were imported from the United States, and extensive agriculture (farming) and mechanised agricultural tools were introduced to Hokkaido (Hokkaido 1989). The system established has persisted in essentials in Hokkaido down to the present and can be seen in most parts of Hokkaido today.

In 1876, the Ainu traditional hunting method, using poisoned arrows, was prohibited; instead rifles were rented to them. The tattooing of Ainu women and the wearing of earrings by Ainu men were also prohibited by the Meiji government (Hokkaido 1989). In the same year, it was prohibited to carry the traditional Japanese sword, which had been a symbol of *Bushi* under the Tokugawa Shogunal government [this proposal was made by foreign representatives in order to reduce the danger of assassination by Japanese '*samurai*' (warriors or vassals) extreme nationalists]. The Tokugawa Shogunal government had refused to yield to this foreign pressure but the Meiji government did it] (Dickins 1894, Hokkaido 1989). Furthermore, the practise of blackening the teeth, general among Japanese women at that time, was prohibited by the Meiji government, as was the distinctive traditional hairstyle of Japanese men. It is evident that it was not only the Ainu but also the Japanese who were forced to give up aspects of their own traditional lifestyle at that time. This is also a time when Japan started to use the solar calendar [which had been adopted in 1872] instead of the lunar calendar (Hokkaido 1989).

Therefore, what needs to be taken into account is the role of Hokkaido during the establishment of a modern nation state — a structure characterised by the centralisation of administrative power — in Japan. It is very important to understand how political discontinuity and the restructuring process at that time has had an enormous affect on the history of the Ainu. In other words, the relationship between the Japanese and the Ainu had already been established in a certain manner before the impact of the Western-modernisation of Japan. To find out the nature of that relationship and to understand upon what that relationship was based on, it is necessary to look further back, using a longer-term historical framework.

1-3 Hokkaido before the Meiji era: *Ezo* under Japanese economic expansion

Hokkaido was called *Ezo* island before the Meiji era, and the people who lived there were also called the *Ezo*. They were the Ainu. To understand the situation in *Ezo* land, conditions in Japan under the Tokugawa Shogunal government in the 17th-18th centuries need to be explained.

The Tokugawa Shogunal government was instituted in 1603, when Ieyasu Tokugawa became shogun as the first generation of Tokugawa. This feudal system was called the *Baku-Han* system, which consisted of the Tokugawa shogun (*Bakufu*) as overlord and under him over 265 *daimyo* (a head family of *Han*) who ruled each *han*. The term '*Han*' (it can be translated as 'domain' or 'fief') refers to the area that each *daimyo* possessed and ruled. There were two classes of *daimyo*: *fudai daimyo* and *tozama daimyo*. The former were those who had declared their allegiance to the Tokugawa before the decisive battle of Sekigahara in 1600, and fought on the Tokugawa side in this battle; the latter were those who declared their allegiance to the Tokugawa after the battle, and became the outer or independent lords.

Tax to be paid to the ruler was based on the crop-growing capacity of each domain. Normally this was assessed in rice. Since the unit of assessment was the *koku*, this was called the '*koku-daka*' system. Rice gathered as tax had been treated as a form of currency in historical Japan since the 7th century AD. The largest domain under the Tokugawa Shogunal government was that of the Maeda-Han in Kaga (the present Ishikawa-ken) with 1,030,000 *koku* (1 *koku* = about 5 bushels or 180 litres). The lowest was that of the Matsumae-Han in *Ezo* (the present Hokkaido) with 10,000 *koku* in 1719 (Kaiho 1989). The Matsumae family became the Matsumae-Han among *tozama daimyo* when the Matsumae-family was recognised as its authorised ruler in *Ezo* by the Tokugawa shogun in 1604. The Matsumae had dominated the Japanese territory of Oshima peninsula in *Ezo* since 1590, although their ancestors, the Kakizaki family, had lived there since around the 13th century AD (see Fig. 1-1).

The Matsumae-Han, however, was a unique and exceptional *han* under the Tokugawa Shogunal government in terms of the ruling system and taxes, because it is said that rice did not grow in the territory of Matsumae under the prevailing climatic conditions. Tribute to the Shogun from the Matsumae-Han took the form not of the products of their territory, but of marine resources and exotic items which were procured in trade with the *Ezo* [Ainu], including bear skins, wings of eagles, and so on.

The Matsumae-Han was also unique in the method of giving stipends to the *samurai* (vassals) who belonged to it. Sixty upper *samurai* received the right to establish and control trading posts (i.e. *akinaiba*) in *Ezo* island instead of receiving a stipend from the Matsumae family.

Akinaiba (later called *basho*) were places where they traded marine resources such as salmon, trout, abalone, tangle weed and other goods with the *Ezo* [the Ainu]. Profit from trade became their stipend. However these *samurai* were not good at making a profit. It was not long before merchants undertook this everyday operation by paying an agreed sum to the *samurai* in return for control over the *akinaiba*.

After 1741, most of the trading posts were held by merchants. This system is called the *Basho-Ukeoi* system, or the contracted trading-post system, because the contract between *samurai* and merchants allowed the latter to trade with the *Ezo* [Ainu] at the trading posts.

Among these merchants, those who came from Omi (now presently in Shiga-ken) were especially powerful; they made systematic inroads into *Ezo* island, with special permission from the Matsumae-Han. The Omi merchants exported products from *Ezo* to Tsuruga and Osaka in Honshu and Nagasaki in Kyushu; and they brought to the Matsumae everyday necessities including rice. This sea route they used along the Japan sea coast was called the *Benzai* trade route, from the name *Benzai-sen*, given to the ships they used. The ports of Fukuyama (the present Matsumae), Hakodate, and Esashi in *Ezo* [Hokkaido] were prosperous at that time (Yamakawa 1983).

Omi merchants introduced new fishing methods and started systematic fishing using the Ainu as labour. Under the contract with the Matsumae, they had to look after and protect the Ainu who belonged to their *Basho*, providing them with food and places to accommodate them (Takakura 1942). They were primarily concerned with the pursuit of profits, however, and consequently the *Ezo* [Ainu] were used as cheap labour and were worked almost like slaves. The *Ezo* [Ainu] were collected from villages, and were forced to live near the *Basho* (ibid.). The work was mostly intensive fishing. The *Ezo* [Ainu] were restrained from leaving during certain seasons, mostly the summer, and only allowed to return to their villages when the season was over. The demands made of them and the treatment they received varied, depending upon the *Basho* and the individual merchants running them. In this respect, the Ainu were strongly involved in Japanese commercial capitalism in the 18th-19th centuries before the Meiji era. In other words, Ainu society was already affected and socially reproduced by Japanese influence, and had been taken into the Japanese framework.

The *Ezo* [Ainu] who were employed by the *Basho* under the Matsumae-Han lost their jobs when the *Basho-Ukeoi* system was broken up by the *Kaitakushi* of the Meiji government, as did the *samurai* who had been employed by each han. The Meiji government insisted that both the redundant *Ezo* [Ainu] and the *samurai* should become farmers, to open up Hokkaido to intensive and ultimately mechanised agriculture like that seen in most parts of Hokkaido today. Now, Hokkaido is very similar to England, the north of United States and the south of Canada, with views of extensive green fields, potato fields and corn fields, and many cows and sheep.

Because of the impact of Western-modernisation in Japan, the Ainu in Hokkaido were integrated into Japan politically without their intention. However, they were already integrated into Japan economically before the Meiji period whether they liked it or not. Under the restructuring process from the Matsumae-Han to the *Kaitakushi*, there was competition among factions which, desirous of increasing their political power, considered forming relations with merchants associated with the former Matsumae-Han and its economic system (Maruyama 1973). What was unfortunate for the Ainu and for Ainu studies was that the people who had worked closely with the Ainu under the Tokugawa

Shogunal government were ousted from their positions. For example, Takeshiro Matsuura, who was one of the inspectors of *Ezo* island and was the person who gave *Ezo* the name of Hokkaido in 1869, travelled widely around the island in order to make inspections and also wrote much about *Ezo*, not only concerning the geography but also about the Ainu. His writings include travel diaries and a great ethnographical study of the Ainu during the 18th century, some of which I cite in this book. These works deserve a thorough re-evaluation, having been entirely ignored by the new officers of the Meiji government and insufficiently appreciated even in more recent Ainu studies.

1-4 The image of the Ainu in Europe

'Ainu' as an ethnic name is fairly well known in Europe. According to Adami (Adami 1991), 1122 pieces of literature in European languages were written on the Ainu between 1565 and 1988. These were written in 13 languages: English, German, Russian, French, Polish, Spanish, Italian, Dutch, Hungarian, Latin, Swedish, Danish, and Portuguese. It is apparent from them that the term 'Ainu' was introduced to Europe as early as 1819 in an article written in German by Johann Severin Vater, entitled "Ainos auch Ainu" (ibid.). Initially, the term was introduced as 'Aino'. In many titles of articles in Adami from this early period the name is written as 'Aino'.

The first European who made a study of the Ainu was Philipp Franz von Siebold, who came to Japan in 1823 as a medical doctor with Dutch traders and was allowed to stay on the island of Dejima in Nagasaki, Japan, under the Shogunal government (he stayed in Japan between 1823 and 1829, and re-entered again between 1859 and 1862). He used the term Ainu in his article 'Mœurs et usages des Aïnos' in the "Journal Asiatic" (Siebold 1828 in Adami 1991). Siebold was the first to suggest that the Ainu were people who were the aboriginal inhabitants of Japan, an idea mentioned in his famous book "Nippon" (Siebold 1854). Unfortunately, he was deported for attempting to smuggle maps of Japan out of the country, but he managed to take many Japanese books back to Europe, including a record of the Ainu language (Terada 1981). This book later became a source for studies of the Ainu, and especially the Ainu language, such as "Über den Bau der Aino-Sprache" by August Pfizmaier, published in 1851 (Kindaichi 1960).

1-4-1 Stolen Skulls

Early European interest in the Ainu is confirmed by an astonishing incident in which Ainu skulls were stolen, by three Englishmen, from Ainu cemeteries in the villages of Mori and Otoshibe, near Hakodate, in 1865 (Hokkaido 1989). This incident is important not only from the political point of view but also from the racial point of view that the skulls led to the interpretation of the Ainu as a white race in Europe.

Hakodate was opened to foreigners in 1859 and was one of three Japanese ports which had already been opened to foreigners before 1868. The Hakodate-Bugyo (the official directly in charge of Ezo island under the Tokugawa Shogunal government) whom the incident was reported by

the local Ainu, dissented from the judgement in Council and requested the English Minister to punish the crime and to pay compensation, and also asked for the return to the Ainu of all the skulls to the Ainu which had already been sent to Britain. The English Minister agreed to this request and paid compensation of a thousand silver coins to 54 Ainu (Koida 1987, Dickins 1894).

According to the biography of Sir Harry Parkes, who was the English Minister in Japan at that time, it was mentioned that:

> Towards the close of 1865 several British subjects resident at Hakodate were accused by the Governor of desecrating Ainu graves for the purpose of procuring skulls — doubtless to satisfy the scientific cravings of some European craniologist. They were tried before the Consul Captain Howard Vyse, and acquitted on the ground the charge was not proven. The assessors, who under the order in Consul regulating criminal justice in Japan sat with the Consul, dissented from the judgement, and the case was referred to the Minister as Consul-General, who found the accused guilty — as they undoubtedly were — and sentenced them to a year's imprisonment in the Hong Kong gaol. He also ordered a thousand silver ichibuns, worth something over one shilling each but in purchasing value very much more, to be distributed among the aggrieved Ainu, each of whom received an equivalent in coins of some twenty-seven shillings, a fortune to the poor Ainu, which they doubtless thought rather easily obtained (Dickins 1894: 67).

Dickins quotes a letter from Parkes to Mr Winchester, Consul at Shanghai, in which Parkes himself noted that:

> Vyse has made a great botch of a disgraceful case that has occurred at Hakodate, in which three Englishmen ...have gone into the country and rifled Ainu tombs of skull and skeletons. Vyse tried the men, but hesitated either to commit or acquit, and the referred the case to me for decision. Afterwards, when all doubt was cleared up by the confession of the prisoners, he again applied to me to sentence the men (ibid. 1894:67).

I presume that the "European craniologist" must have been British, otherwise Parkes, as the British Minister in Japan, would not have paid the 1000 silver coins, even though the criminals were British subjects. According to the Japanese document (Hokkaido 1989), the three British men were members of the Consulate (individual names are given). This incident happened during the period when Parkes was staying at Hakodate between September and November 1865. The first case of theft happened at Mori village in September and the second case in Otoshibe village in October (Koida 1987). Is it just coincidence that both cases happened while Parkes was at Hakodate?

Sir Harry Parkes was a fellow of the Ethnological Society of London, to which he had been elected in 1862. In the *Transactions of the Ethnological Society of London*, vol. VI (1868), there is an article entitled 'Description of an Aino Skull' by George Busk, who was also a fellow of the society, having been elected in 1863, and who was Vice President in 1868. George Busk could have been the

"European craniologist" who received the stolen Ainu skulls from Japan and wrote this article. If so, Parkes and Busk must have known each other at that time. I wonder whether or not Parkes knew of the plan to acquire the skulls.

Busk's article was read in March 1867 and, according to a report from the Hakodate-Bugyo to the Tokugawa Shogunal government in April 1867, three boxes of Ainu skulls and bones which had already been sent to Britain were being returned; they were received from Gower of the Council. Thus this matter was resolved (Hokkaido 1889).

As I mentioned earlier, Ainu studies and the Ainu culture cannot be fully understood without the political framework. In this case, it is noteworthy that the Hakodate-Bugyo, the Shogun's representative, acted on behalf of the Ainu and defended their interests against the British. It is doubtful whether the same action would have been taken under the Meiji government. The respective policies of the Hakodate-Bugyo (an official of the Tokugawa Shogunal government), the Matsumae-Han (a domain within the *Baku-Han* system), and the Meiji government after 1868 were each totally different as regards the Ainu. It is, therefore, important to understand and differentiate the policies of each of these Japanese authorities.

George Busk's article, 'Description of an Aino Skull', is very significant, because in it he suggested that, upon examination, the skull appeared to be similar to European skulls (Busk 1868:109). R.N. John mentioned this in 1873, saying: "they resemble the European race, not only in their features and general contour, but in their expression" and so on (John 1873:248).

Later, in 1909, Alfred Court Haddon stated in his book "The Race of Man" (Haddon 1909, 1929) that the Ainu were a white race: "an ancient mesocephalic group of white cymotrichi" (Haddon 1929:95). His study was then translated into French by A. Van Gennep as "Les Races Humaines" (1927). A French anthropologist, George Montandon, also repeated Haddon's view (Montandon 1931), and the notion that the Ainu were a white race spread all over Europe.

The Ainu thus came to be regarded in Europe as a Caucasoid people. This idea was manipulated when Germany and Japan became allies in 1936. It was argued that the Ainu were the forefathers of the Japanese and, since they were a Caucasoid people, the Japanese too were originally a Caucasoid people like the Germanic races. Therefore, the two should form an alliance. This is a ludicrous idea, but the French anthropologist George Montandon was executed at the end of World War II because he had sided with the Nazis (Obayashi, personal comm.).

It is 124 years since George Busk's significant paper. However, it seems that a notion of this kind still survives in Europe. For example, the issue of the French journal *Archaeologia* published in May 1992 had a cover page that read "Le peuplement par une race blanche il y a 13000 ans" and "Les Ainous du Japon" (Leroi-Gourhan, A. 1992:54).

1-5 The image of the Ainu in Japan

1-5-1 Racial debate

To a great extent the scholars who initiated Ainu studies in Japan were foreigners who had been invited by the Meiji government to introduce Western thought and scientific technology to the Japanese. This constitutes yet another aspect of the Western-modernisation of Japan and the role in it of foreign influence. Thus, these foreign scholars not only initiated Ainu studies but also made a great contribution to anthropological and archaeological thought in general in Japan. One of them was Edward Morse (1838-1925), who arrived in Japan in 1877. He is remembered for the excavation of the Omori shell midden, the first scientific excavation to take place in Japan. This is regarded as representing the beginning of archaeology in Japan. Another foreign pioneer was Neil Gordon Munro, who arrived in Japan in 1893. He was not an invited scholar, but a medical doctor who worked at the general hospital in Yokohama. He introduced the term 'Palaeolithic' to Japanese archaeology. Later he dedicated his life to the study of the Ainu and worked as a medical doctor among the Ainu until his death in Nibutani, Hokkaido (Terada 1981).

Anthropological and archaeological studies were not clearly differentiated at the outset, and, indeed, it was as a result of debate on the Ainu that a clear distinction between them gradually came to be drawn. In other words, the study of archaeology, anthropology, and ethnology in Japan was developed mainly through studies of the Ainu in Hokkaido. Ainu studies played so important a role within the development of Japanese anthropology and archaeology that they constitute a significant part in the history of Japanese archaeological thought.

At the heart of the discussion was a debate about whether the Ainu represented the descendants of the aboriginal inhabitants of the Japanese archipelago or not. There were two different views, one regarding the Ainu as aboriginal and the other arguing that they were not.

Heinrich von Siebold, a son of Philipp Franz von Siebold, arrived in Japan in 1871 and carried out research in order to support his father's idea that the Ainu were the aboriginal natives of Japan. In 1879 he suggested that there were two racial types in Japan and that this was reflected in two different types of archaeological site, one of them being Ainu (Siebold 1879, Terada 1981). An alternative view was that the Ainu were not aboriginal in Japan, and that an earlier race, "pre-Ainu people", had inhabited Japan before them. This idea originated with Edward Morse. Both interpretations, however, suggested that the ancestors of the modern Japanese were not related to the aboriginal inhabitants of Japan.

1-5-2 The Koro-pok-kur debate (Ainu vs. Koro-pok-kur)

The racial debate broke out among Japanese scholars soon after the Anthropological Society of Tokyo was established in 1884. By this time the debate was firmly grounded upon the evidence of data from Hokkaido. Dwelling pits dug into the ground surface were found near Sapporo in Hokkaido. Who were the occupiers of these dwelling pits? Were the Ainu the aboriginal inhabitants of Japan or not? A similar type of dwelling pit had already been found on the main island of Japan. The relationship between the Japanese and the Ainu needed clarification.

Shozaburo Watase suggested in 1886 that the people who had lived in dwelling pits were people called the 'Koro-pok-kur', who had inhabited Hokkaido before the Ainu (Watase 1886). 'Koro-pok-kur' is an Ainu word meaning people who live under butter burs (*Petasites-Japonicus*), and small like a dwarf. They are mentioned in the Ainu oral tradition. Hereby, an interpretation of the Ainu oral tradition became entangled with the debate about racial origins.

According to the Ainu oral tradition, there were people called Koro-pok-kur before the Ainu came, living where the Ainu are now. They were very small and lived in dwelling pits. They used stone tools and pottery which the Ainu do not use. There was trade between them and the Ainu, but they did not like to be seen, so they came in the evening and showed their goods through an entrance or window before exchanges took place. One day some young Ainu men decided to find out what the Koro-pok-kur were like and they caught the hand of one of them as it appeared at a window to exchange goods for trade. The Koro-pok-kur turned out to be a young woman who was small and tattooed around her mouth and hands. She cried so incessantly that the young Ainu men let her go. She went back to her village and told her people how the Ainu had insulted her. Her people became angry and left their village to go elsewhere (Terada 1981).

The idea therefore gained currency that the dwelling pits in Hokkaido had been occupied by the Koro-pok-kur and that the stone tools and pottery had been made and used by them. The tattoos of the Ainu women were also considered to be an imitation of the Koro-pok-kur custom.

A debate about whether the occupants of the dwelling pits were the Ainu or Koro-pok-kur began between Shogoro Tsuboi and Mitsutaro Shirai, both founders of the Anthropological Society of Tokyo. Tsuboi supported the idea that it is possible to consider that the dwelling pits were occupied by the Koro-pok-kur before the coming of the Ainu, whereas Shirai was against the idea. He considered that the Ainu oral tradition lacked credibility and held that the Ainu must be aborigines.

Later, the idea that the Koro-pok-kur were an imaginary people was supported by Yoshikiyo Koganei, and he criticised Tsuboi on the basis of physical anthropological and archaeological data (Koganei 1904).

As the debate continued, the idea that the Ainu were aboriginal came to be accepted by most researchers of the period. Particularly influential in swaying opinion was the evidence suggested by Ryuzo Torii, one of Tsuboi's students. As a result of field work on the Kuril Islands (Chishima), Torii reported that the Ainu had lived in dwelling pits and produced pottery until recently. Moreover, he argued that the Koro-pok-kur oral tradition did not exist in that region.

Despite being a very logical person and a formidable scholar who always defeated his opponents, Tsuboi became increasingly isolated, and the great debate effectively ended with his sudden death in 1913. After his death, the consensus view that the Ainu were aboriginal to Japan prevailed (Terada 1981). It is interesting to note that the only question considered at that time was whether the aborigines of Japan were the Ainu or the Koro-pork-kur. No thought was given to the notion that the aboriginal inhabitants of Japan must include the ancestors of the present day Japanese, who are not Ainu.

However, what was most significant about the debate was that it highlighted the difficulties of interpretation that archaeology is often a prey to when an attempt is made to correlate archaeological material with linguistic and racial evidence. This debate, having occurred as early as the 19th century, led to Japanese archaeology focusing on collecting data and establishing the chronology of a given material culture first and not attempting to place much emphasis on racial interpretation, or to speculative interpretation in the absence of sufficient data. In other words, some scholars had realised that the debate was based on so little data that it was difficult to discuss it meaningfully. This led to the separation of archaeology from anthropology in Japan in 1895. The Archaeological Society was founded in 1896 in order to focus on collecting data and establishing the chronology of the material culture. A knowledge of what Japanese archaeology had learned through the Koro-pok-kur-debate may make it easier to understand the character and tradition of Japanese archaeology down to the present.

However, this characteristic of Japanese archaeology was criticised in 1975 when the annual meeting of the Archaeological Society was held at Sapporo, Hokkaido, because, despite the setting, there was nothing on the agenda relating to the Ainu culture (Fujimoto 1983). Although there was still a big gap between the archaeological data and a racial interpretation, some of the archaeologists in Hokkaido, such as Yoshizaki (Asai et al. 1972), had a vision of an interpretation of Ainu culture and Satsumon culture based on the archaeological data available at that time.

Thus, this book issues a challenge to Japanese archaeology to become much wider in its interpretations of the archaeological evidence, which raises problems common to world archaeology. It aims to contribute to an understanding of the ethnohistorical interpretation of the Ainu culture from an archaeological point of view.

Furthermore, although our understanding of Ainu culture today is much more advanced than in the 19th century and the beginning of the 20th, many questions remain unanswered in the debate about what exactly the Ainu entity is.

1-6. Confusion in academic studies of the Ainu

It has been said that

> It becomes increasingly clear that the correlation of archaeological and linguistic evidence with that provided by physical anthropology and the environmental sciences is the only path leading to

reliable reconstructions of the culture and ethnic processes of the past. However, the merely mechanical correlation of operational and conceptual entities developed in each of these disciplines is methodologically unacceptable (Dolukhanov 1989:267).

1-6-1 Physical Anthropology

The present interpretation of the Ainu in physical anthropology is that they belong to the Mongoloid family. This affiliation is indicated by genetic factors, in particular the study of protein and an enzyme type in the blood and also by the blood type (Haniwara 1993).

According to the physical anthropologist Dodo, morphological studies based on the measurement of skulls analysed by three-dimensional representation of principal co-ordinate analysis based on the distance estimates using the mean measure of divergence (MMD) and nearest-neighbour analysis, indicate that the skulls of the Ainu show similarity to the excavated skulls of the Jomon[2] people (Dodo 1991). Howells also has said: "when we ask, per contra, whether the Ainu were like the Jomon people, the answer seems to be yes; but Ainu affiliations seem to be southern, not northern, as some other considerations would suggest" (Howells 1986).

A scale which is used to measure in order to identify different categories in physical anthropology is not the same as that on the cultural level. In other words, talking about the level of DNA and talking about the level of cultures are totally different things since these fields use different scales of identification. Thus, the formation of the Ainu as a racial group on the basis of physical anthropology is not the same as that of the Ainu as an ethnic group on the basis of these cultural level. Therefore, the Jomon culture and the Ainu culture are different and it should not be assumed that the Ainu culture is similar to the Jomon culture.

1-6-2 Linguistic confusion

The area inhabited by the Ainu in the past is indicated by studies of the distribution of place names in the Ainu language, particularly the distribution of the words *petsu* and *nai* (Kindaiichi 1962, Yamada 1976). This area includes Tohoku, Hokkaido, Sakhalin (Karafuto), and the Kuril Islands (Chishima). Although many scholars think this interpretation seems plausible, it needs to be examined carefully, since the linguistic study has not so far been related to evidence from the material cultural .

For example, it is unlikely that the Celtic culture and the Ainu culture are related, although a phonological study in linguistics indicates some similarity between the Ainu

language and the Celtic language in respect of place names: '*petsu*' in the Ainu language and 'perth' or 'firth' in the Gaelic language are phonetically similar. Moreover, the meaning of these words, both in the Ainu and the Gaelic, indicate the same geological location of the mouth of a river (Naito 1992). If the range of the Ainu is defined by the distribution of the place name *petsu*, it would still be unreasonable to include Ireland and Scotland.

Linguists say that a language exists because of the existence of speakers. However, the language itself does not necessarily relate directly to the material culture of a people or the race to which they belong (Asai 1979).

1-6-3 Ethnological debate

Our image of the Ainu is conditioned by the fact that in most museums Ainu artifacts are exhibited among those of northern peoples like the Oroqens and the Gilyaks. This image is a consequence of the study of the Ainu ethnology, and reflects the fact that their material culture, lifestyle, and customs are very similar to those of northern peoples. The Ainu are considered to be a northern people not only because of their material culture but also because of their mental culture; for example, a notable Ainu custom is the holding of bear feasts, especially bear feasts which involve raising a cub. Hunting and fishing are commonly described as characteristic features of Ainu culture.

To what period does this image of the Ainu, and all the cultural factors associated with it, apply? Although the Ainu have now been assimilated completely into the Japanese population, they are said still to exist and their history is supposed to be continuous. If so, then what is the concept of the Ainu in Ainu ethnology? How does it define the Ainu? Let us take an illustration from outside the academic field and consider the ethnic movement that arose in the 1970s. At that time the Ainu said that although they were no longer hunters, gatherers, and fishermen, that kind of image was perpetuated and led to racial discrimination against them in society. This is not an ethnological problem but a social problem in modern Japanese society that must be solved. However, it is also caused by the fact that the *ethnographic present* is not clearly defined in Ainu ethnology.

Therefore, there must be an examination of the concept of the Ainu which, as I suggested above, considers the problem of their image, and account must be taken of the period in which this image was created and the location of the area where it was researched, since regional differences among the widely dispersed Ainu are great. For this reason, cultural change among the Ainu needs to be examined within its historical framework.

1-6-4 Confusion related to ancient history

The word < 蝦夷 >, as it was written, was pronounced *ebisu* or *emishi* in ancient times. The word was also written as *ezo* in medieval times. Emishi in ancient times was described in the Chronicles of Japan (Nihon Shoki), compiled in 720 AD as the official history of the country. In a chapter on the reign of Keiko Tenno (Emperor Keiko), the Emishi are described as barbarians, who wear clothing made

---

[2]A Japanese archaeological term which defines the period of Jomon pottery, from 10,000 BP until Yayoi pottery appears around 200 BC. The people who produced Jomon pottery are called the Jomon people and their culture is named the Jomon culture.

of furs, and who drink the blood of animals, as also recorded by Takenouchi-no-sukune who came back from a tour of inspection in the East beyond the border of Keiko's territory. He informed Keiko Tenno (Emperor Keiko):

> "In the Eastern wilds there is a country called Hidakami-no-kuni. The People of this country, both men and women, tie up their hair in the form of a mallet, and tattoo their bodies. They were of fierce temper, and their general name is Emishi. Moreover, their land is wide and fertile. We should attack them and take it" (Aston 1972:200; NB. I have corrected the spelling of the Japanese names, Hidakami-no-kuni, and Emishi).

The same character < 蝦夷 >, now pronounced "*ezo*", appears in medieval documents. In Japanese history the island of Hokkaido itself was called *Ezo* before 1869. It is uncertain whether or not the Ainu people who live in Hokkaido at present are the direct descendants of the Emishi of the ancient times.

This has been the subject of eternal debate, generating papers by many scholars. Those who support the idea that Emishi were the Ainu are the historian Teikichi Kida (Kida 1980), the linguist Kyousuke Kindaichi (Kindaichi 1960), Hidezo Yamada (Yamada 1976), and Masaki Kudo (Kudo 1992) among recent scholars. On the other hand, the idea that the Emishi were not the Ainu is supported by Kotondo Hasebe (Hasabe 1917), an anthropologist. The debate still continues and no definitive conclusion has been reached.

According to Japanese historical documents, after the Taika Reform (645) the state-system became more systematically associated with a new departmental system of central government involved with the administration of the smallest unit of local division. In 701, the Taiho Code, equivalent to the Roman Law codes in Europe, was issued and governed administrative practise. This code consisted of two parts: the Ritsu and the Ryo (Regulations and Codes), and the system of government associated with it is called the Ritsu-Ryo system.

Under the Ritsu-Ryo system the Ritsu-Ryo state set up *koori* (counties) successively towards the north (Northern Honshu). This state was concerned about its northern border and the establishment of its authority there. Thus, it built the frontier administrative headquarters of Dewa-no-saku (708 AD), Taga-jo (724 AD), and Akita-jo (723 AD), without making a great military effort. Dewa-koori, Mogami-koori, and Miyagi-koori were also incorporated into the administrative system at the beginning of the 8th century. Then in the early 9th century Izawa-jo (802 AD), and Shiwa-jo (803 AD) were built, and the *oku-roku-gun* (the outer six counties) — comprising Esashi, Izawa, Waka, Hienuki, Shiwa, and Iwate — were established. This period of expansion between the early 8th century and early 9th century constituted the greatest upheaval in the ancient history of the Tohoku region, owing to the resistance of the people who lived in the area (see Fig. 1-2).

The border in the 8th century was a line connecting Taga-jo (on the Pacific side) and Akita-jo (on the Japan Sea side); later, by the beginning of the 9th century, the Ritsu-Ryo

area had expanded to include Izawa-jo and Shiwa-jo, and at that time the area farther northwards was the area of the Non-Ritsu-Ryo system. The people who lived in this Non-Ritsu-Ryo area and who refused to obey the Ritsu-Ryo system were called Emishi by the Ritsu-Ryo people. Takahashi (Takahashi 1982) has pointed out that the word 'Emishi' was used within the Ritsu-Ryo system as a political term. My interpretation of this is that Emishi was recognised by the Ritsu-Ryo people, those who were part of the Ritsu-Ryo system, as distinguishing those who lived outside Ritsu-Ryo territory as Non-Ritsu-Ryo people, who did not want to follow the Ritsu-Ryo system. Once Non-Ritsu-Ryo people had been absorbed into the Ritsu-Ryo system, the term used to refer to them changed from 'Emishi' to '*fushu*' or '*ishu*' (ibid.); and when the Ritsu-Ryo system collapsed, the word Emishi disappeared from Japanese history.

Thus, the Emishi are defined as those people who lived in the Non-Ritsu-Ryo area, and the term cannot be said to refer to a particular race or an ethnic group as it changes in concept over time. On the other hand, the term 'Ainu' is an ethnic name, and I recognise the Ainu as a distinct ethnic group who still exist today.

Therefore, the terms Emishi and Ainu are used to refer to different concepts. The debate over the Emishi and the Ainu has been conducted under circumstances in which these different concepts have been confused.

1-7 Conclusion

Ainu studies started with the assumption or preconception that the Ainu were a pure ethnic group which had preserved its own ethnic identity and had been little influenced by the Japanese or any other people when Hokkaido was integrated into Japanese history in 1869. This impression was largely a misconception caused by major administrative discontinuity based on the political framework which accompanied the establishment of the Meiji government and also by the arrival of foreign scholars who started to explore Hokkaido. Moreover, this was a period when a new school of thought in anthropology and archaeology based on a Western scientific framework was introduced and had just begun. What was discounted or deliberately abandoned was the information which had been accumulated during the previous era and the process of assessing it properly.

Although cultural contact with and interaction between the Ainu and others in the past was noted by Torii as early as 1917 (Torii 1917), it must be emphasised that the Ainu were defined without considering the great influences exerted upon their culture by the policy of the Matsumae-Han (domain) in the 18th century, exemplified by the *Basho-Ukeoi* system. Unless this is taken into account, the concept of the Ainu and their culture must inevitably be distorted.

During the long centuries of the Ainu period, which continues up to the 20th century, it should never be forgotten that cultural contact with and interaction between the Ainu and other people took place. In particular, if cultural contacts between the Ainu and the Japanese are ignored and the historical change in Japanese culture itself is not taken into account, the Ainu culture cannot be fully understood.

Therefore, I examine the Ainu culture from the archaeological point of view in order to discuss cultural contact and the transformation of the material culture, since there is no historical documentation within the Ainu culture itself. I concentrate especially on interaction between the Ainu and the Japanese. In this discussion, terms such as 'medieval' and 'modern', which are valid in Japanese history are used to refer to the Ainu, because the Ainu culture in archaeology is set within the medieval and modern Japanese historical framework. The 'Medieval Ainu period' (around the 12th-16th centuries) and 'Modern Ainu period' (the 17th-19th centuries) are used in the study of Ainu archaeology. The people who produced the Ainu material culture which survives in the archaeological record were the immediate ancestors of the present Ainu.

The Ainu culture in an archaeological sense was formed as a result of a historical process involving contact and interaction with other cultures. I consider that only an understanding of the process of formation of the Ainu culture through the historical sequence can lead us to the answer to the question, "What should be considered as Ainu?".

Fig. 1-1   Map of Matsumae territory (after Kaiho).

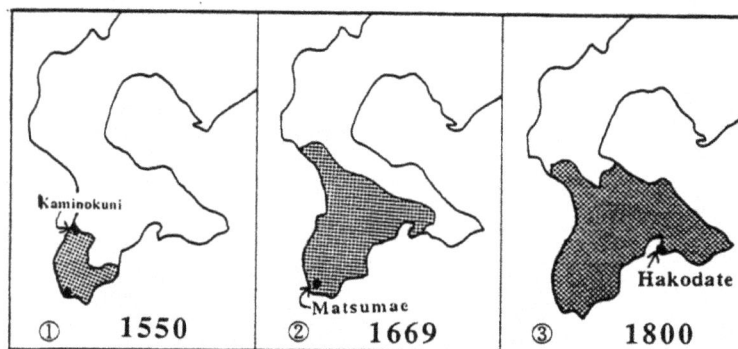

Fig. 1-2   Map of Tohoku expansion in the 7th-9th centuries.

9

Chapter 2

Model-building for Ainu archaeology

2-1 Introduction

In this chapter, I criticise an inappropriate model which caused much misunderstanding of the Ainu culture, by manipulating theory without reality and without consideration of the historical context. In its place, I shall build an alternative model to enable a more substantial discussion of Ainu archaeology.

2-2 Reconsideration of the present model: Criticism of the "Ainu ecosystem" presented by Watanabe

The "Ainu ecosystem" presented by Watanabe in 1972 was based on ethnographic data about the Ainu which he collected by interviewing Ainu informants between 1951 and 1954.

He describes the transition to agriculture in the Ainu culture as being in two stages, and this is used to explain the agricultural transition model from hunter-gatherers to cultivators. In the first stage, men are described as hunters and women as gatherers and cultivators. In the second stage, men become cultivators and women carry on the same role as gatherers and cultivators (or basically cultivators and domestic workers). Watanabe described the two stages of the Ainu transition to agriculture as follows (my translation from the Japanese):

> The first stage was the period before the Meiji government's promotion of a transition to agriculture for the Ainu. It involved an introduction of cereal production by the seed-scattered method using a digging stick. At this stage, cultivation was mainly undertaken by women, and it can be regarded as an extension of a partial plant-collecting (owing to a sharp decrease of wild lilies as farinaceous foods). Thus, there was no change within Ainu society which was regarded as social change. The second stage was the period after the Meiji government's promotion of a transition to agriculture for the Ainu (1899), and involved an introduction of ridge and furrow methods of cultivation with a hoe. At this stage, cultivation also became a task undertaken by men. This led to change not only in the role of men but also in the sexual division of labour (men as hunters and women as cultivators) in traditional Ainu society. This also led to change in their habitation in order to adopt cultivation fields. Thereby their traditional structure of village and kinship relations disintegrated. Therefore, in this stage, the occurrence of structural change can be recognised within the Ainu society (Watanabe 1990:230).

Regarding social change in Ainu society, Watanabe says:

> The transition to agriculture among the Hokkaido Ainu was recognised as the first stage which occurred recently (before the Meiji government). However, this change among the Honshu Ainu took place a very long time ago and had already reached the second stage in the ancient period. In both cases, it is considered that the transition to the second stage involved a structural change within Ainu society which can be recognised by the change in men's role as they became cultivators. This change can be monitored by observing the decrease in hunting activity as an indicator of men's traditional activity; therefore, the trend can be tested archaeologically (ibid.:231).

The logic behind this model is that social change can be embodied in the change of men's role — in that men hunters became men cultivators. It led also to Watanabe's hypothesis that cultivation was an innovation by retired hunters among the men (Watanabe 1987).

In order to assess this two-stage model, I shall examine the way in which the Ainu men as hunters became cultivators after the Meiji government's agricultural promotion policy.

After 1877, when the title deeds for land in Hokkaido were issued by the Meiji government, and particularly following enactment of the Hokkaido Native People Protection Law in 1899, one of the policies of the Meiji government was the policy of transition to agriculture (see Chapter 1) in order to assimilate the Ainu into Japanese society.

According to Article 1 of the Hokkaido Native People Protection Law, "Native people who are engaged in agriculture and who wish to be so engaged are to be given land in Hokkaido up to a maximum of 5cho (49,500m^2) per family, without compensation". Agricultural tools and seed, as well as land, were given free to the Ainu. It should be noted, however, that Article 3 of the same Law states that "If the given land has not been cultivated for 15 years after the year in which it was obtained, it is to be confiscated". In fact, much land which was given to the Ainu was later confiscated under Article 3. This implies that the Meiji government policy of promoting agriculture among the Ainu did not turn Ainu men into cultivators.

For example, according to a simple calculation based on a document which records land granted to the Ainu in Shizunai-cho, Hokkaido, the area later confiscated was 444cho-8tan-23bu (4,448,075.9m^2), out of the total area of land given amounting to 571cho-6tan-8une-23bu (5,716,875.9m^2). This shows that almost 80% of the land was confiscated without having been cultivated. In 1980, 81 years after the enactment of the Hokkaido Native People Protection Law, the remaining portion of land given was only 41cho. This amounts to only 7% of the land which was given under Article 1 of the Hokkaido Native People Protection Law (Pon Fuchi 1992:219). This fact includes many complex problems, so that it is not as simple as this calculation. However, these figures surely suffice to indicate that Ainu men did not become cultivators despite the interference of the Meiji government. Therefore, Watanabe's model of the Ainu ecosystem — involving a transition to agriculture in two stages by the Ainu, as a result of the Meiji government's interference based on the Ainu men's role — simply does not work.

The fact is that Ainu men became cheap day labour, such as unskilled workmen, carriers, porters, and woodcutters at the seashore or in mountains and forests, or cheap migrant workers, in order to obtain cash to live on because they were unable to survive only by cultivation after the interference of the Meiji government. In other words, they were drawn into the cash economy. Moreover, they often became unemployed either because there were no jobs available to them or because they were not able to carry on hunting, due to the fact that Japanese merchants were prohibited from buying or exchanging goods for animal skins at Ainu villages (1875), while, on the other hand, the Ainu were prohibited from catching salmon (1883), and hunting deer (1899) by the Meiji government (Hokkaido 1989). The changes in the character of Ainu society after the interference of the Meiji government were a result of integration into the framework of the modern nation state politically, economically, and socially, whether the Ainu intended it or not.

From the above discussion, it is clear that the two-stage model of the transition to agriculture in Ainu culture does nothing to explain the entity of cultivation within Ainu culture, nor can social change connected with changes in the role of men in the transition to agriculture be substantiated. Further, it does not explain at all the role of cultivation as a subsistence activity, and the role of women as cultivators in Ainu society.

Therefore, the idea of a social change from hunters-gatherers to cultivators in Ainu society needs to be reconsidered in terms of its social meaning, and a new meaning needs to be found within a historical framework. Moreover, since the social change in Ainu society which occurred as a result of the interference of the Meiji government was not a change from hunter-gatherers to cultivators, it is not appropriate to build a generalised evolutionary model, based upon such a social change within Ainu society, to explain the social changes underlying the transition to agriculture in any other society. Because, the model itself does not involve substantiated discussions of the social changes. Thus the Ainu ecosystem is no longer an appropriate model to explain the transition to agriculture in Ainu society. To discuss social change satisfactorily in Ainu culture, the process of its historical development needs to be understood and a framework must be set up based upon understanding such a process; subsequently, the meaning of social change needs to be considered within that framework.

Furthermore, the logic behind this model, in which retired men hunters are seen as innovators of agriculture, leads to a

logic that women are incapable of innovating anything; this cannot be tested. Using an untestable model makes it difficult to formulate substantive hypotheses regarding discussion of the transition to agriculture. In other words, an untestable model leads only to empty theory. Therefore, separate from this kind of model, a model needs to be built based on the setting up of questions to explain the process of change and make logical statements which can be discussed substantively. The significance of the social meaning about gender roles in a society needs to be considered. To build a significant model is to lead to enhanced perception of a social structure; if a model is not based on substantive arguments or is based on preconceptions, then it will lack significance as an archaeological theory. Archaeology as a science should be based upon facts which make it possible to explain and understand society, including entity as one of its component factors.

From the above, it is necessary to consider how the transformation of Ainu culture is to be perceived and explained as a process which leads to substantive discussion. Therefore, a more appropriate model needs to be established based upon evidence, in order to explain the process of social change within Ainu society. In this case, an archaeological model created in conjunction with historical documents and ethnographic evidence can give the most fruitful results.

2-3. Building models for Ainu archaeology

2-3-1 The logic behind the models: a prohibition system in a society

I would like to discuss how a model should be built for studying Ainu culture from an archaeological point of view. A model must be built which makes possible a logical interpretation of the material culture.

A prohibition system is a characteristic phenomenon in a society, or an essential phenomenon which exists within a human group. A prohibition system occurs when preconditioned acts are recognised in a society. It is necessary to understand 'social precondition' as the social phenomenon that the act which needs to be prohibited is recognised by people or groups of people as organisations. For example, "¿¿¿ act is prohibited" means that there are people who practise ¿¿¿ act in a society, and ¿¿¿ act must be recognised by people in a society. If ¿¿¿ act or a person who practises ¿¿¿ act do not exist in a society, it does not need to be prohibited by people; the need to prohibit the ¿¿¿ act would not arise.

A prohibition system involving the imposing of legal controls, or restrictions and laws, occurs always *after* the recognition of the act or the practising of acts within a society. This implies that the existence of the prohibition of a certain kind of act is a result of the social recognition of the act, which leads to the imposition of the prohibition. In other words, to understand the social phenomenon of how the prohibition came to be made in a society is to understand social preconditions. It also needs to be kept in mind that any kind of prohibition system is always associated with acts that breach or violate that prohibition.

By understanding the logic of a society, and applying this logic to explain the structuring of social reality within Ainu culture, it should be possible to explain social phenomena in Ainu society.

Further, social phenomena may be explained and can be interpreted more appropriately by analysing the interrelated positions of each interacting culture within a social and historical context. Interaction between neighbouring societies needs to be taken into account in order to clarify interrelations between cultures which stand face to face. For example, interaction between the Matsumae and Ainu society can be examined in this way.

Therefore, I propose "the prohibition model of cultivation" and "the prohibition model of iron" in order to explain social change in Ainu society.

Then, social preconditions need to be considered to understand how prohibitions came to be imposed on a society. If such social preconditions did not exist, it would not be necessary to prohibit them. Social preconditions are recognised as social phenomena. Thus the social precondition for prohibiting cultivation is the social phenomenon in which cultivation is recognised within a society generally, and the social precondition for prohibiting iron or edged tools is the social phenomenon in which iron tools or iron weapons are recognised within a society generally. These social phenomena are recognised by the people who need to prohibit them; the act of prohibition is then executed as a prohibition system. The prohibitions imposed on the Ainu by the Matsumae were derived from the social phenomena of Ainu society which were recognised by the Matsumae. This implies that cultivation and the use of iron in Ainu culture already existed and were indeed widely disseminated throughout Ainu society, and were already recognised by the Matsumae, otherwise the imposition of prohibitions by the Matsumae would have been superfluous. It also indicates how seriously the Matsumae regarded these social phenomena within Ainu society.

2-3-2 The cultivation-prohibition model

The cultivation-prohibition model hypothesises that cultivation in Ainu culture is one cultural factor as a practical "negotiation" (cf. Shanks and Tilley 1987:72) which was transformed as a result of human agency, being prevented by intentional ideologies, in spite of its existence and extension in Ainu culture since the succeeding Satsumon culture.

Thus, the Ainu culture cannot be fully explained within the framework of the existing model, such as 'a society of hunter-gatherers' or 'a society of cultivators', and it is not appropriate to use such a framework to explain it. It is rather possible to understand it as "practical negotiation" within Ainu society as a historical process. Cultivation in the Ainu culture was transformed as a result of "social reproduction" within Ainu society through interaction between tradition and negotiation which was forced on Ainu society by an outside agency. Thus, the details of this process need to be explained. From this point, this model is intended to enhance our perception of the social phenomenon in Ainu society and to make possible an archaeological interpretation of it. I shall discuss the cultivation-prohibition model from the above point of view, based on Japanese historical and ethnographic documents dating from the 18th-19th centuries.

A historical document dated 1786, which is a report made by an officer of the Tokugawa Shogunal government, Genrokuro Satou, stated: "It is illegal to cultivate cereals in the Ezo island [Hokkaido] from old times" (Hokkaido historiography vol. 7 1969:333-334). My interpretation of this statement is that it is reverse-proof that cereal cultivation was practised in the Ezo island from old times. There is no point in prohibiting cultivation if it had not been practised by the Ezo [Ainu]. Thus, this implies that cereal cultivation was practised before legal action was taken. Satou goes on to say:

> in the previous year, rice was cultivated by the Ezo [Ainu] somewhere in the upper area of the Ishikari River, and rice grew considerably well. However, this fact was heard by the Matsumae, maybe through merchants, and seeds and unhulled rice were taken away by the Matsumae and the rumour says that the Ezo [Ainu] who planted it will be punished with a fine (ibid.).

It is surprising that rice grew well in the upper area of the Ishikari River in Hokkaido. If so, the methods of cultivation would be questioned. However, in a Chinese historical document, the commentary of *Zhou li* written by Zheng Xuan, a Confucian scholar, during the later Han period around 200 AD, rice cultivation is described, employing a seed-scattering method on wetland (Nishijima 1983). It said that if cultivated land is covered by water as a result of previous heavy rain which drowns the weeds, when it has dried up, weeds are mown, and then rice can be grown using the seed-scattering method. In this case, it does not need a complicated process such as constructing wet rice paddy-fields. The area of the upper Ishikari River is a wetland, due to the overflowing of the river, even nowadays. Thus, it is possible to imagine that rice was grown on the wet land by the seed-scattering method.

The report continues:

> ... there are no paddy-fields or fields; however, the Ezo [Ainu] who inhabit a mountain area (i.e. inland) cultivated a little of some millets termed 'munshiro' and 'piyapa'. Although there are no cultivation tools, the Ezo [Ainu] scattered seeds among trees; they harvest quite well and the products are the food of the Ezo [Ainu]. In this area, the Ezo [Ainu] possess mortars and pestles (ibid.).

According to these documents, it can be seen that the Matsumae had some reason for preventing the Ainu from engaging in cultivation by imposing a fine. It is clear that there was a prohibition by the Matsumae.

According to another source, the *Ezo-soshi* (Mogami 1786), "a [Matsumae] law in the area, states that seeds of plants cannot be brought into Ezo [Hokkaido], so cultivation skills are not known" (Yoshida 1965:45). Thus, bringing seeds into Hokkaido was also prohibited by the Matsumae.

Furthermore, ethnographic evidence in the form of a travel record written by Takeshiro Matsuura (Matsuura 1857) states:

. . . beans, kidney beans, millets, glutinous millets, and barnyard millet are cultivated by the Ezo [Ainu] near their houses, and cultivation is women's work. . . The Ezo [Ainu] do not possess hoes, so what they use as a tool for cultivation is a felling axe with a wooden handle instead of a hoe. This is because the Matsumae's policy is that cultivation is prohibited to the Ezo [Ainu], so the Matsumae people do not give any hoes to the Ezo [Ainu]. In the area of Tsuishikari, the Ezo [Ainu] cultivate only the Japanese radish, and when I asked them "why don't you cultivate cereals?", the answer was "there are no seeds and hoes, although we wish to cultivate such cereals" (Matsuura 1857: modern version by Maruyama 1973:24, 72).

It is clear that the Matsumae had a policy of prohibiting cultivation among the Ainu and that they also restricted the supply of agricultural tools. Matsuura continues:

in the area of Totsukubetsuhara, cultivated fields are located away from their houses, somewhere in hidden places, because they are afraid of being seen by the Matsumae (the crops would have been confiscated had they been discovered). Kidney beans, beans, millets, and barnyard millets are cultivated with processed felling axes (ibid.:72).

From this statement, it appears that cultivation was practised in secret among the Ainu, and cultivated fields were at a distance from the houses and villages.

The selection of fields for cultivation by the Ainu was a puzzle for Japanese observers, who were not aware of their situation. For example, Mogami notes that " . . . although there are fields near their houses, they always abandon them; then they go to a valley in distant mountains and cultivate" (Mogami 1808; cited in Takakura 1933). It is also mentioned in *Ezo sangyo zusetsu* that the reason for such irrational activity is not known: "it is not clear how they select land for cultivation from the surface as we observe; however, the Ezo [Ainu] are thoughtful and do not behave rashly, so there must be some underlying rationale, though what it is has not yet been known" (cited in Takakura 1933: 324). The reason why the Ainu selected land at a distance from their houses and went deep into the mountains for cultivation is easy to understand if they did not want to be seen by the Matsumae.

It is very interesting to compare the above statements, dating from the 18th-19th centuries, with ethnographic accounts written in the 20th century after the Meiji-period transformation, though some of them reflect earlier accounts. According to these recent ethnographies, Ainu cultivation was described in terms such as the following: "although there are fertile fields around their houses, . . . a selection of the Ainu's cultivated land is sometimes at a distance of 3-4 ri (11.7-15.5km)" (Arimoto 1916:357); or "it is often more than 1 ri (3.9km) distant, located deep in the forest" (Nara 1928:192). Various interpretations that have been made on the basis of these statements are: 1) that the Ainu chose the cultivation of land along rivers which are located among

mountains; it is not necessary to have a field near their house, or 2) that the Ainu did not care where their cultivation fields were located, or 3) that their selection was related to soil conditions, particularly the softness of the soil because they did not have agricultural tools. This illustrates that an action cannot be interpreted without understanding the intentions of those who carry it out (Hodder 1982).

Even if acts are prohibited, if the degree of necessity for committing such actions is sufficiently high in a society, there are always people who will violate the prohibition. Although cultivation was prohibited by the Matsumae, some of the Ainu desperately needed to cultivate in order to make a living:

"a 14-year-old girl is the only one who can support the family by fishing and gathering, so it is necessary for us to cultivate in order to survive, regardless of what we are told by the Matsumae", and there is a small field in front of their house and beans, millet, and barnyard millet are cultivated. (Matsuura 1857: modern version by Maruyama 1973:74-75)

Further evidence indicates that the Matsumae manipulated the Ainu ideologically to prevent them from cultivating crops:

an Ainu said: "Matsumae's people threatened us that if you sow seeds in the fields, then the gods of the Ezo land get angry and epidemic diseases will spread all over the Ezo land, so that the descendants of the Ezo [Ainu] will die out completely", or they said to the Ezo [Ainu]: " . . . if you want to die from an illness caused by being cursed as a result of cultivation, then you should do it, and if you really wish to cultivate fields in imitation of Shamo [Japanese], then you should shave your beards immediately like the Nishipa [the master or Shogun in Japanese] in Edo [present Tokyo], and speak Japanese. The names of Ezo [Ainu] who speak Japanese will be written down on a sheet of paper and burnt in front of Bentensama [a Japanese god or spirit], then you will die immediately" (ibid.:73).

These statements, implying ideological manipulation of Ainu society, indicate the strength of the Matsumae attitude to Ainu attempts at cultivation and how seriously they tried to prevent cultivation among the Ainu. It can also be understood that, for the Ainu, cultivation was important for survival.

A further interesting fact is that, over 100 years later, this ideological manipulation by the Matsumae is reflected in the common ideology of the Sakhalin Ainu, as Watanabe reveals from his ethnographic data. He said :

Among the Sakhalin Ainu, it was said that if land was cultivated rashly, then those who did it would get ill, and their action would bring misfortune upon their descendants. So, it is necessary to understand the basic mentality of hunter-gatherers (Watanabe, conversation in Anzai & others 1990:61).

It would be impossible to understand the basic mentality of the hunters-gatherers if his data were based on a story derived from Matsumae's manipulation propaganda as described above. However, these data would be very useful for clarifying how such manipulation had affected the peripheral zone of the Ainu culture. By searching for this kind of ethnographic data, which might already have been collected elsewhere in the past, it may be possible to trace back the diffusion of ideological manipulation.

The sentence from the above paragraph which may raise the question of gender roles for cultivation is: "if you really wish to cultivate fields in imitation of Shamo [Japanese], then shave your beards immediately like the Nishipa [master or Shogun in Japanese] in Edo [present Tokyo], and speak Japanese". It should be noted that the phrase "shave your beard immediately" would only make sense in the context of an audience of Ainu men.

It has been thought that "cultivation in the Ainu culture is women's work, as a part of domestic work in small-scale fields with digging sticks" (Hayashi 1969, Watanabe 1990). If this was the case, what was the most appropriate reason for the Matsumae's prohibition policy, involving both threats and attempts to control the Ainu ideologically? The Matsumae would not have needed to prevent just small-scale women's work. The pressure applied by the Matsumae rather implies that because the women's role as cultivators was so significant in Ainu society that cultivation needed to be prohibited. It also implies that interpretations made about Ainu cultivation based on recent ethnographic data are the result of social reproduction within the Ainu culture which was affected by the prohibition of cultivation from the 17th to the mid-19th centuries.

A study based on the historical records gives the area of cultivated fields in an Ainu village indicates that the average area of cultivated field per household decreased from 68.0 tsubo (224.4m^2) to 33.3 tsubo (109.89m^2) between 1800 and 1858 in the Tokachi area. This is despite the fact that the Tokachi area is located in the south-east of Hokkaido, some distance from the Matsumae. The area of cultivation thus almost halved in the period under consideration (Hatano 1981:180). This provides strong evidence that a decrease in the area under cultivation was taking place in Ainu society at that time.

According to a calculation for a given cultivated area of barnyard millet, it was stated that "in order to feed one person for a year on barnyard millet, an area of 500m^2 needs to be cultivated, so, for a household of 5 persons for a year, an area of 3000m^2 would suffice to supply their needs" (*Biratori mura soto hakkasonshi*, cited in Takakura 1933:328). It is also estimated, based on the above calculation, that:

> barnyard millet produces 450 litres per 1000m^2. Although barnyard millet would not have been the sole item in the diet, 1350 litres is required in order to feed one person for a year. A skilled woman harvesting for 6 hours by picking ears of barnyard millet can gather 90 litres of barnyard millet, covering an area of 200-300m^2. Assuming 3000m^2 of barnyard millet to have

been cultivated, and that 2 skilled women were involved in harvesting it, then only 5-8 days work would have been required to harvest enough to feed the 5 persons in the average household (Segawa 1989:81).

This calculation suggests that barnyard millet could easily have been the main food of the Ainu, without any need to cultivate a large area.

The reason why the Matsumae prohibited cultivation among the Ainu is "presumably that, if the Ezo [Ainu] worked hard at cultivation, the products of fishing would decrease; then, as a result, trade for merchants would also be reduced, then the tax yield for the Matsumae would be reduced as well" (Mogami, modern version by Yoshida 1965:45); or, the only way to survive for the Matsumae under the Baku-Han system was "to force the Ainu to labour" (Kaiho 1991:80), because the Matsumae's income was largely based on their ability to control the *basho* in Ezo land. In addition, the Matsumae's tribute to the Tokugawa Shogunal government was in the form of exotic goods which were obtained though the Ainu. If the existence of the Matsumae under the Shogunal government was based on the exploitation of Ainu labour, particularly in the fishing industry, within the Basho-Ukeoi system, then the prohibition of cultivation among the Ainu was aimed at acquiring Ainu women's labour as well as that of the men. Consequently, this implies that cultivation in Ainu society before the prohibition must have been more significant and extensive than is suggested by interpretations based on recent ethnographic data (see Chapter 3 for the archaeological evidence).

From the above discussion it is clear that for an understanding and explanation of the entity of Ainu culture, neither human agency and intentions nor factors which were affected by such an agency can be ignored. It makes us more aware of the significance of the historical process and social change, rather than the ecosystem, in the Ainu culture. Needless to say, ethnographic data which have been collected from informants need to be examined within their social and historical contexts. Furthermore, the informants on whom ethnologists rely for their information need to be understood within the context of the period and conditions in which they live.

2-3-3 The iron-prohibition model

Iron, as indicated by Bismarck's statement that "iron is a state" (Bismarck, speech in 1862), has always been considered to be related to a state or a nation in all ages and countries. However, recent ethnohistorical and archaeometallurgical studies of the Inuit in Greenland suggest that they were an ethnic group that produced iron products from meteoric iron and carried out an extensive trade in iron products despite the lack of a developed state system and the belief that they had no iron technology (Buchwald & Mosdal 1985). The role of iron in human history is so important, and its value is so great as a superior raw material, that everybody desires to possess it.

The iron-prohibition model is based on a policy according to which iron, such an important materials for human beings, is prohibited from being traded. It is designed to perceive the substantive phenomenon that those people who possess iron are afraid of the outflow of iron, and to perceive the ways in which people who do not possess iron obtain it. The iron-prohibition policy is operated by people who posses iron in order to control different peripheral ethnic groups or populations. However, by the time the prohibition policy was implemented, iron had already spread to the people who were though not to possess it. Moreover, this model also takes into account the phenomenon of iron outflows in spite of the existence of an iron-prohibition policy.

Further, I shall include in this prohibition model the technological aspects of iron, since both iron production and iron use are associated with technology. The technology which produces iron from the raw materials of iron, the technology which produces iron products, and the technology which processes iron are all relevant here.

Thus this model allows us to perceive these phenomena and to make archaeological interpretations from the above point of view. These phenomena can be seen frequently in history, so that it is possible to give some examples on which to base this model of the use of iron-prohibition as a method of controlling other peripheral ethnic groups or populations. Iron played a very important role in the interaction and cultural contact between different ethnic groups in East Asia. Here I shall discuss the following case studies: the Xiongnu, the Jürchen, the Emishi, and the Ainu. In spite of the different historical and social context in each of these cases, it is still possible to build an iron-prohibition model.

(1) The case of the Xiongnu

The interaction between the Han dynasty and the Xiongnu, who were northern barbarians from the Chinese point of view, had a long history. The Han policy which controlled the Xiongnu was described in Han documents. One of the most interesting documents for understanding not only the Han policy for the Xiongnu but also the economic policy of the Han dynasty, which was also linked with and affected the control of the Xiongnu, concerns the salt and iron industries, which were centralised government monopolies under the Former Han dynasty.

Scholars have based their studies of the salt and iron monopolies on the interpretation of a document entitled *The discourses on salt and iron*. The aim of these studies has been to understand the Han dynasty historically, economically, and politically. The role of iron at the time of the Han dynasty can be elucidated by studying this historical document.

The discourses on salt and iron is a record of the debate about state control of commerce and industry in ancient China which was presented by Huan K'uan, a scholar of Hsuan-ti's time (73-49 BC). The debate is said to have taken place in 81 BC in the Shin-Yuan era of the Emperor Chao (86-81 BC).

A prolonged argument ensued between the Lord Grand Secretary of the Han government, the statesman and economist Sang Hung Yang, who defended his policies against the demands of the recommended sixty representatives of the Literati and Worthy classes. They were summoned to present criticisms to the effect that the government monopoly was inferior and unsuitable. They also asked for a return from the policy of a centralised government monopoly to the policy of earlier times (Gale 1931).

Although one of the central topics of the discourses was how to work out the best policy for dealing with the Xiongnu, the emphasis was on easing the financial problems caused by the Xiongnu, rather than on the supply of weapons which were supposed to be required near the border with the Xiongnu.

Kageyama (1984) points out that this might be interpreted as indicating that the iron monopoly was related only to iron agricultural tools which were produced by the iron casting technique, but not to iron weapons, which were made of steel and produced by the forging technique. He discusses the technological differences between iron agricultural tools and iron weapons, noting that the characteristic of Chinese iron technology was that the casting technique was developed around the 7th-6th centuries BC, earlier than the practice of steel forging, which developed around the 3rd-4th centuries BC.

The main reason why iron came under state control was that the state wanted to acquire from private enterprise the great profits, which associated with the high demand for iron agricultural tools by farmers, who had increased in number due to economic activity on the land after the Era of War.

The production of iron weapons, therefore, might already have been controlled by the state before the iron monopoly was set up. It is natural to assume that weapons would be controlled by the state because of their nature and purpose. According to the *Han Shu*, "it is said that bronze weapons were produced under the state" (*Han Shu*, vol. 76). This suggests that iron weapons were also produced under aegis of the state.

In addition to the iron monopoly as a means of financial support, iron as prohibited goods for barbarians, and the prohibition of trade in iron products are described in the *Han Shu* and the *Ho Han Shu*. According to the law of the Han, weapons and iron were prohibited goods that were not to be taken into barbarian territory. Under Empress Lu (187-180 BC), "metal, especially iron, iron pans, and agricultural tools were prohibited goods for all the barbarians (including those of the North, West, and South)" (Yü 1967). "According to the prohibition, it is not allowed to export weapons, grain, horses, oxen, and sheep". All the items were prohibited goods mentioned several times in the Han imperial edicts (ibid. 129). Moreover, the *Han Shu* says: "in the barbarian market, officials as well as common people are not allowed to carry weapons and iron beyond the frontier barriers" (*Han Shu*, vol. 50). Thus, it is clear that the iron-prohibition policy was applied to the Xiongnu by the Han dynasty. The prohibitions were enacted primarily on account of political and military considerations rather than on economic grounds.

One of the policies the Han operated in order to win over the Xiongnu was to open markets for trade near the border and exchange goods and agricultural products which the Xiongnu desperately wanted to have, as it says: "the Xiongnu very much liked Han food" (*Han Shu*, vol. 94, & *Shiji*, vol. 110). Peace between them was maintained in this way.

The Han merchants who were involved in this trade are described in records of the economy and geography of North China (*Shiji*, vol. 129). In this trade, merchants dealt not only with goods which were permitted but also with prohibited goods as contraband, described as "*kan-lan ch'u-wu*" (*Shiji*, vol. 110) and "*lan-ch'u ts'ai wu*" (*Shiji*, vol. 120, and *Han Shu* vol. 50). Yü (1967) discusses the existence of the contraband trade, stating that

> the barbarians could obtain weapons and iron pans neither from the Han government as "gifts" nor from the barbarian markets as exchange goods, the most likely channel through which such things went all the way from interior China and got beyond the border was probably contraband trade (Yü 1967:130).

However, at a place beyond the northern frontier, a large number of iron weapons and implements have been recovered, and identified as of Han origin. These include swords, double-edged swords, axes, spades, knives, etc. Yü mentioned that a Russian archaeologist, Rudenko, has pointed out that the barbarians not only obtained iron from China but also knew how to smelt iron and forge iron implements. However it is rather difficult to distinguish the Han imports from the native products among such finds (ibid.:168). In this connection, archaeological finds can be most fruitfully studied in conjunction with literary sources in order to test the iron-prohibition model.

(2) The case of the Jürchen

The Ming dynasty (1368-1644) executed an iron-prohibition policy against a peripheral ethnic group, the Jürchen, from the 15th century through to the 17th century. There were three groups of Jürchen people. One was the Yeren Jürchen, who did not cultivate; their subsistence was based on hunting-gathering. The second was the Haixi Jürchen, who settled and cultivated the ground. The third was the Jianzhou Jürchen, who were almost the same as the Chinese in what they ate and wore.

In 1439, the Ming Emperor decided to prohibit the exchange of iron because of an officer's word that

> barbarians (including the Jürchen) bring back fabrics, cattle, and copper and iron products from our markets to their home territory to meet all the needs of their territory. The barbarians process copper and iron and use them as source materials. Therefore, we should cease to exchange goods which are made from iron and copper (Ming; *Eiso-Sillok*, vol. 54).

The Emperor accepted this proposal and ordered a prohibition of iron trading in the markets, saying "if anyone breaches the rule, their action will be punished" (Ming; *Eiso-Sillok*, vol. 54).

However, the policy of prohibition was not effective since, 30 years later in 1476, prohibition was ordered again in response to reports that

> much exchange of iron is still carried on by the army and people when the Koreans and barbarians come to give tribute to the Ming. It

was considered that this did not benefit the country, and should be stopped, by closing the cross-border roads and setting up interpreters in order to ask visitors what reason they had for entering the country. (Ming, vol. 159).

The government decided not to export iron and cattle.

The interaction between the Ming and the Jürchen started around 1403, as a tribute relationship in the usual Chinese way. In 1406, a frontier headquarters office was set up and horse markets were opened. The number of Jürchen coming to the market ranged from 10 people at the smallest to the largest as many as 2-3000 people. The Jürchen received a great amount of iron from the Ming by exchanging it for horses, which they had obtained from the Mongolians. The Jürchen people went to the city of the Ming with tribute goods of horses, sable, and ginseng. In this way the Jürchen obtained iron from the Ming. The Ming dynasty taxed goods at the rate of an iron pot for one *bun* of silver in order to receive a large amount of exchange tax from the Jürchen.

The Ming dynasty knew that the Jurchen used iron and felt threatened because the Jürchen were becoming powerful. The Ming manipulated this fact in order to exert control over the Jürchen politically by controlling iron exchange. This was the reason for instituting the iron-prohibition.

Not only the Ming dynasty but also another neighbouring country — the Korean dynasty — tried to control the flow of iron to the Jürchen. The Jürchen also had interactions with Korea in order to exchange their goods for iron. According to Korean historical documents known as the *Yijo Sillok*, it is said that

> it was not to our country's benefit that any iron goods are going to the Jürchen territory (*Yijo Sillok*, vol. 276).
> Cattle and iron goods had been exchanged for sable fur, which the Jürchen brought in; however, cattles and iron goods are flowing out to their territory; this needs to be prohibited (*Yijo Sillok*, vol. 52).

or,

> there is a statement that in order to prohibit the exchange of iron for sable fur, the Korean government prohibited the wearing of sable fur coats which caused problems (*Yijo Sillok*, vol. 25).

Moreover,

> Gifts or presents of fur coats are prohibited, and also prohibited is the receipt of tribute in sable fur from 5 villages in border area. If anyone received or permitted receipt of such furs, they would be punished severely (*Yijo Sillok*, vol. 276).

From the above it is clear that the Korean dynasty also had executed an iron-prohibition policy. The Koreans realised how serious the situation was when any kind of iron goods could be processed into iron weapons. Once the Jürchen became powerful, then they would become a threat and peace would be at risk.

From around 1474, sable fur became so popular and such a precious item that everybody in Korea wanted to have it. Sable coats were worn especially by the Royal family and aristocracy, and they were very pleased to receive them as tribute or gifts. Under these circumstances, one could not go out without a sable coat because it was too shameful (*Yijo Sillok*, vol. 29).

The Jürchen decided on a policy that sable skins should not be exchanged for anything but iron (*Yijo Sillok*, vol. 228). Garrisons of Jürchen on the border were in charge of dealing with this exchange between the Jürchen and the Koreans. Then sable became very valuable and brought high profits. The Korean government decided to prohibit the wearing of sable coats and the paying of tribute in sable, with severe penalties for breaking the regulations.

Another policy aimed at obtaining iron was to deal in Korean captives (*Yijo Sillok*, vol. 282). Korean captives were returned in exchange for iron objects. One captive was equivalent to thirty cattle, one horse, an iron helmet, ten iron pans, ten agricultural tools, ten hoes, ten axes, five brass bowls, and five brass hubs (*Yijo Sillok*, vol. 282). Thus it is clear that many iron objects entered Jürchen territory.

As we have seen, there were preconditions for the iron-prohibition policy of the Ming and the Korean dynasties before the execution of iron-prohibition policy.

Although the prohibition policy made things difficult in Jürchen society and delayed the development of Jürchen production and their standard of living, there are indications that there was contraband trade in this case as well. It was said by a Jürchen leather trader that "previously, such iron goods were hidden in order to exchange them, but nowadays there is open exchange not only of agricultural tools but also of weapons" (*Yijo Sillok*, vol. 52). This reflected the resigned attitude of Korea in that there was no way to stop iron flowing into Jürchen territory. The iron-prohibition was the policy of the Ming and the Koreans, it did not necessarily follow that iron did not flow into the Jürchen territory. For example, prohibition of iron exports by the Ming specifically referred to iron weapons but did not include iron agricultural tools such as hoes and spades.

It is quite clear that a certain amount of iron flowed into Jürchen territory. The Jürchen processed the iron in the following way: broken iron pans were melted down and then the iron was reproduced to make iron goods and weapons. Therefore, the demand for iron in Jürchen society was satisfied from within that society.

It is very interesting to consider the development of the Jürchen iron industry under the iron-prohibition policy. Historical documents indicate that, despite iron-prohibition, the development of the iron industry in Jürchen society was an example of a success story. The Jürchen were forced to initiate developments within their own society in order to alleviate this serious lack of iron. This led to the production of iron in order to satisfy consumer demand for iron to use in everyday life and war.

Although iron tools were initially introduced to Jürchen society from the Ming through the medium exchange, at an earlier period the Jürchen did not know how to use iron. According to historical documents (*Yijo Sillok*, vol. 57), the iron industry among the Jürchen gradually developed in the late 15th century. A document of 1475 describes a blacksmith and craftspeople who produced bows in a village. According to a document of 1483, when the Jürchen (Jianzhou and Yeren) were invited to court, they were asked several questions. "How do you make greetings when men receive their wives?" "Men bring some gifts to the wife's family." "What are the gifts?" "Men bring weapons to the wife's family." "What are the weapons made of?" "They are made of iron." "How do you make iron?" "Iron is made on ground-hearths." "Are there any smiths?" "There are many."

According to Li (Li 1984), the Jürchen did not know about *liantie* (wrought iron). They only knew *seitetsu*, which was the technique of reprocessing iron goods. The process of the reproduction of iron goods was progressing at that time in Jürchen society, but they did not know how to produce *liantie* directly from iron ore. *Seitetsu* implies that reproduction relied on availability of material from the Ming and from the Korea (ibid.).

The technical process of this stage was established in their society although it was still the processing stage. Korean documents indicate that there were already blacksmiths in the Jürchen territory. According to the Korean documents of 1494, "there were 70 Jürchen people at Funnei; in 1480, they escaped from Korean territory, but in 1481 some of them went back to Korean territory, where a number of them stayed, and the people who stayed started to produce weapons". This clearly indicates that the Jürchen were blacksmiths, and also implies that their iron techniques were very advanced, due to the influence of the Ming and the Koreans (ibid.).

The Jürchen already possessed tuyeres. This implies that high temperatures could be produced inside the hearths, which led to the production of high quality iron in large quantities. The documents also record that red hot iron was immediately dipped into water. This implies that the heat treatment technique was used in order to enhance the hardness and sharpness of the products. The Jürchen iron industry could be described as an armaments industry, producing armour and helmets for wars against external enemies and for internal wars (ibid.).

In the 16th century, under Nurhaci's leadership, the pace of development of the Jürchen iron industry accelerated. In 1599, Nurhaci ordered the exploitation of iron sand ores and the opening of mines. Nurhaci was in Hetu-ala at that time, and the mining town was within 400 km of Hetu-ala. Jürchen territory was not only rich in raw materials such as iron ore and coal, but also many of the Jürchen were skilled smiths who had already mastered the techniques of using tuyeres and of quenching (ibid.).

According to Korean historical documents of 1594, a report of a messenger who went to Hetu-ala, there were 16 craftspeople who produced arms, 50 craftspeople for arrows, 30 craftspeople for bows, and 15 blacksmiths. These were all foreigners, but not Chinese or Koreans; they were barbarians of the North (i.e. the Jürchen). Specialised craftspeople already existed and they understood how to produce iron from iron ore. Thus, the Jürchen iron industry had developed from the 16th century to the early 17th century as the technique reached the level of producing and smithing iron, whereas before it involved only reprocessing iron from used iron objects (ibid.).

Nurhaci regarded iron production as important and treated the blacksmiths very well. According to a record of 1601, when a battle between Korea and the Jürchen had taken place in the north of Korea, a number of Koreans including skilled smiths were captured. At that time in Jürchen territory, there were not enough iron goods such as iron balls, arms, axes, and sickles. Once smiths entered Jürchen territory, Nurhaci was very pleased and welcomed them, giving them gifts, including cattle and horses. In general, Nurhaci treated Korean smiths very well and the Jürchen smiths even better. Thus, development of the iron industry was given priority in Jürchen society (ibid.).

According to the Korean eyewitness report of 1620, there were all kinds of craftspeople for silver, iron, leather, and wood; in particular, the techniques of the blacksmiths were excellent.

According to socio-historical research conducted in this area in 1980, a farmer said that before 1949 a large quantity of raw iron was found and was carried away in two carts. Furthermore, after 1949 in the same area, much raw iron and iron slag was found. These material remains, including iron ingots, iron swords, iron tools, iron helmets, and iron files in a wide range of variety and quality, all of which can now be seen in the museum, indicate that the level of the iron technique among the Jürchen was very advanced (ibid.).

The fact is that in 1619 the historic war of Sarfû led to a change of dynasty in China, with the Ming being replaced by the Ching, who were in fact the Jürchen people led by Nurhaci (Kawauchi 1992). Their power was fully supported with iron weapons made by the Jürchen people.

The Jürchen iron industry progressed under Nurhaci's rule and his policy. Although the Ming dynasty and the Koreans had intended to control the Jürchen through the prohibition of iron, the end result was rather the opposite of their intentions and put them in a difficult position. The prohibition policy caused the Jürchen to develop their own iron industry to satisfy the demand for iron, instead of relying on the iron which they previously obtained from the Ming and Koreans.

(3) The case of the Emishi

According to Japanese historical documents, after the Taika Reform (645) the state-system became more systematically associated with a new departmental system of central government involved with the administration of the smallest units of local division. In 701, the Taiho Code (equivalent in some ways to Roman Law in Europe) was set up and implemented as administrative practice. This consisted of two parts, the Ritsu and the Ryo (Regulations and Code), and is

therefore called the Ritsu-Ryo system, and the state of that times is called the Ritsu-Ryo state (see Chapter 1).

By studying of the Ritsu-Ryo regulations it is possible to gain an insight into the peripheral situation and the interaction between those people who lived on the periphery and beyond the boundaries.

Among the regulations in the Ritsu-Ryo, in volume 10 of the Ryo, Article 27 for weapons under "*the rule of barriers and markets*" (Inoue et al. 1976) says: "arrows, bows and weapons are not allowed to be exchanged with foreigners. It is prohibited to place smelting installations in the East direction and the North direction". According to the interpretation of this rule by Inoue and others, this is a rule to "prohibit exchange of weapons with foreigners and the location of smelting installations in the East direction and the North direction" (ibid.). "The East periphery and the North periphery" means the peripheral area facing the Emishi. It also says "around what is called Mutsu and Dewa, etc." according to the "Old note" (i.e. annotation). The "Old note" (i.e. annotation) says for smelting installations "installations in which iron is smelted" (ibid. 442). According to the "Anaki" (i.e. annotation), "to prohibit iron smelting installations includes of course the transfer of iron technology and exchange of material made of metal" (ibid. 442). Thus, it is clear that there was an iron-prohibition policy against the Emishi, prohibiting smelting installations in the East and North peripheries. This implies that there must have been some reason to keep smelting techniques away from this peripheral zone of the Ritsu-Ryo state. My interpretation of this statement is that its existence obviously indicates that much iron material must have passed beyond the boundary of the state.

I assume that 'smelting installation' here implies iron smelting furnaces and the associated workshop area, and also includes craftspeople. The social precondition which led to the institution of the iron-prohibition policy in the Ritsu-Ryo state can be seen as a social phenomenon: namely that iron smelting furnaces were already in existence and iron was already being produced before the rule came into existence. However, there must have been some problem which was particularly connected with the smelting installations. This inconvenience must have led the Ritsu-Ryo state to institute the rule.

The prohibition of iron-smelting installations also implies that there are raw materials for producing iron near the border with the Emishi. It would be unnecessary to institute such a rule where there was no raw material for iron; besides, it is impossible to prohibit the existence of raw material as a natural resource. However, a natural resource in the area near the border with the Emishi can be shared equally with the Emishi. From the above, it is possible to assume that the purpose of the rule made by the Ritsu-Ryo state was either to control the technology which made it possible to produce iron, or to prevent the plunder of iron which was produced near the border. Thus, it would be a problem for the Ritsu-Ryo state if the Emishi acquired the iron-smelting technology of the Ritsu-Ryo state, and also if the iron produced was plundered by the Emishi, although raw materials for iron were found in the East and the North peripheries.

Since the iron technology prohibition was instituted by the Ritsu-Ryo state, social phenomena such as iron technology passing to the Emishi or iron being plundered by the Emishi must have been perceived by the Ritsu-Ryo state. If the Ritsu-Ryo state did not stop these phenomena, they would cause very serious problems. Thus as a social precondition for the iron technological prohibition, iron technology, or iron must have passed to the Emishi.

If the social phenomenon was that the Emishi wanted to have iron products, then the Emishi must have known already how to process iron; while if it was the technology, then the Emishi must have possessed iron smelting technology already by the 8th century, since the Ritsu-Ryo was instituted at the beginning of the 8th century. It follows that the Emishi could have mastered iron smelting technology as early as the 8th century.

As I have mentioned in the case of the Jürchen, craftspeople were captured in order to transmit technological processes; thus, a similar situation could have occurred in the Emishi case. For example, volume 6 of the Ryo, containing "the rule of living and habitat in the East direction" says "people who live on the periphery around the East, the North, and the West directions, should all live in 'saku' (hill forts)" (ibid.: 338). This rule was instituted under "*living on the periphery, agriculture, and repair of hill forts due to their security*" and to ensure that life on the periphery should be secure. This implies that there must have been reasons for insecurity, such as kidnapping.

Furthermore, contraband exchange occurred also in this case, as in the other cases. In 787, the Ritsu-Ryo government prohibited trade with the Emishi in the following terms: "it is forbidden both for government officers and farmers to exchange any goods with the Emishi" (*Ruiju sandai kyaku*, cited in Takahashi Takashi 1986:172). The existence of this renewed prohibition presupposes that contraband exchange had been carried out not only by farmers but also by government officers. Besides this, there were "pieces of cotton turned into the Emishi's clothes, iron armour processed into the Emishi's agricultural tools" (ibid. 173). This implies that the Emishi wanted to acquire agricultural tools, iron armour, and cloth. What the government officers and farmers wanted from the Emishi was horses and *nuhi* (the word can be translated as 'slaves' or 'servants' — a concept which needs to be defined within the framework of Japanese ancient history but will not be considered in this book). From this historical document, it is clear that the Emishi had already obtained iron and also the technique for processing iron products.

The above discussion can be correlated and evaluated with the archaeological evidence from the Tohoku area of northern Honshu. In particular, the recent discoveries of iron smelting, refining, and forging sites in the northern area of Akita-ken and also Iwate-ken dating from around the 8th century, and the associated studies based on archaeometallurgical analysis, corroborate my argument. These finds will be discussed detail in Chapter 4.

(4) The case of the Ainu

Although I mentioned elsewhere (Fukasawa 1989:251) my assumption, on the basis of the ancient historical documents discussed above that iron was prohibited in the Ainu culture, I was unable to find specific details of legislation to this effect in the official records of the Matsumae-Han (domain), which chronicle the history of the Matsumae family under the Tokugawa-Shogunal government in the 17th-18th centuries. However, I did find a statement in a travel diary written by Koshoken Furukawa (1788): "there is a rule made by the Matsumae that it was forbidden to give any kind of iron to the Ezo [Ainu], without permission; do not exchange or trade any kind of edged tool including those of iron and steel; these are strictly forbidden" (Furukawa 1788, modern version by Ofuji 1964). Thus I confirmed that there was a prohibition policy operated by the Matsumae. Moreover, I found the following sentence in the historical documents: "in old times, there were many edged tools, arms, and weapons, and also many other tools. These seemed to have been gradually brought in one after another from Japan. After an uprising by the Ezo [i.e. Shakushain's revolt in 1669], all the edged tools were completely taken away by the Matsumae" (*Kaifumaru Ezo Monsho* 1688, cited in Kodama 1971:459). It is, thus, clear that many iron tools and weapons existed in Ainu society before Shakushain's revolt in 1669; however, after this revolt the Matsumae executed the iron-prohibition policy with regard to the Ainu which prohibited the giving of any iron products to the Ainu.

The prohibition policy of the Matsumae was prompted by Shakushain's revolt. It is assumed as a social precondition that the Ainu used many iron weapons in this revolt, so the Matsumae perceived there was a dangerous situation in the increase of Ainu power based on the increased use of iron products and iron weapons which were supplied to the Ainu by trade. This social phenomenon, according to which iron products, or some associated technology, had been extended to Ainu society, is not contradicted by the archaeological evidence from the Saru area before 1667, which indicates the existence of iron-working hearths in the context of Ainu sites, as discussed in Chapter 5.

Further, Furukawa says:

> although it was strictly forbidden by the Matsumae to give iron material to the Ezo [Ainu], many iron products, including carpenters' tools, had been passing to the Ezo [Ainu] for a long time. Such products were always of low quality but when the Ezo [Ainu] received them they transformed them into ones of higher quality. It is difficult to believe this story, but I heard it from people who lived in the Matsumae territory, so I record this fact (Furukawa 1788, modern version by Ofuji 1964:166).

This historical document is very important for understanding the Ainu social phenomenon of iron technology within Ainu culture. The quotation ended: "It is difficult to believe this story but I heard it from the people who lived in the Matsumae territory so I record this fact". That Furukawa heard this in Matsumae is realistic. Moreover, from the statement that "although it was strictly forbidden by the Matsumae. . . . many iron products, including carpenters' tools, had been passing to the Ainu for a long time", it can be inferred that contraband exchange had occurred frequently and that there were people who did such things in secret in spite of the prohibition policy. Iron is a material which has always flowed in this way.

Further, the phase "when the Ainu received them they transformed them into ones of higher quality" can be interpreted as meaning that the Ainu could already transform dull, blunt, and low quality iron objects into higher quality iron, such as steel. Thus there were Ainu blacksmiths who had great knowledge of iron technology. Although Furukawa did not believe this story that he had heard in Matsumae, he honestly recorded the story as it was, even mentioning his opinion that he, as a representative of the Japanese at that time, did not believe the story. If the iron products made by the Ainu had been of low quality, as the Japanese expected, then no one would have talked about the quality of iron material made by the Ainu. It is logical to suppose that the only reason this story had become a rumour among the people in Matsumae is that the Ainu were able to transform low quality iron into iron of higher quality (for more detailed archaeological discussion of this is offered in Chapter 5).

Therefore, the prohibition on giving iron to the Ainu can be interpreted as a method of controlling the Ainu. Iron technology in the Ainu culture declined after the prohibition policy of the Matsumae as compared with previous times, leading to changes in Ainu society. However, there is a possibility that the technology with which the Ainu culture was already equipped was continued on a small-scale, or maybe in secret, with iron acquired through the contraband trade.

From the above four examples, it is clear that the iron-prohibition model is significant for perceiving certain social phenomena by analysing the interaction between different ethnic groups and central and peripheral peoples in order to understand both cultural contexts. Therefore, this model can be significant for archaeological interpretation in order to explain the process of social change by analysing archaeological data and then obtaining an understanding of substantive social phenomena.

2-4 Conclusion

I have built the prohibition model of cultivation and the prohibition model of iron for Ainu archaeology in order to interpret archaeological data and to confirm substantive social changes within Ainu culture by setting up a model which perceives social change as a social phenomenon.

The next consideration will be how to approach the matter archaeologically in order to explain and to understand the substantive nature of Ainu society through its material culture. The methodological approach to this question needs to be discussed in relation to Ainu archaeology. However, it raises questions to be solved in Ainu archaeology as well as in archaeology in general.

Chapter 3

Chronology and archaeological data in Hokkaido and Tohoku

3-1 Introduction

Having established the models for Ainu archaeology in the previous chapter, I would like now to focus on archaeological data.

The archaeological data which I examine in this study was obtained from excavations in Hokkaido and Tohoku. In this chapter I discuss the chronological sequence within which excavated sites can be correlated and dated by volcanic ash; the volcanoes erupted in historical times and the exact date of each ash fall can be determined. Discussion of the material culture is based upon these chronological sequences. A table for tephrochronology and the chronological sequence of Tohoku and Hokkaido is given at the end of this chapter (see Table 3-1). The excavated Ainu sites are correlated by the volcanic ash which fell in 1667. There is potential for understanding the Ainu culture before 1667, in the first half of the 17th century. It is most significant that this period predates the influence of the *Basho-Ukeoi* system discussed in Chapter 1. Hence this was a time before the Ainu culture was influenced by commercial capitalism.

It is very important to take into account cultural factors such as cultivation and the metal industry when considering cultural changes in Ainu society in terms of the models which I built in the previous chapter.

3-2 Chronology

There is no doubt that dating is the most important aspect of archaeology, whether it is absolute or relative. In Japan, which is a volcanic country, the method of tephrochronology has been studied for a long time in archaeology; it has been developed and applied to take advantage of the volcanic evidence. Areas have been correlated by the succession of volcanic ash deposits, so that it is fairly easy to understand chronological relationships and to correlate the existence of pumice or volcanic ash as very useful key layers within stratigraphic layers at site and to correlate among sites. Such pumice or volcanic ash studies involve quantitative analysis and are carried out by volcanic geologists. Various aspects, such as gravity, chemical components, and an index of refraction etc. in laboratories, as well as morphological features and observation in the field, are examined in order to identify the source volcano and the distribution of the same kind of ash across space.

Tephrochronology in Hokkaido, particularly in the south-west area of Hokkaido and the northern area of Tohoku, will be explained for understanding of chronological sequence of those areas (Tokui 1989:197). There are three main volcanic mountains in the south-west of Hokkaido, and ash has erupted from them in the past (see Fig. 3-1 a, b, and c). These eruptions can be identified to the exact year, having been recorded in Japanese historical documents. One of the big volcanic mountains which has erupted a number of times in history is Tarumae-san (1,024m). The volcanic ash from Tarumae in 1667 was found to cover a fairly large area up the east side of Hokkaido. This is called Tarumae-b (Ta-b), and

the upper layer of the ash from Tarumae in 1739 is called Tarumae-a (Ta-a). The volcanic ash from Usu-san (737m) in 1663 is called Usu-b2 (Us-b2). The ash from Komagatake (1,133m) in 1640 is called Komagatake-d2 (Ko-d2), and the 1694 ash is called Komagatake-c2 (Ko-c2).

It is very significant that the dating of each ash layer is identified at the site, so that structures at the site which are sandwiched between volcanic ash which originated in different eruptions can be identified and the duration of time at which these existed can be determined.

There is also an important deposit of volcanic ash which can be correlated in both Hokkaido and the Tohoku area of Honshu (Machida 1986). It erupted from the Changbaishan (Baegdusan) volcano, located on the Chinese-North Korean border. The ash from this large-scale eruption is called Baegdusan-Tomakomai ash (B-Tm) and is found widely spread over an area of $50km^3$ including northern Japan and the Sea of Japan (see Fig 3-2). The date of the eruption has been examined by stratigraphic observations and some radiocarbon determinations. It is also supported by chronological and archaeological data from north Japan, indicating that B-Tm ash occurred between 915 AD and 1334 AD (Machida et al. 1981). Recent archaeological data and its stratigraphic relations with the overlying 915 AD Towada ash from northern Tohoku suggest that the eruption occurred sometime in the 10th century (Machida 1986).

In northern Tohoku, ash layers which have been identified include that of Towada-a (To-a) ash, which is dated to 915; Akita Yakiyama ash, which was found covering a ditch at Shiwa-Jo (built in 803 AD) and is dated to 807, on the basis of a historical document; Izawa ash, which covers the remains of Izawa-Jo (built in 802 AD) and was deposited at the beginning of the 9th century (Inoue and Yamada 1982).

The dating of archaeological sites is correlated with evidence which is cross-checked with the stratigraphic observations associated with this ash and also with historical documents of between the 8th and 10th centuries relating to Tohoku, Honshu.

3-3 The Ainu culture in archaeology

3-3-1 Ainu archaeology

No historical documentation was recorded by the Ainu themselves because they had no written language. Tangible evidence available from them consists solely of their material culture as archaeological data, including artifacts and structures. It is appropriate to apply archaeological methods in order to set up a chronology of their material culture and reconstruct their society. There have been some attempts by archaeologists to define the concept of the Ainu culture from the archaeological point of view and to place the archaeological cultures in Hokkaido in a chronological order. Notable work has been done by Utagawa (Utagawa 1988), Koshida (Koshida 1988), Kono (Explanation panel at Utari association, Sapporo), and Nishimoto (Nishimoto 1989).

Within the archaeological sequence of cultures in Hokkaido, the emergence of the Ainu culture is recognised after the disappearance of Satsumon pottery, although it is still not certain when the Satsumon period terminated on account of regional differences. It is considered to have ended about the 11th or the 12th century (Kikuchi 1980, Miura 1991). The Satsumon culture, which precedes the Ainu culture in archaeological terms, is equivalent to the pre-medieval period in Japanese history. The Ainu culture in archaeology is set within the medieval and modern period of Japanese history. This periodisation is valid in Japanese history and it is applied appropriately to the Ainu as well, because it would be difficult to discuss the Ainu without taking account of cultural contact with the Japanese culture and its historical change. The people who produced the Ainu culture were the immediate ancestors of the present Ainu. Ainu archaeology seeks the significance of cultural changes and cultural contacts through historical change and attempts to reconstruct Ainu society.

3-3-2 The material culture of Ainu archaeology

Relatively numerous Ainu sites such as *chashi* (i.e. a place which is divided by a man-made structure such as a ditch or conveniently located on a higher level geologically; its function is still debatable as it had multiple functions), burials, and shell mounds have been found. The recent large-scale excavations at *chashi* and settlements have revealed Ainu material such as houses with central hearths, forging hearths, heaps of small pebbles, animal remains, and other organic remains such as millet, barn-yard millet (Japanese millet), and rice. These data can be useful for understanding the structure of the village and for reconstructing the social side of Ainu culture, although they are insufficient to allow complete reconstruction. Volcanic ash (Tarumae-b; Ta-b), which fell in 1667 and covered a fairly large area up the east side of Hokkaido was found especially in the area of Chitose and Hidaka.

The basic material culture which defines the archaeological concept of the Ainu culture was divided into two categories by Hiroshi Utagawa. One is "material of the Ainu's own making" and the other is "material of Japanese making and distributed to the northern area" (Utagawa 1989). However, I would like to suggest a further category: that of material which was modified by the Ainu; this I term the "material of the Ainu's own processing". Hence I categorise three types of basic material culture which define the concept of Ainu culture. There are two reasons why I have created a third category, "material of the Ainu's own processing". One reason is that the cultural context in which each artifact was used is significant. The second reason is that the technical context — that is, the processing technology used in the Ainu culture — is significant. It is important to understand archaeologically these cultural factors in the Ainu culture.

Material of the Ainu's own processing is that material which lost its original meaning when used in the Ainu cultural context and was transformed by Ainu techniques. For example, the *tamasai* (necklace) uses an ornament which was originally a *wa-kyo* (Japanese mirror); coins also became ornaments in the Ainu culture, and the top of a hoe became a chisel, and so on. It is necessary to deal separately with processed goods and the processing of material, but I shall discuss this point in Chapter 5.

Material of the Ainu's own making is that material which originated within the Ainu culture or was transmitted as a tradition from the previous culture, and includes, for example, clay pots with inside hook handles, small clay balls, tuyeres, *makiri* (small knives), *kite* (fishing tools), *marekku* or *marec* (fishing tools), bone tools, hooks, *pipa* (cultivation tools), and *pi* (weaving tools).

Within the category of material imported by the Ainu, there is a difference between imported goods that the Ainu kept as treasure and the goods which they used in the same context as in the culture from which they originated. For example, goods with the same use were iron pots with inside hook handles, iron pots with hanging hooks, a coarse type of china ware, porcelain, beads, and *kiseru* (pipes); objects kept as treasure include lacquered wares.

The concept of the Ainu culture in archaeology is defined by the assemblage of these artifacts and their cultural context. It needs to be examined whether some artifacts can be traced back to the culture which existed before the formation of the Ainu culture.

3-4 The relationship between the Ainu culture and the Satsumon culture

The cultural change from the Satsumon to the Ainu has long been a problem, due to the fact that the archaeological evidence for each culture is very different. For example, the type of house structure is very different: there is a square-shaped dwelling pit with oven and chimney in the Satsumon culture and a square-shaped house built on the ground surface like a hut in the Ainu culture. The archaeological record does not clearly show continuity between the Ainu culture and the Satsumon culture. Moreover, there is no archaeological evidence recorded so far which can be dated to the 14th and 15th centuries.

As the study of the Satsumon progresses, it is gradually being understood that highly suggestive links in material culture do exist between the Satsumon and the Ainu. This material is especially related to fishing equipment, as most settlement sites of the Satsumon culture are found beside rivers. For instance, implements called *marekku* or *marec* (fishing tools) in the Ainu culture have been found in a very similar form in the Satsumon culture (the Sakushukotoni site, the Toyotomi site, etc.). *Teshi* is a type of fish trap made in a river, consisting of posts set in a line across a river in order to catch anadromous fishes (salmon and trout) in the Ainu culture. A structure which has exactly the same form as a *teshi* trap was found at a site of the Satsumon culture (the Sakushukotoni site). At this site, a *marec*, mentioned above, was also found. It is suggested that this fishing method, used in the Ainu culture, can be traced back to the Satsumon culture, and its existence is indicated by the presence of the *teshi* and *marec* as a set (Yokoyama 1990).

The process of changing from the dwelling pit to the surface house can be seen by analysing the overlapping structures which were found at the Satsumae site. The dwelling pit in the Satsumon culture is very similar in type to that associated with the Haji culture in Tohoku: an oven and chimney occur in a rectangular dwelling. Many organic remains, comprising cultivated products such as millet, Japanese millet, Indian millet, buckwheat, and beans are found within the dwelling pit.

The Satsumon culture is characterised by the disappearance of stone tools and the increasing use of iron products. Most iron products have been recovered from burials as grave goods. Among these burial goods, sickles, hoes, and spades (which indicate cultivation) are found. It is interesting to note this fact when considering the character of the Satsumon culture.

In spite of research on cultivation in the Ainu culture carried out by Yoshishige Hayashi (Hayashi 1969), cultivation as a cultural factor of the Ainu has not been significantly assessed, and it has been thought that the Ainu culture is defined rather by the disappearance of cultivation than by its existence. However, the cultivation prohibition model, discussed in Chapter 2, is corroborated by the results from a recent excavation at the Pipaushi site, which revealed that the cultivated millet found at this 17th-century Ainu site was exactly the same type of cultivated millet which was found at the end of the Satsumon culture (the Okawa site), (Yamada and Tsubakizaka, forthcoming). This can be interpreted as demonstrating that cultivation continued from the Satsumon culture until at least the 17th century in the Ainu culture. This indicates that cultivation as a cultural factor was intentionally suppressed by the Japanese.

Cultivated millet (*Echinochloa utilis=Nanbu-bie*) was found as the result of flotation at the sites of Okawa and Pipaushi. The flotation technique in Japan has been developed since 1971 (Tokyo-to Kyoiku-iinkai, cf. the site reports of Nakazanya: 1973, Maehara: 1975, and Shinbashi: 1977), beginning immediately after the publication of Higgs's *Paleoeconomy* (Higgs 1971). It is now used on many excavations in most parts of Japan, particularly in Hokkaido, and provides us with many interesting results.

Many organic remains, comprising cultivated products such as millet, broomcorn millet (*Panicum miliaceum*), Indian millet (*Holcus sorghum*), foxtail millet (*Setaria italica* Beauv.) buckwheat, barley, and beans, have been found within excavated Satsumon dwelling pits, demonstrating cultivation (Crawford and Yoshizaki 1987). The results from the excavation at the Pipaushi site, an Ainu site of 17th-century date, revealed a similar kind of complex of cultivated seeds of the Satsumon culture: finds included millet, broomcorn millet (*Panicum miliaceum*), Indian millet (*Holcus sorghum*), foxtail millet (*Setaria italica* Beauv.), and beans (*leguminosae*). Buckwheat and barley were not found yet, however (Yamada and Tsubakizaka, forthcoming).

The evidence from oral tradition, a story of Okikurumi, has been virtually ignored. The story narrates that Okikurumi stole seeds of millet when he came down to our world from the holy land. Therefore, millets were cultivated from the time of the creation of the Ainu world. And also in Ainu belief, millets are symbolised as marital foods and are linked to a genesis myth (Yahata 1956).

Many iron products have been found in excavations of Satsumon sites (Kikuchi 1979, Amano 1983, Segawa 1989). These iron products include knives, arrowheads, swords, axes, sickles, spades, drills, needles, ornaments, pieces of iron, pieces of iron pot, and fishing hooks. The estimated quantity of iron in the Satsumon culture might be calculated from the number of dwelling pits and the amount of iron each household possessed. It has been calculated that almost 90 kg of iron was consumed per year in the Satsumon culture, a figure which converts into 3600 small knives (*makiri*) and 100 axes (Amano 1989).

The increased use of iron in the Satsumon culture can be demonstrated by the existence of evidence for iron technology in the form of hearths, tuyeres, slag, and by-products of the forging technique such as hammering scale found at sites. It is recognised that tuyeres in the Satsumon bear the same decorative pattern as on the Satsumon pottery (the Horonaipo site). It is possible to see chronological change in tuyeres within the Satsumon, and tuyeres used in the later stage of the Satsumon (the Okawa site) is typologically very similar to the tuyeres which were found at an Ainu site of 17th-century date (the Pipaushi site). A more detailed discussion of this will be given in Chapter 4. At the sites of Okawa and Pipaushi, the same type of cultivated millet (*Echinochloa utilis=Nanbu-bie*) was found, as noted above. This suggests that there is a possibility of continuity in respect of iron technology, as well as the existence of cultivation.

3-5 The Satsumon culture

The Satsumon culture is defined by the existence of Satsumon pottery. The form of Satsumon pottery exhibits a combination of two different types of pottery: one retains the tradition of Haji pottery as regards vessel shape and techniques of manufacture, while the other retains the Zoku-Jomon pottery tradition as regards decoration, having lines, parallel lines, and geometric and incised patterns. This means that these cultures influenced each other.

The emergence of Satsumon pottery occurred around the 8th century (Kikuchi 1989). It is very similar to Haji pottery, not only in shape and method of manufacture but also in the presence of a set of vessels like pots, jars, pedestaled bowls, and unfooted bowls. This assemblage indicates strong Haji influence, since a similar set occurs in Haji pottery. The similar structure of dwellings also demonstrates influence.

In the period of the Satsumon culture, along the lowlands of the Ishikari River there were burials called the "Hokkaido Kofun" type (Ishizuki 1962). They consist of mounds, but the central part of the mound is just a burial pit of a square shape. It was pointed out that this type of burial is very similar to the type found in the north part of the Tohoku area, in the last stage of the Kofun period (around the 7th-8th centuries), and the burial goods which were found in both types of burial are very similar, too (Ishizuki 1966). They include iron products such as sickles, *warabiteto* (i.e. swords with fern-frond-shaped handles) and knives. Furthermore, in the lowlands of the Ishikari River there is another type of burial characterised by only a burial pit and no mound but exactly the same type of burial goods, including Zoku-Jomon pottery. The affinities of the people who were buried in these burials and what kind of cultures they belonged to are still problematic.

From all these aspects, it is possible to understand that the Satsumon culture and the Haji culture of Tohoku had strong cultural contact and influenced each other.

The distribution of Satsumon pottery covers the whole of Hokkaido except the Shiretoko peninsula, and the north part of Tohoku (Yokoyama 1990), especially down to the Yoneshiro River (Akita-ken) on the Japan Sea side and the Mabuchi River (the border between Aomori-ken and Iwate-ken) on the Pacific Ocean side.

3-6 The material culture of the Tohoku area in the 8th-10th centuries

The diffusion of Haji ware in the Tohoku region occurred during the stage of non-wheelmade Haji, which is characterised by incised lines at the neck of the Haji vessel shape. It is called the first type of Sakurai (equivalent to Kokubunji lower type in southern Tohoku) in the chronological sequence established by Kiyohiko Sakurai (Sakurai 1979). The existence of the pottery, which has marks of unhulled grain on the bottom, and also the presence of carbonised rice, indicate that the subsistence base involved rice cultivation. Satsumon pottery is also associated with these Haji settlements. In Hokkaido, Satsumon settlements are mainly composed of Satsumon pottery with some associated Haji ware; on the other hand, in Tohoku, the settlements were composed mainly of Haji ware, but some sites had associated Satsumon pottery as well. The existence of Satsumon pottery marked with unhulled grain on the bottom (the Yomogida-Odate site, the Tsuijikan site) indicate that this Satsumon pottery was probably made in Tohoku because evidence for rice cultivation has not been found in Hokkaido. Although the existence of rice was known in Hokkaido, it is unlikely that Satsumon pottery with marks of unhulled grain on the bottom was produced there and brought into Tohoku.

According to the results of recent excavations, settlement sites consisting of 15-16 dwellings have been found and, among those, two types of settlement can be recognised from analysis of the structure of the dwellings. One type indicates sedentary settlement of long duration, and the other indicates short-term settlement. The short-term settlement can be interpreted as based on non-rice cultivation, but cereal cultivation is indicated because millets, rape, and *shiso* are found, as well as a small amount of rice (Miura 1991).

The percentage of iron artifacts among all those recovered from settlement sites by excavations in Akita-ken is as follows: 25% of all artifacts from the 8th-9th-century sites are iron, 78% of all artifacts from the 10th-century sites are iron, and 90% of all artifacts from the 11th-century sites are iron. According to a proportional increase through time, the uses of iron artifacts shows that the proportion of cultivation tools is very high (Kumagaya 1989). These results may be explained by the fact that a number of iron-working sites have been found, including not only forging sites but also production sites. The distribution of iron production sites in Tohoku covers the area of central Akita-ken (the Sakanoue-E

site) an up-river district (the Samukawa site), and the lower reaches (the Kanninzawa site) of the Yoneshiro River, at the foot of Mt. Iwaki in Tsugaru district, Aomori-ken (the Mokusawa site, the Ohirano site), and the coast of Iwate-ken (the Wandai site, the Kamimura site). These sites are located in areas beyond the Ritsu-Ryo system. This means that iron production was being practised by people who lived outside the Ritsu-Ryo system.

These furnaces are classified as semi-underground shaft-type (see Glossary), which are found mostly in the north-east part of Japan. Some differences among the sites can be seen, such as the numbers of furnaces and associated facilities. Satsumon pottery was found at the Mokusawa site; however, the Satsumon sites in Hokkaido which have produced evidence of iron production have only the forging hearth, forging equipment such as tuyeres, and by-products of the forging technique, such as slag and hammering scale. There are no records of iron production sites in the Satsumon proper. This implies that the scale of production and operation were different and could reflect different social contexts in the area. A society which needs iron as a production system and a society which needs iron as a processing system constitute very different social contexts. It follows that the Satsumon culture and the Haji culture exhibit different social contexts, although there some characteristics were shared. A more detailed discussion and examination is given in Chapter 4.

3-7 Conclusion

Taking account of the background of the material culture in Tohoku and Hokkaido in terms of cultural contact and transformation of the material culture, data from recent excavations may be used to challenge previous views of Ainu culture as well as the theoretical framework.

The emergence of the Ainu culture is recognised after the disappearance of Satsumon pottery. Such an approach to the concept of culture forms the basis of much archaeological thought in Japan, since the disappearance of pottery in archaeology implies that the concept of culture, which is elaborated by all kinds of information including artifacts and structures associated with that pottery, has changed. Thus, an archaeological culture is a cultural identity which can be recognised from the distinctive features of archaeological material such as pottery (Childe 1956).

However, this definition of culture has been shifted to a concept of culture which includes the common code of a people based on the intentions of human agency who acted and presented that action within a society (Hodder 1982). Under these circumstances, I consider that the concept of culture of the Satsumon and of the Ainu in the context of Hokkaido archaeology to be in question and that there is a need to reconsider it within a current theoretical framework. I therefore attempt to change this idea in order to create a new interpretation of the concept of this cultural distinction in Chapter 8.

By looking at this archaeological evidence, which indicates some continuity from the Satsumon to the Ainu, it may be possible to define the Satsumon culture as a proto-type of the Ainu culture.

Fig. 3-1-a   A distribution map of Tarumae-b (Ta-b: 1667) (after Tokui 1989:199).

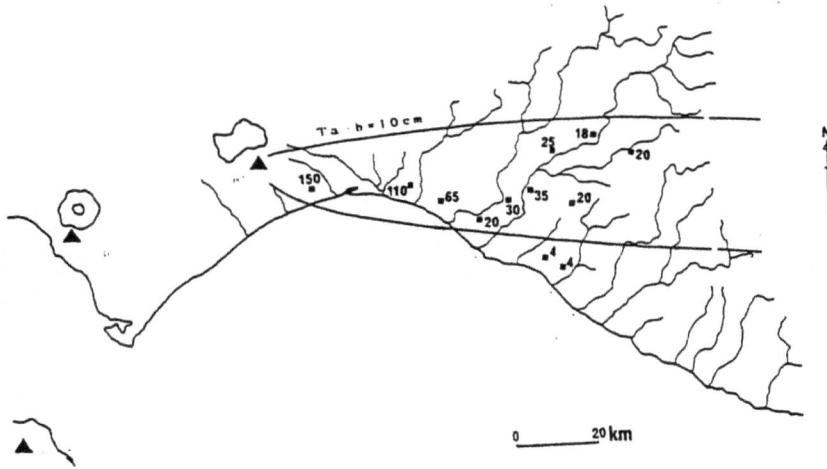

Fig. 3-1-b   A distribution map of Tarumae-a (Ta-a:1739) and Komagatake-c2 (Koc2:1694) (after Tokui 1989:201). :
Ta-a and Ko-c2 are found. : Ta-a is found. : Ko-c2 is found.
* indicates mountains.
1. Komagatake, 2. Tarumaesan, 3. Tokachidake, 4. Asahidake, 5. Meakandake

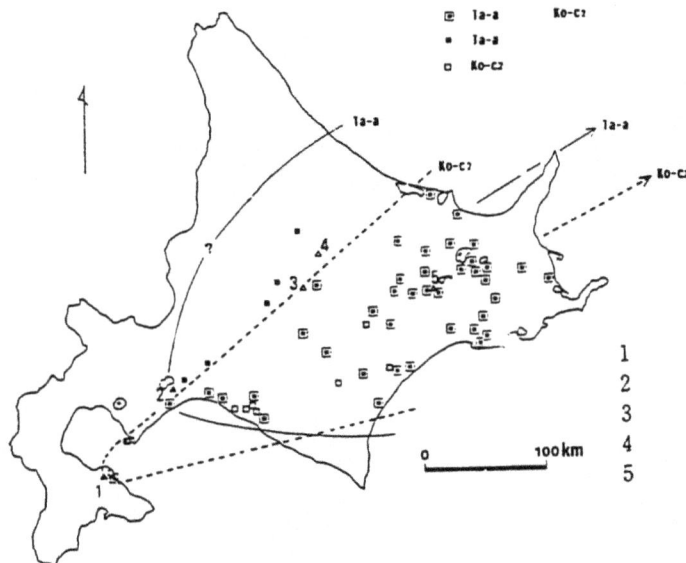

Fig. 3-1-c   A distribution map of Usu-b (Us-b: 1663) (after Tokui (1989:202).
              Figures refer to the thickness of this pumice.

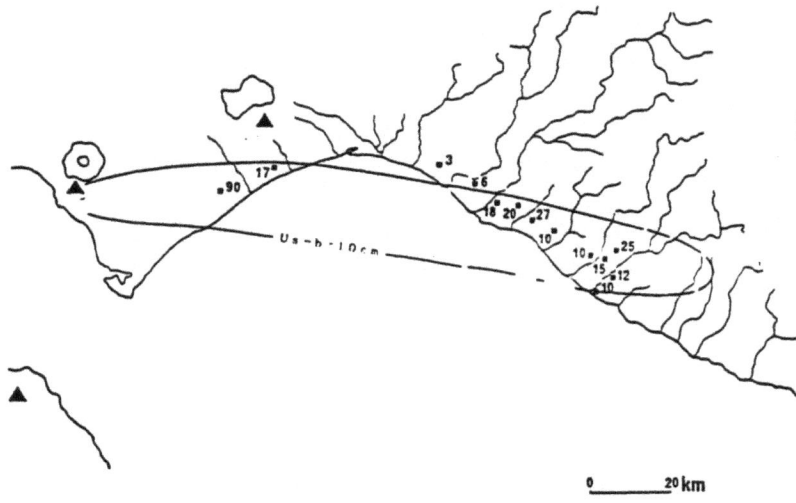

Fig. 3-2   A distribution map of Baegudusan-Tomakomai ash (B-Tm) (after Machida 1986).

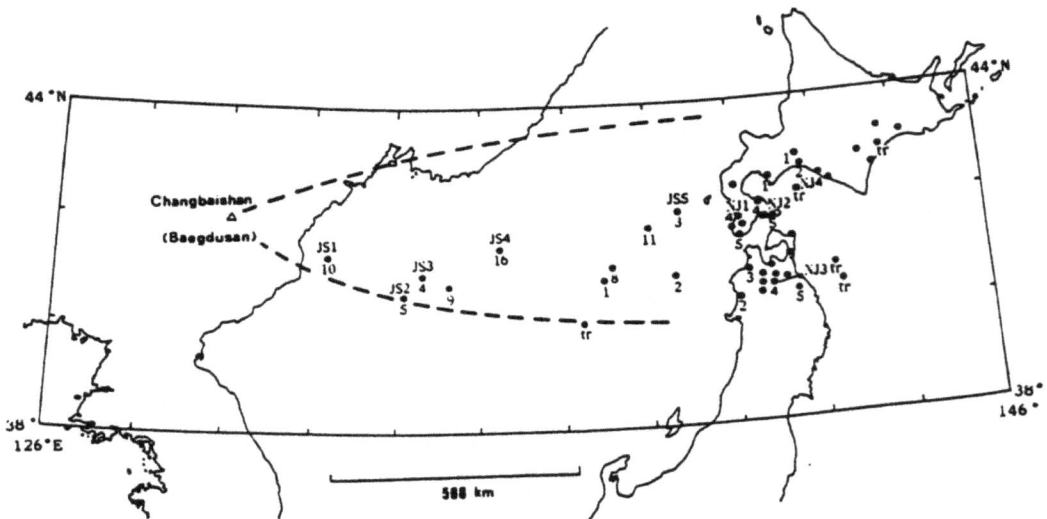

Table 3-1

Tephrochronology and the chronological sequences of Tohoku and Hokkaido

	Tohoku		Hokkaido	
20C	**Tohoku**	|	**Hokkaido**	
	Japanese		Japanese	Ainu

----------M E I J I---G O V E R N M E N T (1868)-------------

19C		|	**Ezo-island**	
	Wajin	|	Wajin	Ezo
18C		|Tarumae-a (1739)		Osatsu site (Ainu)
				Bibi-8 site (Ainu)
		|Komagatake-c2 (1694)		
		|*TARUMAE-b (1667)*		Yukanboshi site (Ainu)
17C		| *USU-b (1663)*		Pipaushi site (Ainu)
		|		Iruekashi site (Ainu)
				Yuoi and Poromoi site (Ainu)
16C		|Kaminokuni site (Wajin)(Ainu)		
15C		|Shinori site (Wajin)		
14C		|Sunadate site (Wajin)		
13C	Sakaizeki site	|		Okawa site (Satsumon)
		|		Aonae site (Satsumon)
		|		
12C	Namioka-Jo	|		Satsumae site (Satsumon)
11C	Furudate site			
				Suehiro site IH-35 (Satsumon)
	Yomogida site (Haji&Satsumon)|			Suehiro site IH-93 (Satsumon)
	Mokusawa site (Haji&Satsumon)|			Satsumae site-36 (Satsumon)

Hakutousan-Tomakomai-ash(10c-11c)

10C	Asahiyama site	|		
	Kumanodo site	|		
Towada-a-ash (10c-11c)		|		
Akitayakiyama-pumice (9c-10c)|				
Izawa-ash (9c)		|		
	Shiwa-Jo(R) Nagase site(NR)	|		Ranshima site (Satsumon)
9C	Izawa-Jo(R) Sekizawaguchi site	|		
		|		Nakajimamatsu site (Satsumon)
8C	Taga-Jo (Ritsu-Ryou state)	|		

27

Chapter 4

Discussion of iron technology in the Hokkaido and Tohoku districts in relation to Ainu iron technology

4-1 Introduction

This discussion of iron metallurgy is placed within the context of one of the three categories of Ainu material culture which I defined in Chapter 3, the category of material which was modified by the Ainu; this I termed "material of the Ainu's own processing".

The technical context — that is the processing technology used in the Ainu culture — is significant. It is important to understand archaeologically these cultural factors in Ainu society.

Until recently, there was no archaeological evidence for whether or not metal technology existed in Ainu culture, although iron materials do exist which were obtained through direct and indirect contacts with other cultures. These materials were thus thought to be present in the Ainu context as a result of trade. Because of this, and also because of the lack of historical documents which refer to Ainu metal technology, or because of the lack of any real assessment of its existence, it had been thought that the Ainu did not practise metal technology despite the fact there is already some evidence for metal technology in the form of iron products, slag, tuyeres and so on in the preceding Satsumon culture in the Hokkaido chronological sequence, as discussed in Chapter 3.

The data in this study, which were provided by the excavation in the Saru River valley carried out by the author at Nibutani village, Biratori-cho, Hokkaido, in 1988 and 1990, have led to a reconsideration of the previous interpretation of the Ainu culture. I would like to examine the question of how and when metal technology entered the Ainu culture and also try to reconstruct the Ainu metal technology from the results of metallurgical analyses, discussing them in relation to Ainu society.

For this reason, I have to expand my field of study in time and space in order to understand the technological context within the historical context and the chronological sequence and the cultural contact between the Ainu and outsiders. Thus, the preceding Satsumon culture (from approximately the 8th century to the 11th-12th centuries) in Hokkaido and the Japanese culture from the 8th century to the 15th-16th centuries in Tohoku are taken into account in the discussion. In this chapter, I discuss how I approach iron technology and the difficulties of reconstructing iron technology, and also the peripheral factors affecting Ainu iron technology. I have also attempted to create a hypothetical reconstruction of the distribution network based on the present understanding of the study of iron technology and its interpretation at the end of this chapter (see Flow diagram 4-1). Although Flow diagram 4-1 associated with the Ainu iron technology, the main discussion of Ainu iron technology is in Chapter 5.

4-2 Iron technology and difficulties inherent in its study

To study technology which reflects the economic and social structure, one needs to understand the whole structure of the material culture, including the process of raw material — production — consumption. A technology functions between raw material and production, and distribution functions between production and consumption within material culture (cf. Leroi-Gourhan 1964). Moreover, a processing technology can be encountered in the use of secondary material for reprocessing to make new objects for consumption. From this perspective on the material culture, the present study takes into account processing technology from the aspects of technology and distribution.

The reason why iron technology is of such significance for indicating social aspects of society is that it reflects a complex combination of the technological, economic and sociological factors which I mentioned above. Although iron technology is a social factor which is of significance as an indicator of certain aspects of culture, it is difficult to reconstruct this a technology from the archaeological evidence available at the beginning of this research. Two aspects of history should be taken into account. One is iron technology as a complete process in a system, from which it is possible to reconstruct the progress of or the diversity of the history of technology. The other is localised uniqueness, which is a result of a combination of the availability of raw material, and the adaptability and manipulation of the technological process, from which it is possible to reconstruct the cultural side of history (Iida 1982a).

As a result of the combination of the above aspects, a great diversity of techniques is used in iron-production around the world which may still not be fully known. Therefore, iron technology needs to be examined by dealing with those aspects which form an interface between technology and local culture.

Moreover, because of the great diversity of iron technology, there are also different frameworks for study which are based on the tradition and history of iron-production. In particular, terms and definitions which are used in metallurgy do not correlate directly between countries. For example, cast iron could not be produced in Europe until the 14th century, due to the structure of the furnaces used, whilst in China a casting method was used as early as 600 BC (Hara 1988). To understand the cultural side of history, its technological process needs to be explained as precisely as possible. I try to explain Japanese terms by English terms in using parentheses, the words within them indicating English terminology. However, it is very confusing that the terms used in English do not seem to correlate well with terms used in Japanese iron technology; this is because the terms and definitions used in Japan are based on Japanese iron technology, and archaeological interpretations of iron technology in Japanese archaeology are different from those of both China and the West. Therefore, traditional terms and definitions which may be difficult to express in English within the western framework will be used to explain the iron technology in this study.

For example, in the Japanese case, when technological aspects are taken into account for reconstruction of the iron-production process within an archaeological and historical framework, the ideas and terminology relating to the traditional technological process, *tatara* iron-production, are commonly used even though modern Western metallurgy was introduced in the 19th century and the traditional Japanese method was completely replaced by it for industrial production. This change within Japanese iron technology also causes difficulties in Japanese archaeometallurgy because the traditional method is no longer practised. Furthermore, earlier ancient types of iron technology, studied archaeologically from which the *tatara* method might have derived, can be expected to be more difficult to reconstruct than the traditional *tatara* method. Modern Japanese metallurgists still have difficulties in reconstructing fully the process of this traditional and earlier ancient iron technology in Japan.

The reconstruction of the iron technology of the prehistoric and historical periods in Japan has been conducted since the beginning of the 20th century, especially on the basis of iron artefacts such as the Japanese sword and raw material such as iron ingots which were found in tombs. The *tatara* method, which was the traditional iron-production method using iron sand in the 18th century, has been studied in order to reconstruct the process of iron-production (Iida 1982 b).

Since 1957, under the aegis of the Tatara Study Society, which is an interdisciplinary society established to study traditional Japanese smelting methods, research has involved metallurgy, history and archaeology. However, the term archaeometallurgy, which in Japan is based on a scientific analytical approach in post excavation archaeological study, has not been considered part of archaeological study, so that most analytical work has been undertaken by metallurgical scientists who work in the field of the history of metallurgy or who are interested in its history. Although archaeometallurgy is part of archaeology, which should take this aspect seriously into account, the archaeological approach does not fully integrate the process of archaeometallurgy into Japanese archaeology. 'Archaeological' here means results from empirical, morphological and typological studies of material associated with other archaeological contexts. On the other hand, 'archeometallurgical' here means study based on the result of metallurgical analysis such as chemical composition and metallographical examination. Therefore, comprehensive and systematic interdisciplinary studies of archaeometallurgy need to be fully expressed in Japanese archaeology. In the discussion of my approach, the archaeological and archaeometallurgical aspects will be dealt with separately. The reason the discussion is ordered in this way is that it demonstrates the significance of carrying out archaeometallurgical analysis for the interpretation of archaeological sites and evidence.

The geographical area studied, which provides evidence resulting in the advance of the study, is the western part of Japan, since the density of evidence such as iron objects from tombs and *tatara* sites is higher than in the eastern part of Japan. In contrast, in the area of the present study, which covers Hokkaido and Tohoku in north-eastern Japan, there are not many sites identified as iron-production sites (these are located only in Tohoku), although there are many sites at which artefacts associated with iron-production, such as tuyeres (see Glossary), have been found. This may imply that evidence remains to be discovered in eastern Japan.

Under these circumstances, I would like to discuss how the question can be approached in order to understand iron technology in Japan.

4-3 The evidence of iron technology at sites

Although it is not always easy to interpret pieces of evidence from excavations, the existence of a set of data such as a hearth, tuyeres, slag, hammer scale, etc. can be recognised as resulting from some form of activity relating to iron technology, as the whole process of iron-production is known at present, such as smelting, refining, casting, and forging. These four different processes may be regarded as the basis of the iron-production process (Table 4-1).

Smelting is an iron-production process, proceeding from the raw material of iron, such as iron ore and iron sand, to iron. Refining is a fining process which produces steel. Casting is an iron-production method which is carried out by pouring iron in an molten state into a mould. Forging is an iron-shaping method which is carried out by hammering softer iron.

It should be possible to recognise the kind of evidence which is the result of carrying out each of these processes in iron technology. Evidence from archaeological sites can be discussed and compared with these processes in order to reconstruct the technology which might have been carried on at the site. It should be possible at least to interpret the evidence as indicating that one site could be a smelting site or another could be a forging site, etc.

The basic requirements of the process of iron-production include not only the evidence which may be expected to survive at sites, but also archaeologically invisible aspects that have to be considered such as water, air, labour and transport for distribution, which have to be taken into account. However, I shall concentrate particularly on the direct evidence obtained from archaeological sites in this study.

4-3-1 The basic evidence for identifying the iron-working sites

The basic evidence for the process of iron-production is as follows: raw materials for iron, such as iron ore and iron sand. Secondary raw materials are items such as iron ingots, iron bars, a lump of iron, pieces of iron, nails, and so on. Fuel is material such as charcoal or coal. Although I concentrate particularly on the evidence of the type of the hearth present, furnace types include the Tatara furnace, box type furnace, semi-underground shaft type and forging type which I call a hole-in-the-ground type. Tuyeres, which normally occur as incomplete items, i.e. as shards of tuyeres, are counted. Craft tools include moulds, crucibles, anvils, hammers, tongs, whetstones and so on. By-products comprise material such as slag, including the flowed type, tap slag, and a bottom-of-bowl-shaped slag and hammer scale. Additives such as shell and ash are also included. These basic requirements as evidence for the process of iron-production are listed in Table 4-1. This indicates where these factors are present or absent in each metallurgical process, and they are next considered individually in detail.

Table 4-1   The basic evidence for identifying iron-working on sites in Japan.

Numbers in parentheses refer to the numbers in Table 4-2 [referring to the types of evidence for iron technology].

Factors	Smelting	Refining	Casting	Forging
(1) Raw material	√			
(2) Sec. Raw material		√	√	√
(3) Fuel	√	√	√	√
(4) Tatara furnace	√			
Shaft furnace	√	√	√	
Hearth		√		√
(5) Tuyeres	√	√	√	√
(6) Craft tools	√	√	√	√
mould			√	
crucibles			√	
anvil		√		√
hammers		√		√
tongs		√		√
whetstones				√
(7) Slag	√	√	√	√
flowed type, tap slag	√			
bowl-bottom slag		√		√
(8) Hammer scale		√		√
(9) Additives		√		√

(1) Raw material for iron

In Japanese metallurgy, ore was mainly divided into two categories according to the size of ore, rock type, and sand type. In this book, the term 'iron ore' means rock origin, and 'iron sand' means sand origin.

Both iron ore and iron sand were used as raw material for producing iron in Japan. Of these, iron sand was frequently used as a raw material. This is the most characteristic feature of iron-production in Japan. Iron sand was classified into three types — mountain iron sand, river iron sand, and beach iron sand — according to the environment in which it was found. In ancient times, iron sand was obtained mainly from recent river and beach deposits, whilst mountain iron sand was obtained by the specific-gravity method using water, called *kan na nagashi* (Hayama 1992).

(2) Secondary raw material: Iron products as iron source material

Secondary raw material can be divided into two categories: on the one hand, there is basic material such as iron ingots, iron bars, or a lump of iron which might be distributed as a form of raw material for producing iron products. On the other hand, there are some other iron products which also might have been used as a source of iron material; these were probably made of wrought iron and include such things as nails, armor scales, clamps, and miscellaneous pieces of iron such as shaped bars and plates. These might have been refined and some made into small iron products such as knives, daggers, and fish hooks. In an area where it is difficult to obtain smelted iron locally, an external source of iron material might be used pieces of iron products which had been imported or collected for the reworking of iron objects.

The possibility of material for reworking derived from pieces of cast iron pots must be considered as well. Therefore, the origin of iron material needs to be investigated.

(3) Charcoal

Charcoal as a fuel is an important factor in all metallurgical processes: smelting, refining, casting, and forging. There is evidence for charcoal production near the iron-production furnaces, such as charcoal kilns which have many local variations. The concentration of charcoal or a pile of charcoal as fuel near the forging hearth is also an important factor in the forging process. From the study of charcoal it is possible to determine the species of tree used to produce it, and hence its place of origin. Systematic iron-production indicates the selection of charcoal from a region, and it might be possible to see some kind of trade. In the case of *tatara* smelting, pine charcoal was particularly selected, and the area where it was produced is known.

(4) Furnace/Hearth

The evidence from furnace or hearths is the most important information for understanding iron technology, as all metallurgical processes require either a furnace or a hearth. Their structural function is clearly different, so it is easy to determine which process might have been used: at least it is possible to identify whether smelting or forging took place.

However, the process of refining might require both types. The degree of development of iron technology from a primitive stage to a more advanced stage, or complexity of technology can be seen in the different types of hearth: the location of a hearth at a site, whether it is within a dwelling or open field, indicates the character of the site and the degree of specialisation. The size of the hearth and the frequency of its use are good indications of function, from which to interpret whether it was used as a smelting furnace, a melting furnace, refining furnace, refining hearth, or forging hearth etc. The number of furnaces/hearths indicates the scale of activities and so helps to determine the functions of sites. Therefore, the evidence from furnaces/hearths is the most reliable for identifying the process of metallurgy.

(5) Tuyeres

Tuyeres are attachments to bellows which blow the air into furnaces or hearths. Since all metallurgical processes require air, tuyeres are used in all metallurgical processes: smelting, refining, casting, and smithing. They are the item most frequently found in archaeological excavations, so they are good indicators of the existence of any metallurgical process, although they are usually found in fragments. Different shapes of tuyere may indicate use in different processes. Complete shapes of tuyeres can be reconstructed by refitting the pieces of tuyeres. Counting the number of diagnostic parts of the tuyeres indicates the number of tuyeres used. The useful life of a tuyere depends on the process carried out; if the process of producing iron was associated with a very high temperature, then the rate of attrition is very high. It is possible to estimate the frequency of use and the period of use of the hearth by qualitative analyses of tuyeres, and it is also possible to estimate the complexity of the iron-working process at the forging hearth by quantitative analyses. For example, tuyeres can be made of clay mixed with a grass temper in order to make them stronger, i.e. less subject to thermal shock, and this thick type of tuyere indicates the existence of an iron-working technique which requires a high temperature.

(6) Craft tools

Different types of craft tools need to be used in all metallurgical processes: smelting, refining, casting, and smithing. The existence of craft tools and tools associated with iron-working at sites is a significant indication of iron-working sites.

However, particular types of tools are associated with the certain specific processes. If tools such as anvils, hammers, tongs, rasps, and chisels and whetstones are found, the site might have been for the process of forging. If it was a site related to the process of casting iron, moulds and crucibles would be found.

Although a set of these artefacts is unlikely to be found at an archaeological site, some of them have survived well.

(7) Slag

To a greater or lesser degree, slag is an essentially unwanted by-product of all metallurgical processes: smelting, refining, casting, and smithing. As slag is the remains of the final stage of the iron-production process, its presence implies definitely that activity connected with iron technological processes took place. It can often be found more easily than the hearth itself, which normally can be found only by excavation. The shape of slag and the morphological condition of slag, such as a bottom-of-bowl-shaped slag or a flowed type of slag, also indicates particular stages or methods of the process of iron-production.

(8) Hammer scales

When iron or steel is heated in air, iron and oxygen react to form a coating of iron oxide on the surface of iron; this is called 'scale', which is normally 0.5mm-1.0mm in size. Scale which was produced during hammering in the process of forging is called 'hammering scale'.

Hammer scales definitely indicate only evidence of a forging or smithing process. A concentration of hammer scales inside or outside a dwelling indicate exactly where hammering took place within a space. The duration of the hammering process can be estimated by the quantitative study of hammer scales.

(9) Additives

Additives such as iron sand, pieces of iron ore, shell and ash are associated with a certain process of iron technology. It is a significant indication which identifies the process of iron technology. Although these are very rarely found, such evidence indicates a distinctive process of iron technology, such as reduction or decarburisation.

4-4 Discussions based on the archaeological evidence

4-4-1 The archaeological evidence from the excavated sites

The archaeological evidence at excavated sites is listed in Table 4-2. From this, it is possible to interpret the existence of activities relating to iron technology. The types of evidence referred to are those already given in Table 4-1 in order to confirm the basic requirements of the evidence for iron technology.

Brief summaries of the findings at each site are given in
Appendix 1, in the following order: A. The Hokkaido
district, and B. The Tohoku district.

Table 4-2   The archaeological evidence at excavated sites.

(1) Raw material for iron, (2) Secondary raw material, (3) Fuel, (4) Furnace/hearth structure, (5) Tuyeres, (6) Craft tools,
 (7) Slag, (8) Hammer scale, (9) Additives.

The site numbers given here are used for cross-reference in the text. However these numbers refer only to technological sites
which have been identified archaeologically (i.e. the basic evidence was found as detailed in Table 4-1).The sites are described
under these numbers in Appendix-1.

Hokkaido

	site name	(1)	(2)	(3)	(4)	(5)	(6)	(7)	(8)	(9)
1	Iruekashi		√		√	√		√	√	
2	Pipaushi		√	√	√	√	√	√	√	
3	Yukanboshi		√		√	√	√	√	√	
4	Setanaichiashi						√			
5	Katsuyamadate		√		√	√		√		
6	Satsumae		√		√	√		√		
7	Miyukicho				√	√		√		
8	Nishikicho 5				√	√		√		
9	Ranshima				√	√			√	
10	Suehiro IP-89					√		√		
10	Suehiro IH-35					√				
10	Suehiro IH-97					√				
11	Nakajimamatsu 6					√				
11	Nakajimamatsu 7								√	
12	Sakushukotoni					√		√		
13	Okawa					√		√		
14	Genwa							√		
15	Aonae					√		√		
16	Attusabukawaguchi							√		
17	Horonaipo					√		√		
18	Minamimachi C					√				
19	Kagawasansen					√		√		
20	Takasago BH-54					√		√		
20	Takasago 2-5					√				
21	Higashihirosato					√		√		
22	Tanaka							√		
23	Watenbetsu							√		
24	Tapukopu					√				
25	Hokkema					√				
26	Tokachibuto				√	√				
27	Kawagichi					√		√		
28	Nishitsukigaoka					√				
29	Tokorochiashi					√				
30	Sudou					√				
31	Gifu					√				
32	Shintotsugawa					√				
33	Kabukai					√				

Tohoku

	site name	(1)	(2)	(3)	(4)	(5)	(6)	(7)	(8)	(9)
34	Namiokajo		√							
35	Hamadoori				√	√				
36	Mokusawa	√		√	√	√		√		√
37	Kitsuneno				√	√		√		
38	Furudate				√	√	√			
39	Chokaisan		√		√	√	√	√		
40	Hagurodaira				√	√		√		
41	Uchiebisawa					√		√		
42	Sumodaiyasuhara					√		√		
43	Botandairaminami	√				√		√		√
44	Hatchazawa		√			√		√		
45	Odate							√		
46	Kodate				√			√		
47	Asahiyama					√		√		
48	Itadome 2					√		√		
49	Shimoyachi					√		√		
50	Takagi					√		√		
51	Niwagamae					√		√		
52	Yaedaira					√		√		
53	Kamimura	√			√	√		√	√	√
54	Wandai				√	√		√		
55	Natsumoto				√	√		√	√	
56	Rozawa				√	√		√		
57	Kadowakizawa	√			√					
58	Shiwajo		√	√	√	√		√		
59	Shimohaba				√			√		
60	Osegawa A				√					
61	Aozaru									
62	Asukadaichi				√	√				
63	Sekisawaguchi				√	√				
64	Komayakiba				√		√	√	√	
65	Harimadate		√	√	√	√	√	√	√	
66	Uwano				√	√	√		√	
67	Samukawa				√	√		√		
68	Kaninzawa	√			√	√				√
69	Ryugesawa			√	√	√	√	√		
70	Odateno				√	√				
71	Junibayashi				√	√				
72	Sakanoue E				√					
72	Sakanoue F					√				
73	Nakadai				√					
74	Shironaganedate				√	√		√		
75	Kitazawa	√	√	√	√			√		

4-4-2 Discussion

The discussion is set out according to geological area in order to establish whether or not it is possible to see: 1) technological development through the Satsumon to the Ainu in Hokkaido, and 2) the period at which it may be considered that technological diffusion from Tohoku into Hokkaido took place; moreover, 3) the extent to which the archaeological evidence fits into the model of the iron prohibition which I discussed in Chapter 2, in relation to the Emishi in Tohoku. Site numbers in parentheses refer to Table 4-2 and descriptions are given in Appendix-1.

A. The Hokkaido district

(1) A provisional chronological ordering of tuyeres

The chronology of Satsumon pottery is still debatable due to the fact that the interpretation of typological studies depends on individual researchers and regional differences. For this reason I cannot rely too much on the pottery chronology.

Although I had thought that it would be difficult to set up a chronological order from material like tuyeres before having studied and seen them, I did in fact see some variations amongst tuyeres in the Satsumon which may be chronological and/or functional.

I have attempted to establish a provisional chronological order of tuyeres based on stratigraphic evidence, mainly depending on tephrochronology, and on the style of tuyere. I have tried to relate dwellings which show clear stratigraphic relationships, but I have not taken into account any regional differences for the present. I divide the Satsumon into three stages; a fourth stage would be the Ainu period.

The 1st stage: Before the 11th century

Hakutosan tephra erupted between the late 10th century and the early 11th century. This stage includes everything before the Hakutosan tephra. Tuyeres found at the following sites are included in this stage: Ranshima (9), Suehiro IP-89 (10) and Aonae (15). Tuyeres from Ranshima and Suehiro both have, remarkably, a similar trumpet shape which is also found on Haji ware: thin and fine. Aomae site and Suehiro IP-89 (10) dwellings are both located below the Hakutousan tephra layer according to stratigraphic observations.

The 2nd stage: the 11th century onwards

This stage comprises the period after the Hakutousan eruption. Tuyeres which were found in the dwellings at several locations at Suehiro (10) are included in this stage: IH-97, IH-93, IH-35. From stratigraphic observations, Suehiro IH-97 occurs immediately above the Hakutosan. Suehiro IH-93 and IH-35 occur above Suehiro IH-97. The shape of the tuyeres is fairly small but fine, and it seems as if these were made by someone who knew how to make Satsumon pottery.

The 3rd stage

Tuyeres which were found at the Satsumae (6) and Okawa (13) sites are included in this stage. The tuyeres are big and coarse, and they have become thicker.

The 4th stage: approximately the 17th century (before 1667)

Tarumae-b tephra was deposited in 1667. This stage runs from the end of the Satsumon, which is not clearly delineated but was sometime around the 11th-13th centuries to the Ainu period. Tuyeres which were found at the following sites are included in this stage: Iruekashi (1), Pipaushi (2), and Yukanboshi (3). Pipaushi is dated between 1663 and 1667 because the iron-working hearth was sandwiched between Usu-b tephra which was deposited in 1663 and Tarumae-b tephra which was deposited in 1667. The site looks as if it was abandoned because of the eruption; for example, the beam from one of the houses was in situ within Tarumae-b tephra. On the other hand at Iruekashi, which was also completely covered by Tarumae-b tephra, the site appeared from the observations during excavation, as if it had already been abandoned when Tarumae-b tephra was deposited.

Summary of tuyeres in Hokkaido

It is possible to observe morphological differences in tuyeres of the Satsumon culture which indicate that the tuyeres became larger and thicker through the Satsumon period. For example, tuyeres at Horonaipo (17), and Miyukicho (7) are more similar than those from Satsumae and Okawa. The former ones are a rather compact type made of fine clay, and the latter ones are a roly-poly style type which were made of clay with temper and baked. Although the tuyere at Okawa is in the final stage of the Satsumon, which is definitely within the Satsumon context, it is very similar to ones at Pipaushi in an Ainu context. The clay of both seems to have been baked. From these observations, it may be possible to say that there was some kind of technological connection between the Satsumon and the Ainu.

Fig. 4-1
Tuyeres in Hokkaido.
Numbers are the site numbers given in Table 4-2 and Appendix 1.

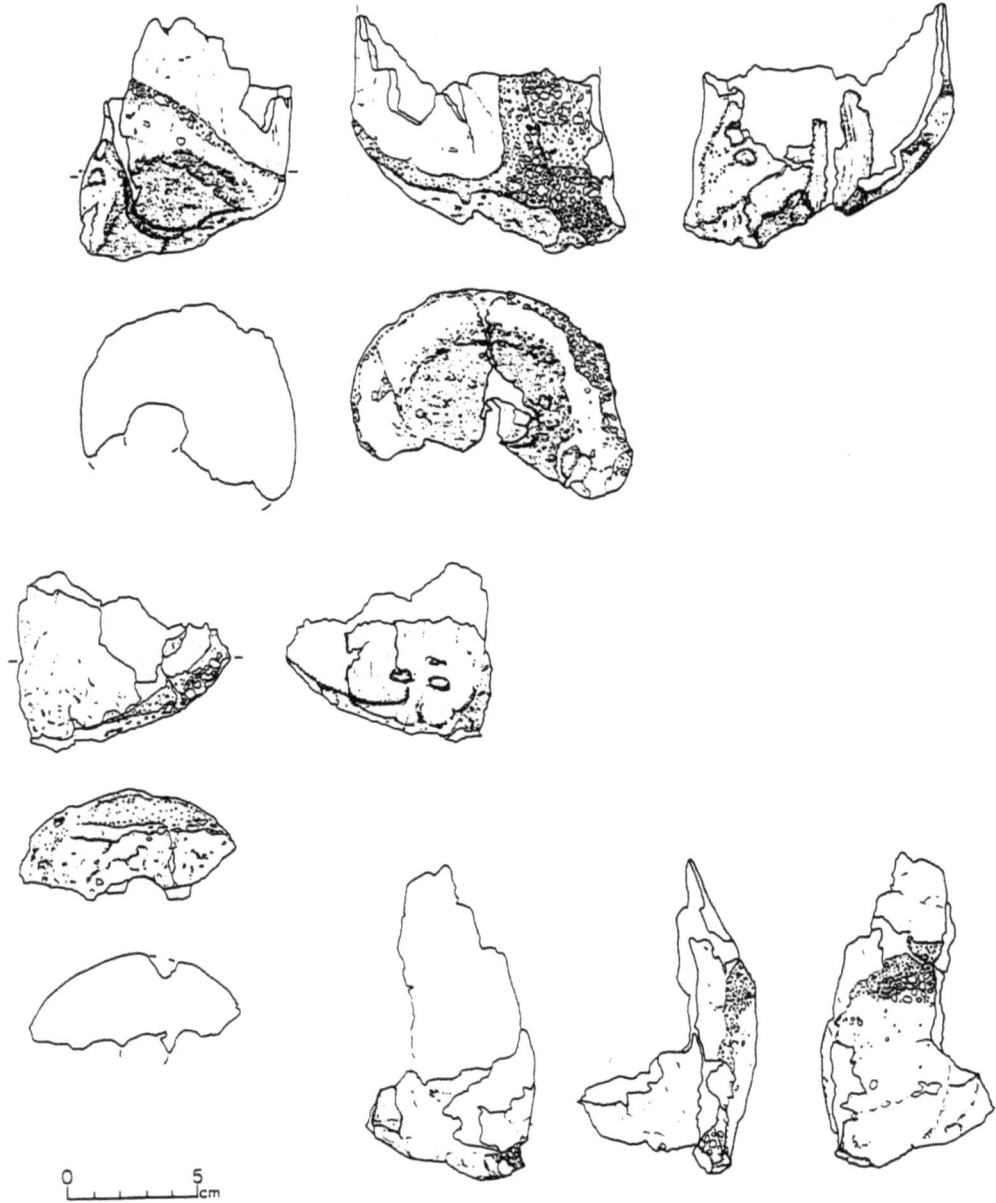

1　Iruekashi

Fig. 4-1 cont.

5 Katsuyamadate

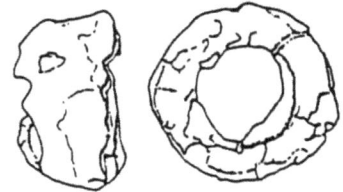

7 Miyukicho

0   10

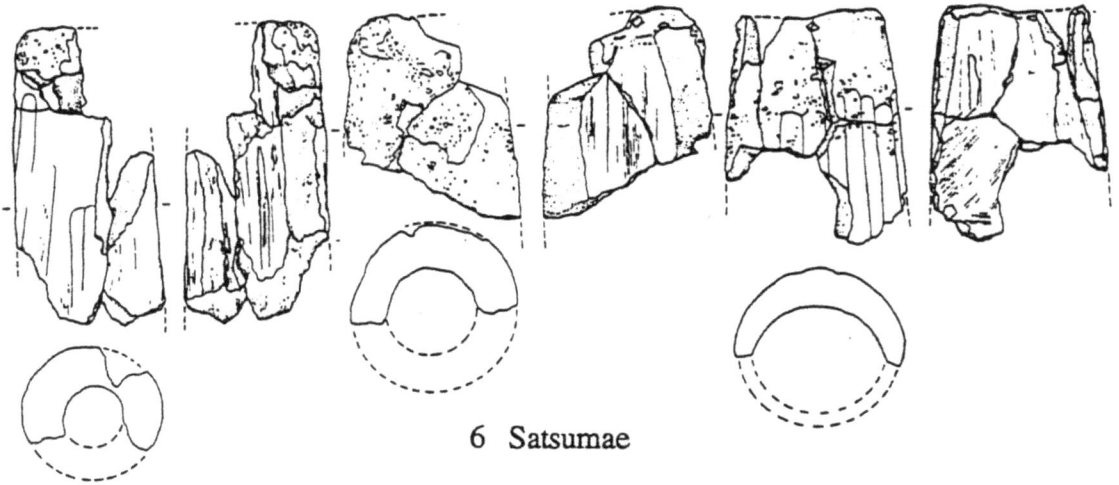

6 Satsumae

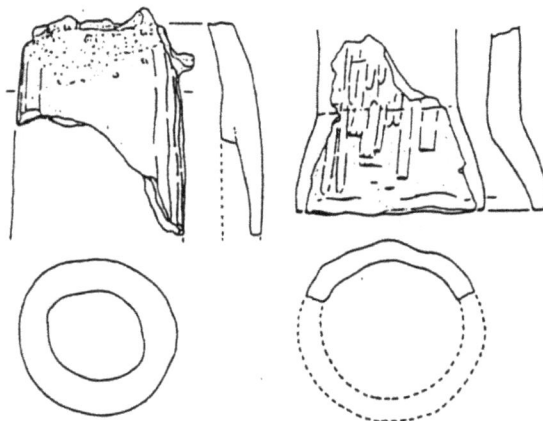

8 Nishikicho 5

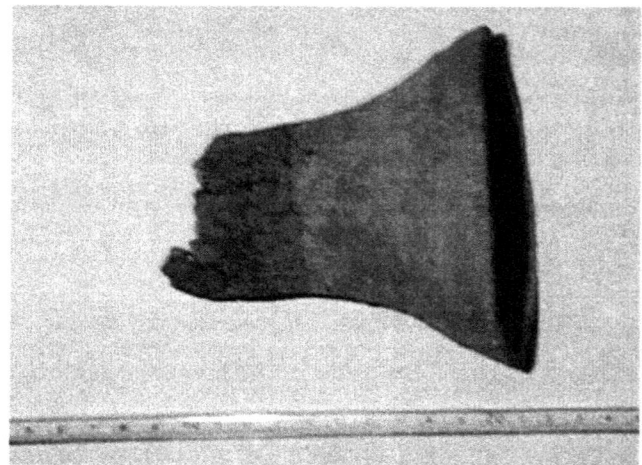

9 Ranshima

Fig. 4-1 cont.

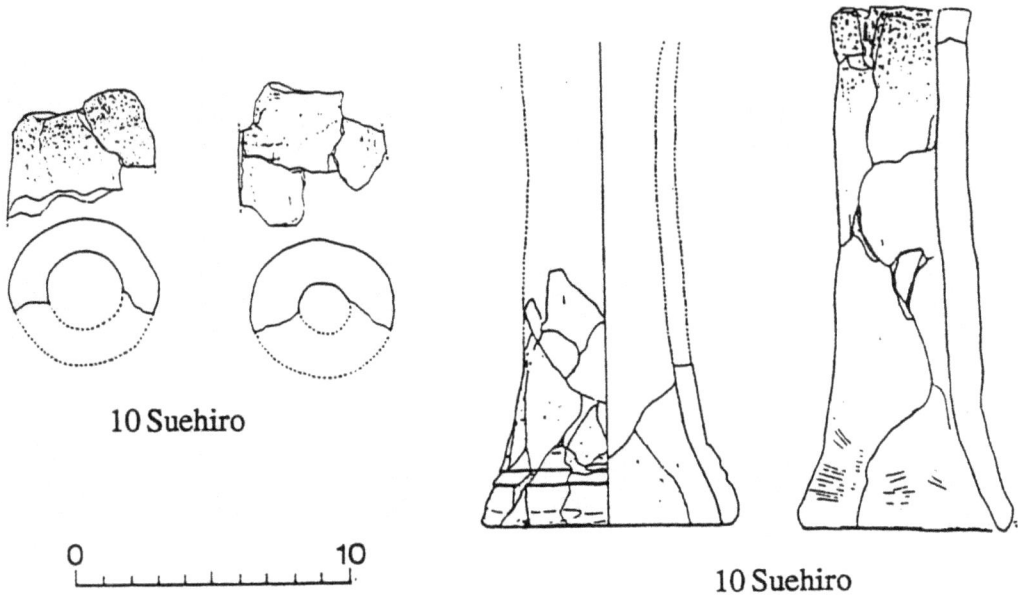

10 Suehiro

10 Suehiro

0   10

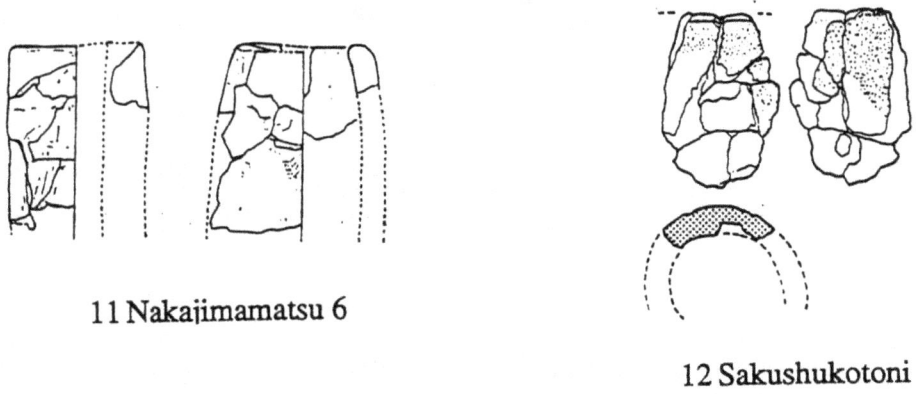

11 Nakajimamatsu 6

12 Sakushukotoni

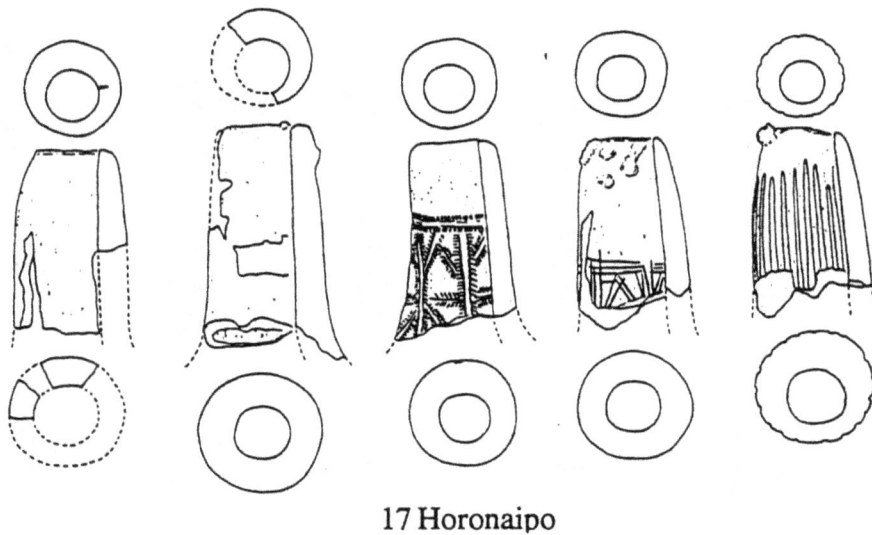

17 Horonaipo

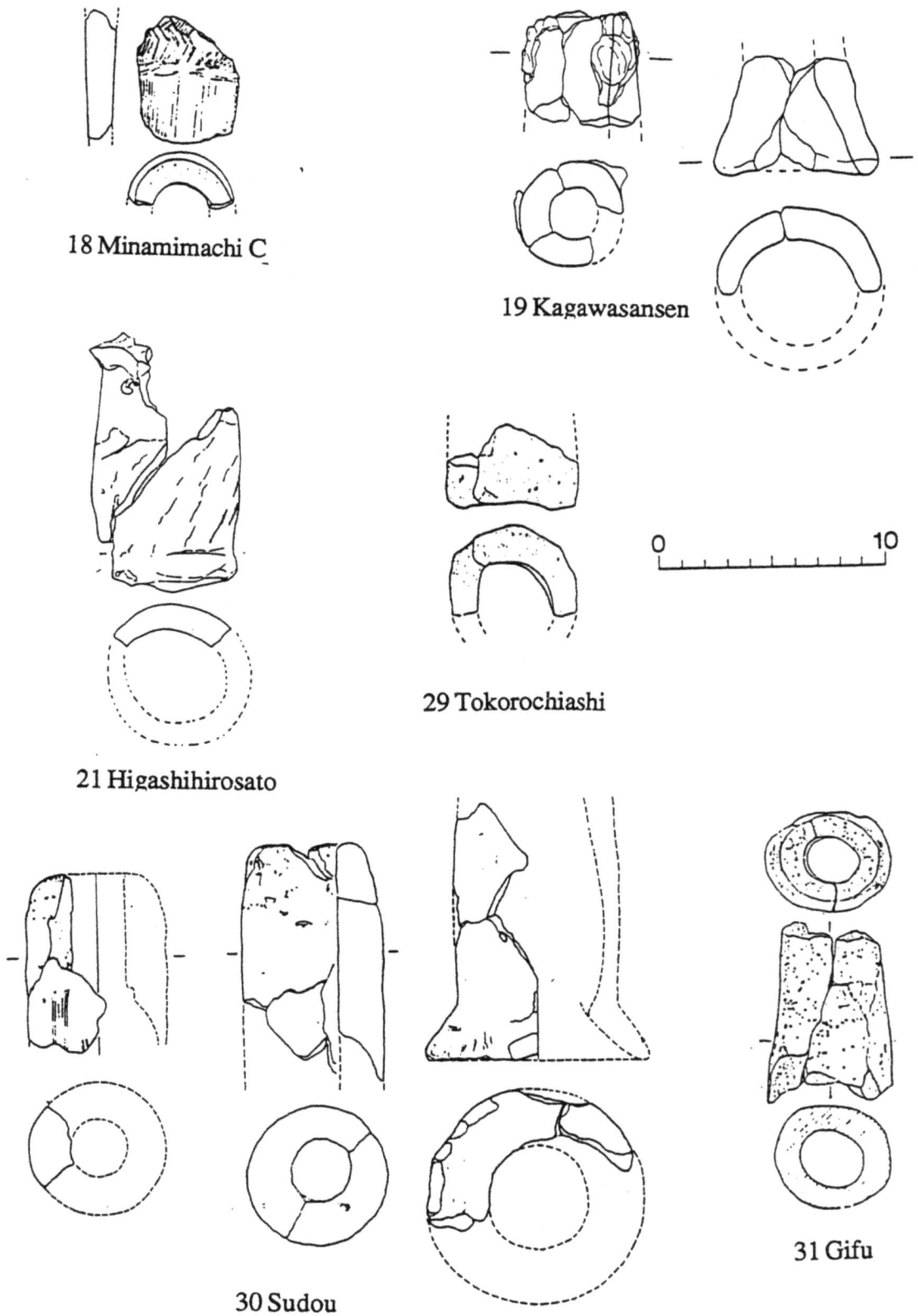

Fig. 4-1 cont.

18 Minamimachi C

19 Kagawasansen

21 Higashihirosato

29 Tokorochiashi

0   10

30 Sudou

31 Gifu

B. The Tohoku district

(1) Furnaces

There are two different categories of furnace structure which can be distinguished in the Tohoku district: a rectangular box furnace and a semi-underground shaft furnace (see Glossary). These two types of furnace can also be classified according to the incline of the bottom of the furnace: a semi-underground shaft furnace with an inclined bottom and a rectangular box furnace without an inclined base. These features relate to the iron technology and the functional differences of the furnace, such as strength and direction of the wind, and the liquidity of the iron in the molten state.

A type of rectangular box furnace seems to have appeared around the 7th century, and a type of semi-underground shaft furnace seems to have appeared around the 8th century onwards.

In the Non Ritsu-Ryo area, around the 8th century, there are rectangular box furnaces at the Osegawa A site (60) (Terashima 1991) along the Kitakami River, in the inland area; on the other hand there are semi-underground furnaces at the Kamimura (53) (1994), Rozawa (56) (Sasaki 1990), and Kadowakizawa (57) (Sasaki 1990) sites in the coastal area on the Pacific Ocean side. The Wandai site (54) which is located near the Kamimura site on the Pacific Ocean side, has a rectangular box furnace probably of 9th-10th century date. All of them are being interpreted as smelting sites.

On the Japan Sea side, there are semi-underground furnaces at Sakanoue E site (72) along the Omono River, and further north, along the Yonashiro River, at the Samukawa (67), Ryugesawa (69), and Kanninnzawa (68) sites.

However there are also semi-underground furnaces without inclined bases in this area, as at the Odateno site (70).

These sites are located in areas beyond the borders of the Ritsu-Ryo state. This means that iron-production was practised by people who lived outside the Ritsu-Ryo system.

These furnaces are classified as semi-underground shaft-type, which are found mostly in the north-east part of Japan. Some differences among the sites can be seen, such as the numbers of furnaces and associated facilities. Satsumon pottery was found at the Mokusawa site (36); however the Satsumon sites in Hokkaido which shows evidence iron-production have only the forging hearth, forging equipment such as tuyeres, and by-products of the forging technique such as slag and hammering scale. There are no records of iron-production sites in the Satsumon proper. This implies that the extent of production and operation is different and could demonstrate different social contexts in the area. A society which needs iron as a production system and a society which needs iron as a processing system are very different social contexts. This implies that the Satsumon culture and the Haji culture exhibit different social contexts, although there are some similarities.

4-5 The limitations of archaeological observation based on the evidence from the sites

Although there is much evidence from excavations such as the existence of tuyeres and slag which can definitely be interpreted as the result of activity connected with iron technology, these data do not provide details of the technological process within which to set their technological level, such as smelting refining and forging.

As I have noted, there are many factors in Table 4-1 which overlap within the technological process, and one cannot decide based only on the evidence available at sites whether smelting or refining, and whether refining or forging have been carried out.

To reconstruct the iron technology certainly require more detailed study if we are to understand how this technology was used. Therefore, archaeologists should be aware of the limitations of the archaeological observation of data.

In archaeology particularly, although archaeologists and metallurgical scientists co-operate to understand the technological process from the evidence derived from excavations, there is still a gap between archaeologists and metallurgical scientists due to the lack of knowledge of each other's subject. Archaeologists tend to be passive and accept the data which derive from the metallurgists' analyses. However, at the least it is important to read what the data represent within the mechanism of metallurgy.

Among metallurgical scientists, methodological debate is still open and depends on which chemical processes are given priority in making interpretations. Different interpretations of the same site depend on who analyses material from it. This kind of debate needs to be resolved.

It is interesting to note that, for example, two different interpretations were reported as a result of two different groups of metallurgists analysing the materials at the site of Kitazawa (75). One said that the site was a smelting site, and the other said that the site was a refining site; both verdicts were based on archaeometallurgical analysis. This debate may lead to further different interpretations of the trade network of that period.

Although the archaeologist of the Kitazawa site put forward the interpretation of a refining site (Niigata-ken Toyoura-cho Kyoiku-iinkai 1992:150-151), the report shows evidence of confusion. This, however, is a good example of the current debate about iron-working sites in Japanese archaeometallurgical study.

4-6 Approach from metallurgical analysis

4-6-1 Analytical methods

(1) Chemical composition analysis

The chemical composition of the iron is very important; in particular, the amount of carbon, silicon, sulphur, and phosphorus greatly affect the mechanical properties of the product. According to the amount of carbon, iron is divided into two different categories, such as steel and cast iron. There is, however, wrought iron which contains a smaller amount of carbon than steel. The amount of copper, manganese, titanium, and phosphorus can help in determining the kind of raw materials that were used, such as iron ore or iron sand.

The chemical composition of slag is also important to understand the process of iron technology. The amount of copper, manganese, titanium, and phosphorus is useful components to identify what kind of raw materials were used. The existence of silica, aluminium, and magnesium can help in determining that these might be contaminated from the wall of the furnace or impurities from imperfectly clean ore. Important technical details of the iron-production process will emerge from a more careful study of the chemical composition of iron products (Akanuma, personal communication).

(2) Metallographic analysis

Metallographic analysis shows structurally and also gives evidence of treatment of the iron. The micro-structure can be viewed by optical microscope or SEM (Scanning Electron Microscope), without chemical analysis. The micro-structure of the mineralogical components can be observed under EPMA (Electron Probe Micro Analyser). The distinction between steel and pig iron is based on the amount of carbon within samples as a component; however, it is also a useful indication to observe ledeburite in the micro-structure which exists in cast iron. The presence or absence of titanium-compounds indicate whether the raw material was iron ore or iron sand. If the main compound consists of wustite and fayalite in slag samples, it indicates reducing conditions and that it was made at a low temperature. A slag sample consisting mainly of glass and silica compounds probably indicates slag which was running out of the furnace, and the reducing condition can be estimated based on the amount of iron oxide present. If the amount of iron oxide, which was deoxidised at a low temperature is high, then steel might have been produced. If it is low and consists of glass compounds, then the temperature was high and pig iron might have been produced (Akanuma, personal communication).

4-6-2 Analytical results and discussions

(1) Slag
(the results of the analysis of slag are shown in Table 4-3):

Although the technique is still controversial, the examination of slag from an iron-working site is potentially very useful in the identification of the process employed at the site. Therefore, the initial stage of the present study was to seek slag which had been kept in museums from other contemporary excavations in order to conduct metallurgical analyses and compare them with slag from the Ainu sites. Here, I discuss how the results can be read in order to identify whether slag was a by-product of the process of smelting, refining and forging. Discussion which further relates to Ainu iron technology, particularly on the

Iruekashi site (1), Pipaushi site (2), and Yukanboshi site (3), is given in Chapter 5.

Metallurgical analyses of slag in order to see its chemical composition and micro-structure provide a valuable source of information for all metallurgical processes. Particularly, in the Japanese case, which may differ from other cases, the use of iron sand is frequent, so that inclusions which contain titanium-compounds can be identified in the slag. Slag from the process of smelting iron ore otherwise includes FeO, Fe_2O_3, and silicate (SiO_2) glass, generally without the presence of titanium-compounds. Therefore, it is possible to determine whether the raw material used was iron ore or iron sand.

The interpretation of the Kamimura (53) (around the 8th century), Mokusawa (36) (around the 10th century), and Kitazawa (75) (around the 13th century) sites, indicate that two different processes — smelting and refining — may have taken place. For example, interpretation of the Mokusawa site has concerned whether it was a smelting site or a refining site. It has been interpreted as a smelting site for producing iron from iron sand due to the fact that morphological observation of the slag indicates it to be a tap slag. According to the chemical analysis, the slag contains a high proportion of titanium (TiO_2), which probably has its origin in iron sand. The iron sand may have been the original raw material for smelting or the additive in a refining process. The original interpretation is that iron was smelted from iron sand.

However, it is also possible to make the interpretation that iron sand was used as an additive for refining *sentetsu* (see Glossary) in order to carry out decarburisation as part of the process, so that the slag also contains a high proportion of titanium (TiO_2). Akanuma (1991) interprets the Mokusawa site as a refining site, suggesting that iron sand was used in the refining process due to the fact that the structure of iron sand particles of local origin is different from the structure of iron sand particles found in the slag. In the case of the Kitazawa site, there are almost the same problems on account of the presence of certain titanium-compounds in slag and recovered at the site. These debates all affect the interpretation of the existence of *sentetsu*, and how it is decarburised to produce steel. This leads also to the discussion of the distribution network for both the raw materials and the refined iron at that time. Slag sample No. 27 (Table 4-3) from the Harimadate site (65), was identified by Akanuma (Akanuma 1993) as in the middle of the transforming process by decarburisation from *sentetsu* to steel as it contained titanium-compounds. This is truly a lump of iron rather than slag.

Moreover, one of the processes — that of decarburising cast iron in a liquid state to produce steel — can also be indicated by the presence of iron sand; but in this case, a furnace is needed because the metal is heated, oxidised and stirred in a furnace to reduce the carbon content. Hence the existence of a furnace and crucible is required.

At the Satsumae site (6) (Satsumon period), metallurgical examination of the slag indicated that the refining process may have been practised at this site because iron sand particle

Table 4-3   The chemical composition of slag (Hokkaido).
The following data are compiled from the excavation reports listed in Appendix-1.
The site numbers given here are used for cross-reference in the text. However these numbers refer only to technological sites which have been identified archaeologically (i.e. the basic evidence was found as detailed in Table 4-1). The sites are described under these numbers in Appendix-1.

No. & Site Name	T.Fe	FeO	Fe2O	SiO2	Al2O3	CaO	TiO2	Mn	P	S
1 Iruekashi K-26-3	10.20	6.61	54.02	14.76	8.77	0.30		0.34	0.0016	
1 " K-26-4	28.05	28.46	38.31	9.37	8.45	0.73		0.32	0.023	
1 " K-27-9	49.13	54.55		20.64	4.61	3.34	3.24	0.22	0.070	
1 " L-27-2	41.73	30.4		9.59	2.52	5.22	0.15	0.05	0.375	0.173
1 " T-30-6	57.03	37.10		3.53	0.70	0.27	0.03	0.03	0.383	0.107
1 " T-34-3	45.26	9.58		5.79	0.85	0.52	0.04	0.01	0.262	0.080
2 Pipaushi G-12-8	45.39	25.46		16.57	4.06	8.42	0.22	0.23	0.650	0.025
2 Pipaushi G-13-5-2	61.43	43.19		10.25	2.07	1.28	0.15	0.060	0.175	0.014
3 Yukan- 4055-83	68.73	66.18	24.82	0.64	0.97	0.45	0.049	0.021	0.157	0.001
3 -boshi 4042-1	37.36	36.66	12.69	37.00	3.18	4.18	0.117	0.127	0.282	0.009
3 " 4055-133	71.92	71.36	23.55	0.99	0.74	0.66	0.066	0.013	0.165	0.002
5 Katsuya- UEN-1	58.3	59.3	17.40	14.92	3.97	2.38	0.30	0.052	0.40	0.026
5 -madate UEN-2	42.9	40.4	16.43	28.9	5.43	2.69	0.27	0.062	0.54	0.124
5 " UEN-3	68.0	59.5	31.1	5.90	1.61	0.77	0.11	0.023	0.19	0.020
5 " UEN-5	4.65	3.74	2.49	55.6	12.28	11.75	0.55	0.19	5.05	0.079
5 " UEN-6	29.0	27.7	10.64	34.5	11.96	6.30	0.57	0.31	0.88	0.074
5 " UEN-7	60.5	62.8	16.71	11.10	3.59	2.17	1.44	0.098	0.34	0.026
5 UEN-11	62.6	57.8	25.2	9.20	2.83	1.71	1.29	0.077	0.27	0.051
6 Satsumae SAT-1	47.30	43.90	4.86	20.10	5.03	2.66	0.28	0.043	0.013	0.030
6 " SAT-2	8.78	7.19	2.27	48.00	15.60	4.57	0.77	0.160	0.020	0.023
6 " SAT-20	8.04	8.05	0.01	45.60	17.30	4.22	0.87	0.140	0.016	0.032
6 " ST-1	8.07	6.97	4.69	54.8	17.38	5.77	0.88	0.18	0.33	0.011
6 " ST-2	10.70	11.14	2.97	55.6	21.26	1.96	1.04	0.12	0.24	0.009
6 " ST-3	32.5	26.30	17.24	34.6	10.77	3.18	0.55	0.097	0.65	0.045
6 " ST-5	11.00	11.78	2.63	51.9	19.93	4.77	0.90	0.17	0.47	0.005
6 " ST-6	35.9	22.85	25.93	32.8	9.64	5.04	0.43	0.10	0.48	0.020
6 " ST-7	49.4	53.9	10.73	23.48	6.33	2.48	0.33	0.071	0.36	0.010
6 " 21H 1-18	26.5	27.6	7.27	57.2	8.97	6.72	0.44	0.10	0.86	0.008
6 " M1B2S1	7.75	7.13	3.16	13.82	20.88	4.06	0.96	0.18	0.83	0.029
ShizuuraD ST-8	9.55	8.69	4.00	51.1	21.54	4.41	0.77	0.21	0.80	0.008
7Miyukicho MIK1	47.60	27.80	28.31	18.00	5.59	1.86	0.200	0.055	0.020	0.053
8 Nishiki- ZW841	9.15	8.48	3.66	56.5	16.63	4.97	0.57	0.12	0.52	0.017
8 -cho SE32H844	59.0	58.6	19.15	13.40	4.12	2.70	0.30	0.032	0.31	0.059
10 Suehiro B-851	56.6	50.3	25.02	13.82	5.67	3.39	0.23	0.05	0.36	0.068
10 " B-852	68.3	57.1	34.2	3.54	2.13	1.29	0.15	0.08	0.14	0.033
10 " 8u-852	65.1	59.6	26.8	6.70	4.23	2.01	0.15	0.036	0.55	0.004
13 Okawa OKW-1	32.10	22.40	13.87	32.50	8.88	1.98	0.510	0.100	0.044	0.043
13 " OKW-2	18.00	15.20	8.49	44.20	11.40	2.80	0.750	0.110	0.360	0.042
13 " OKW-3	45.40	51.60		21.80	5.58	1.29	0.370	0.037	0.400	0.050
13 " OKW-4	9.16	7.56	4.52	55.90	13.10	3.14	0.920	0.120	0.320	0.020
13 " OKW-5	53.10	53.70	18.70	3.50	1.14	0.70	0.060	0.360	0.052	
13 " OKW-6	46.40	18.90	36.50	7.97	3.24	0.640	0.120	0.570	0.037	
16Atsusabu ASB1	12.20	4.64	10.81	51.50	13.60	1.55	0.400	0.084	0.01	0.011
17Horonaipo A-90	44.50		27.90	6.51	0.80	0.32				
33 Kabukai A	35.92	28.85	17.91	35.11	6.16	2.73	1.14			
33 " B	30.44	12.63	29.47	37.82	7.47	2.01				

Table 4-3 cont.   The chemical composition of slag (Tohoku).
The following data are compiled from the excavation reports listed in Appendix-1.

No. & Site Name	T.Fe	FeO	Fe$_2$O	SiO$_2$	Al$_2$O$_3$	CaO	TiO$_2$	Mn	P	S
36MokusawaMS-1	23.20	28.60		27.00	9.64	5.66	23.30	1.240	0.170	0.060
36 " MS-2	26.10	31.10		27.10	4.93	2.87	19.30	1.030	0.110	0.049
36 " MS-3	39.20	6.56		12.10	4.53	2.40	8.54	0.380	0.230	0.065
36 " MS-4	43.30	48.00		21.10	5.67	1.84	7.87	0.510	0.180	0.043
36 " 1-4	25.47		12.4	2.97	2.84	7.35	0.629	0.162		
36 " 2-5	15.33		18.68	6.88	2.21	3.65	0.408	0.195		
36 " 3-6	21.16	18.13		16.28	4.71	3.24	8.85	0.76	0.095	0.036
36 " 4-7	36.80		11.89	4.21	2.51	5.09	0.225	0.217	0.118	
36 " 5-1	24.74		12.88	4.37	2.27	8.08	0.60	0.156	0.087	
36 " 6-2	35.45	41.25		10.50	3.05	2.64	8.29	0.67	0.190	0.03
36 " 7-3	28.48	28.56		12.26	4.09	3.36	9.76	0.75	0.185	0.040
37Kitsuneno80811	21.32	20.26	7.97	21.20	6.12	2.30	35.96	0.91	0.034	0.015
41 Uchiebisawa 1	62.12	7.40	79.79	2.03	0.42	0.01	0.02	0.03	0.060	0.055
41 " 2	43.11	17.42	41.22	15.40	3.65	0.62	5.58	0.36	0.120	0.065
41 " 3	59.12	8.58	69.13	3.96	0.98	0.11	0.26	0.04	0.061	0.726
41 " 4	72.37	29.29	10.99	2.07	0.68	0.08	0.21	0.05	0.129	0.657
42 Sumodai- 1	24.01	13.35	19.49	41.67	11.24	3.77	1.24	0.21	0.054	0.129
42 -shimoya- 2-1	9.33	8.17	4.26	63.62	13.44	2.45	1.20	0.25	0.020	0.020
42 -suhara 2-2	45.16	30.43	30.75	18.99	6.23	1.62	3.25	0.20	0.102	0.064
42 " 3-1	4.72	4.93	1.27	62.74	16.31	4.62	0.82	0.04	0.021	0.013
42 " 3-2	45.71	49.84	9.97	17.56	6.33	2.68	7.08	0.41	0.99	0.033
42 " 4	34.08	39.97	4.30	25.08	9.73	3.04	11.85	0.70	0.180	0.037
42 " 5	41.08		14.85	2.10	0.17	0.12	0.42	0.290	0.096	
42 " 6	34.19		19.34	5.12	0.18	0.22	0.46	0.221	0.136	
42 " 10	38.65		16.52	4.61	0.36	0.15	0.44	0.480	0.142	
53Kamimura KM1	60.40	51.60	12.50	14.20	5.96	2.59	1.830	0.320	0.026	0.021
53 " KM2	47.90	44.60	4.72	18.10	4.36	2.05	1.400	0.270	0.022	0.024
53 " KM3	39.20	38.80	0.57	27.60	7.07	4.84	2.480	0.480	0.028	0.017
53 " KM5	62.00	25.30	29.35	4.70	1.93	0.41	0.530	0.148	0.117	0.007
53 " KM10	46.2	58.5	0.55	22.2	5.99	1.93	1.63	0.58	0.31	
53 " KM11	57.9	68.6	5.90	13.5	3.61	1.52	1.43	0.42	0.31	
53 " KM12	49.1	56.0	0.02	20.4	5.46	3.80	2.20	0.59	0.83	
53 " KM13	44.9	57.0	0.45	23.6	6.37	1.56	1.89	0.49	0.26	
53 " KM14	42.3	54.1	0.11	24.3	6.90	2.45	1.56	0.47	0.82	
53 " KM15	53.4	57.3	12.4	16.3	4.52	1.38	1.26	0.40	0.25	
53 " KM16	51.6	37.6	31.7	13.1	3.93	1.42	1.65	0.34	0.33	
53 " KM17	50.7	61.1	3.87	17.8	5.33	2.29	1.43	0.54	0.92	
53 " KM18	50.2	61.1	3.56	15.4	4.34	3.16	2.15	0.54	1.20	
53 " KM19	42.3	44.9	10.1	24.2	7.25	1.81	1.29	0.40	0.73	
53 " KM20	59.2	66.7	10.1	11.0	2.90	1.62	1.74	0.42	0.57	
53 " KM21	58.8	65.9	10.4	13.2	3.74	0.93	0.76	0.21	0.36	
53 " KM22	45.9	55.2	3.96	25.3	6.43	2.18	2.41	0.67	0.38	

Table 4-3 cont.   The chemical composition of slag (Tohoku)

No. & Site Name	T.Fe	FeO	Fe2O	SiO2	Al2O3	CaO	TiO2	Mn	P	S
52 Wandai WD-1	41.40	47.40		25.80	8.05	3.51	2.600	0.420	0.350	0.029
52 " WD-2	43.50	50.00		22.70	5.98	4.64	2.510	0.470	0.350	0.028
52 " WD-3	42.70	50.20		22.40	7.20	5.10	3.790	0.600	0.280	0.028
52 " WD-4	47.00	56.20		21.80	6.26	3.73	2.570	0.480	0.280	0.030
52 " WD-5	40.00	11.70		20.10	5.52	2.11	1.020	0.120	0.210	0.087
52 " WD-6	50.40	56.50		18.80	5.52	2.57	1.210	0.380	0.160	0.028
52 " No.10	45.62			1.45	0.349	3.58	0.392	0.429	16.0	
52 " No.11	70.16			0.698	0.092	0.86	0.247	0.209	1.68	
52 " No.12	69.91	0.001		0.803	0.095	1.29	0.252	0.269	3.48	
52 " No.13	63.89			0.963	0.060	1.85	0.331	0.263	5.27	
52 " No.14	64.59			0.086	0.022	0.361	0.080	0.125	1.16	
52 " No.15	62.24	0.001		0.548	0.177	1.90	0.206	0.164	4.26	
52 " No.16	69.99			0.965	0.081	1.10	0.275	0.341	3.21	
52 " No.17	58.05			1.91	0.231	2.72	0.383	0.396	12.4	
52 " No.19	65.82	0.001		0.436	0.061	0.965	0.136	0.159	3.86	
Kawaidate 4	49.73			23.0	3.18	1.32	0.192	0.066	0.081	
" 5	68.91			3.52	0.58	2.27	11.22	0.007	0.087	
" 6	29.44			44.3	5.90	1.23	0.327	0.086	0.116	
" 7	55.91			20.8	2.32	1.10	0.230	0.050	0.019	
55 Natsumoto S-1	55.29			17.88	4.38	0.68	0.674	0.08	0.14	
55 " S-2	54.79			16.26	4.65	0.82	0.981	0.09	0.13	
55 " S-3	54.10			10.50	3.55	0.29	0.320	0.05	0.09	
65 Harimadate 12	40.26			4.56	3.59	1.11	12.04	0.54	0.13	
65 " 25	10.74			23.26	8.60	1.76	2.77	0.35	0.11	
65 " 27	56.61			2.58	1.33	0.15	0.45	0.042	0.093	
68 Kanninzawa 1			57.84	15.03	4.84	2.61	13.30	0.62	0.87	
68 " 2			51.82	19.28	6.41	2.89	13.05	0.65	1.05	
68 " 3			50.97	20.27	7.44	2.21	13.36	0.64	0.76	
68 " 4			51.82	19.28	6.41	2.89	13.05	0.65	1.05	
68 " 5			53.27	18.29	4.44	2.61	14.44	0.70	0.83	
68 " 6			46.38	24.30	6.90	3.03	12.77	0.58	0.75	
72 Sakanoue E 1			48.60	25.40	5.69	0.75	15.22			
72 " 2			56.75	17.18	3.23	0.64	18.00			
72 " 3			50.88	24.20	4.80	0.62	15.61			
74 Shiranagane- 1			40.40	27.23	5.54	4.31	15.31			
74 -date 2			47.62	23.57	5.009	3.38	15.31			
74 " 3			39.48	28.50	5.76	4.35	15.36			
Takou			60.52	12.45	3.11	2.46	19.59			
75 Kitazawa6-No6			13.00	20.18	6.260	1.590	16.09	0.780	0.079	0.015
75 " 7-No8			7.110	28.33	7.440	1.420	14.82	0.730	0.047	0.005
75 " 8-GX22				42.05	7.01	1.96	23.2	1.16	0.064	

were observed in the slag samples. This was interpreted as being a result of decarburisation using iron sand. Although furnaces of the kind required for refining were not found at this site, it is suggested that the refining method was used (Osawa 1985).

On the other hand, at the Nishikicho site (5), metallurgical examination of the slag indicated that it was forging slag by the fact that it contains mainly silica and magnetite, and the chemical composition analysis indicates 59% of total Fe, which was high and 0.3% of titanium (TiO2) which was low. At the Suehiro site (10) (Satsumon period), the results indicated that it was forging slag by the fact that samples contain mainly silica and magnetite, and chemical composition analysis indicates 65.1% of total Fe, which was high, and 0.15% of titanium (TiO2), which was low (Osawa 1982). Also at the Horonaipo site (17) (Satsumon period), forging slag was identified from the fact that it contained mainly silicate and magnetite, and the chemical composition indicated 44.50% of total Fe, which was high, and 0.32% of titanium (TiO2), which was low (Osawa 1983).

Slag at the Miyukicho (7), Okawa (13), and Genwa (14) sites has been identified as forging slag on the basis of metallographic analysis.

The existence of iron sand particles indicates that the refining process was carried on by reaction of iron sand, and this can be evidence that decarburisation has been carried out by the addition of iron sand during the melting process. This suggests that the technique is not as simple as just forging but a more advanced stage characterised by specific techniques to produce steel products. It is very important to understand whether iron technology had already reached the level of steel-production.

(2) Hammer scale
(the results of the analysis of hammer scale are shown in Table 4-4)

Metallurgical examination was carried out on hammer scale found at the Ranshima (9) and Suehiro (10) sites.

Discussion on the Pipaushi site (2) and the Yukanboshi site (3) will be given in Chapter 5.

Table 4-4　　The chemical composition of hammer scale.
The following data are compiled from the excavation reports listed in Appendix-1.
Shadowing indicates data analysed specially for this book by a metallurgical analyst, K. Ito.

	Site name Sample no	T.Fe	FeO	Fe2O3	SiO2	Al2O3	CaO	TiO2	MnO	P	*
2	Pipaushi 1		61.0	32.8	2.53	0.70	0.46	0.12	0.20		3.89
2	Pipaushi 2	67.1	59.7	28.1	5.35	1.39	0.77	0.27	0.35		7.86
2	Pipaushi 3	51.3	11.8	59.6	7.84	2.51	0.68	0.13	0.73		11.76
2	Pipaushi 4	62.8	52.8	29.4	7.63	2.24	1.00	0.20	0.44		11.31
3	Yukanboshi 1	68.04	46.82	45.28				0.028			2.42
3	Yukanboshi 3	67.98	42.60	49.88				0.021			1.33
3	Yukanboshi 4	69.93	63.26	29.75				0.033			1.66
3	Yukanboshi 5	66.60	61.91	26.45				0.100			8.87
3	Yukanboshi 6	64.20	57.52	27.89				0.071			4.91
3	Yukanboshi 8	65.56	59.0	28.12				0.048			4.38
3	Yukanboshi 9	66.20	64.88	22.58				0.067			5.30
9	Ranshima	57.36			13.42	4.34	0.94	0.28	0.07	0.09	
55	Natsumoto	72.66	58.52	37.89	1.50	0.02		0.037	0.02	0.03	
53	Kamimura 8	68.6	55.8	35.7	5.29	0.91	<0.1	0.11	<0.1	0.05	
53	Kamimura 9	68.8	61.8	29.4	4.25	1.13	<0.1	0.23	<0.1	0.07	

(3) Iron products
(the results of the analysis of iron products are shown in Table 4-5)

According to the proportion of carbon which iron products contain, 1.7% carbon is defined as the dividing line between steel and *chutetsu* in Japanese metallurgy (Nishizawa et al. 1979). Metallurgical discussions in Japan are based on this definition; I therefore follow this definition.

Iron pots are frequently found at sites in Hokkaido and Tohoku dating from the 11th century onwards. It is not known where they were produced or how they were distributed in the north of Japan. Therefore, it is significant to study the result of metallurgical analysis on the material in order to understand the source and distribution network.

All iron pots exhibit evidence of ledeburite in the metallographic results and high carbon as a chemical component. They are made of cast iron. Among chemical components, particularly copper (Cu) and phosphorus (P), or titanium (Ti) are good indicators to understand the original iron raw material, whether it was copper-containing iron ore or phosphorus-containing iron ore. According to Akanuma (1989:196), if the calculation based on phosphorus/total Fe (T.Fe) is more than 0.1%, then the proportion of phosphorus is high. Most samples have high proportions of phosphorus, which indicate that the original iron ore was phosphorus-containing magnetite. On the other hand, it is interesting that titanium is not significant, as it has always been thought that iron sand containing titanium was the traditional raw material for iron products in Japan.

There are some other iron products containing less than 1.7% carbon that are made from soft steel or forged iron products, such as daggers, nails, fishing hooks, harpoons and miscellaneous pieces of iron.

At the Katsuyamadate site (5) (around 15th-16th century), a non-metallic inclusion of *kozane* (iron lamellae for armour) indicates no evidence of titanium-compound and a low proportion of titanium thus it was made of iron ore. On the other hand, a non-metallic inclusion in nails and harpoons indicates evidence of titanium-compounds, so it can be said that iron sand was used for the production of the raw material from which these iron products were made.

More detailed discussion on iron products at the Iruekashi and Yukanboshi sites will be given in Chapter 5.

Table 4-5   The chemical composition of iron products.
              The following data were analysed by H. Akanuma for the forthcoming reports.

	Site name Sample no	T.Fe			Si	Cu	Ca	Ti	Mn	P	S
3	Yukanboshi 9566-3	61.24			0.542	0.226	0.066	0.007	0.010	0.085	
3	Yukanboshi 9566-8	62.32			0.417	0.014	0.042	0.009	0.015	0.095	0.073
5	Katsuyamadate kozane	63.38				0.010	0.064	0.003	0.005	0.141	
5	Katsuyamadate T 67	96.47			nd	0.015	0.003	0.018	0.0011	0.035	
		M			0.061	0.014	0.009	0.056	0.003	0.030	
5	Katsuyamadate T 70	M				0.008	0.002	0.006	0.001	0.017	
		92.89				0.012	0.006	0.019	0.011	0.024	
5	Katsuyamadate T 68	61.44			1.12	0.011	0.080	0.061	0.011	0.027	
					0.034	0.014	0.002	0.008	0.001	0.027	
5	Katsuyamadate T 71				0.181	0.014	0.015	0.088	0.004	0.008	
					0.176	0.015	0.010	0.065	0.004	0.015	

(4) Lumps of iron material
(the results of the analysis of lumps of iron are shown in Table 4-6)

A semicircular shape of iron material, weighing 5kg and found at Katsuyamadate site (5) (around the 15th-16th centuries), was analysed by a metallurgist (Akanuma 1993). It contains less than 1.7% carbon, suggesting that it is soft steel. According to tests for non-metallic inclusions in this soft steel, titanium-compounds were found, indicating that iron sand was used in the process of production of the steel. The components of non-metallic inclusion of the steel are similar components to those of non-metallic inclusion of the T 68, T 70, and T 71 samples from the same site, which I mentioned just above (see also Table 4-4). It may be said that these iron products were made from the same type of steel at the site. However, it is not known whether the semicircular shape of steel was produced at the site or not. It might have been produced there, as archaeological evidence indicates complex features of iron technology at this site — such as an extraordinarily large type of tuyeres and tuyeres made of stone(s), and the existence of a crucible. The semicircular shape of steel could just as well have been brought into the site through the distribution network.

Two out of 30 iron bars which were together in a bundle from Namiokajo site (around the 15th-16th century) were analysed. They contain 0.3-0.4% and 0.6-0.8% carbon, so that they are steel. They also indicate a high proportion of phosphorus. Titanium compound in a non-metallic inclusion indicates that iron sand was used in the process. Akanuma (1993) suggests that this can be interpreted as evidence for the indirect steel-production method: that is *sentetsu* which contains high phosphorus was used as the material, and iron sand was used for decarburisation in order to make steel. Sasaki (1989) also mentions a similar type of find from Fukushima-ken, Tohoku; analysis shows that it is a soft steel. There is an example in China which might be interesting to note in terms of the production process and distribution of this kind of iron bar. An example is figure 13, "bar iron produced by traditional methods in Hunan" in Wagner (1985). It is possible to say that the figure which shows iron bars 3x3x11cm in size which look very similar to ones from Namiokajo site (34). Such iron bars in China are produced in the indirect steel-production method, termed *chao* in Chinese, translated 'fining'. Generally 30-40 wrought iron bars are produced (the photograph on p.26 in Wagner 1985, shows 30-40 iron bars together in a bundle in Hunan). Similar iron bars in Henan in China indicate the proportion of carbon is 0.34% and the chemical components of the example are as follows: Fe = 98.68%, Si = 0.37%, P = 0.16%, and S = 0.045% (Wagner 1993).

Table 4-6   The chemical composition of a lump of iron.
             Shadowing indicates data analysed by K. Ito, and the rest were analysed by H. Akanuma (1993).

	Site name, Sample no	T.Fe	FeO	Fe_2O_3	SiO	Al_2O_3	CaO	TiO	Mn	P	C%
2	Pipaushi	65.90	<0.01		4.83	1.48	0.400	0.068	0.040	0.600	
5	Katsuyamadate				<0.01	<0.002	<0.001	0.004	<0.01	0.018	<1.7
34	Namiokajo F3	58.76			0.412		0.098	0.001	0.005	0.283	0.3-0.4
34	Namiokajo F	63.63			0.258	0.012	0.016	0.004	0.002	0.162	0.6-0.8

4-7   A hypothetical reconstruction of iron-working in northern Japan

Diagram 4-1 (pp. 49-50) shows expected archaeological finds superimposed on a flow diagram of a hypothetical reconstruction of possible processes of iron technology for iron material production within the Japanese network and the Ainu network, with special reference to the understanding of distribution ways to Ainu society for the Ainu's iron technology.

For example, if moulds are found at a site, then the archaeological reconstruction of iron technology falls within the consideration of the technological process of cast iron as I have mentioned in Table 4-1. However, if slag is found at a site, there are many possible processes of iron technology which may be reconstructed. Therefore, it is necessary to consider the slag both within the archaeological context, such as other archaeological finds, including furnace, hearth, tools, raw material and products etc., and within the technological context based on the metallurgical study including chemical components and micro-structure, in order to narrow down the possibilities and identify more precisely the process of iron technology involved — for example, whether the slag was left as a result of the process of smelting, refining, or forging. Then this process can be interpreted within a social context in order to reconstruct the iron technology at that site and to give a reasonable explanation for the role of the site within the society to which the site belonged.

Therefore, it is possible to reconstruct a flow diagram of the iron-production process, based on the process of iron-production as known at present. Three stages can be identified: smelting, refining, and forging. It is possible to see the kind of evidence which results from carrying out each of these processes in iron technology. Then evidence from archaeological sites can be discussed and compared with these hypothetical processes in order to reconstruct the technology which might have been operating at the site.

Basic requirements for smelting are raw materials such as iron ore and iron sand, fuel such as charcoal or coal, and a furnace, although water, air, labour, and some other considerations should be taken into account. I concentrate particularly on the evidence of the type of hearth present, and the products and by-products, in order to identify the available evidence.

When technological aspects are taken into account for reconstruction of iron-production processes within an archaeological and historical framework in Japan, particularly, an aspect of the technological process of the *tatara* methods is commonly take into account. Thus, this aspect is taken into account on the diagram.

In this discussion, I also consider a variety of possible ways in which iron may have been distributed to a market. There are four such ways as follows: [1] Cast iron products such as iron pots are produced and distributed to a market. [2] It is possible to distribute lumps or bars of *sentetsu* to a market. [3] Steel iron bars or lumps of steel can be distributed to a market. [4] Forged iron products can be distributed to a market.

It is very important to understand the range of physical conditions of iron itself, from raw materials to product, as it changes condition during the process from a solid state to a liquid state by melting and again becomes solid depending on its temperature. It is also important to understand the chemical reactions occurring in the solid state, gaseous state, and liquid state. The whole process occurs according to the combination and range of chemical reactions and physical principles.

In this smelting process, the form of furnace required is one acting as a container which holds liquid iron, such as a smelting furnace. Different degrees of the physical state of iron — for instance, molten or half-molten, according to the proportion of contained carbon — which is defined by metallurgists as the product, and slag, defined as the by-product, are produced.

With respect to [1], the molten state of liquid iron is called *zuku* or *sentetsu*, and if this liquid iron is poured into a mould, it is *chutetsu* (cast iron). A cast iron product such as an iron pot is produced and distributed to a market. According to this process, some form of ladle such as a crucible melting pot and a frame which contains liquid iron, such as a clay mould are required. Remains of these artefacts need to be found at a site for the identification of *chutetsu*.

Although iron pots are found at many sites in Tohoku and Hokkaido, it is not known yet where they were produced. According to the micro-structure of the iron, these iron pots are definitely cast iron products due to the existence of the

46

ledeburite in the micro-structure. The chemical composition indicates that the raw material was possibly phosphorus-containing iron (Akanuma 1989).

With respect to [2], iron in a half-molten state is also called *sentetsu*. A lump of *sentetsu* is in the solid state after cooling down from the half-molten state as products are produced. It is possible to distribute such a lump or a bar to a market.

The refining stage can be identified by many different methods which may indicate the scale of production. For refining this *sentetsu*, a refining furnace is required and refining slag is produced by this process.

A similar process for making an iron product with iron sand was still practised around 1958 in China (Wagner 1985). In China, this process is termed 'chao', or 'fining' in English, which indicates a more specific process than that implied by the general terms for the refining process.

The refining process which transform a lump of *sentetsu* into steel or wrought iron can be divided into four different kinds of processes according to the kind of reaction between the state of the iron and the state of the additives: A) a reaction between *sentetsu* in a solid state and oxygen in air in a gaseous state. B) a reaction between *sentetsu* in a solid state and iron sand or iron ore in a solid state. C) a reaction between *chutetsu* (cast iron) in a liquid state and iron sand or iron ore in a solid state. D) a reaction between cast iron in a pasty or liquid state and oxygen in air in a gaseous state.

From the above reactions, when these are carried out in reactions in furnaces, two different types of furnace forms can be considered depending on the range of temperature reached. When circumstances allow a high temperature to be achieved, a furnace type which has a structure incorporating a container to hold liquid *sentetsu* is needed; if not, a hole-in-the-ground-hearth type is required to heat a lump of solid *sentetsu*. Both types produce refining slag, but the morphological features of the slag are different depending on the different reactions which have taken place.

Hence, some confusion arises in the archaeological identification of the refining processes. The existence or not of furnaces which are in the form of containers for liquid *sentetsu* indicates whether they are smelting furnaces or refining furnaces.

For example, interpretations of the Mokusawa site (36) are concerned with whether it is a smelting site or a refining site. It has been interpreted as a smelting site for producing iron from iron sand due to the fact that the slag morphology is of the tap type and because of archaeological evidence such as the presence of semi-underground shaft furnaces. According to chemical component analysis, the slag contains a high proportion of TiO_2, which indicates some connections with iron sand — whether as a raw material or an additive. For this reason, the interpretation was made that iron was produced from iron sand.

However, it is also possible to make the interpretation that iron sand was used as an additive for refining in order to carry out decarburisation as part of the process. In this case, the slag also contains a high proportion of TiO_2. Akanuma interprets the Mokusawa site as a refining site, suggesting that iron sand was used for the refining process due to the fact that the chemical composition of iron sand particles of local origin is different from chemical composition of the slag. There is another example at the Kitazawa site (75).

Sentetsu in a solid state becomes steel through a refining process. In this process, a lump of *sentetsu* is heated in a hole-in-the-ground hearth, and material for decarburisation is required to be added. It is a very simple process, but it does not produce as large an amount of steel as other methods. It needs much labour, which means it is a low-production process.

The refining process requires a knowledge of how to control carbon in iron because, as a result of this process, a different state of iron is produced. At present, metallurgists define steel as having less than 1.7% carbon, and the definition of *sentetsu* is metal containing more than 1.7% carbon.

With respect to [3], it is possible to produce steel directly by the smelting process, and this is termed the direct method. Steel iron bars or lumps of steel can be distributed to a market. The archaeological evidence includes 30 iron bars found in a group from Namioka-jo site (34) (Aomori-ken), and a similar type of bar from Iizaka-cho (Fukushima-ken), which were interpreted as being possibly soft steel (Sasaki 1898). The lump of iron of semicircular shape and 5 kg in weight found at Katsuyamadate site contained less than 1.7% carbon, suggesting that it is also a soft steel iron lump. The structure of iron artifacts — including iron arrows, fish spears, fishing hooks, and harpoons — is similar to that of the steel iron lump, which indicates that they may have been produced at Katsuyamadate by the forging process.

It is possible to interpret these examples as indicating the existence of steel iron bars in Tohoku during the 15th-16th centuries, and also it is possible to hypothesise that these lumps of steel might have been distributed within a certain network in society.

With respect to [4], mentioned above, forged iron products can be distributed to a market. Steel iron bars or a lumps of steel are prepared in order to form forged iron objects such as nails and clamps by hammering during a forging process. A forging hearth in the form of a hole-in-the-ground hearth is required to heat the material and to make steel iron soft. Many kinds of iron craft tools such as hammers, rasps, and chisels are required, and remains of them need to be found at a site for the identification of the forging process. Slag and hammering scale as by-products are also required and need to be found at a site for the identification of this process. The shape of slag which is made in a hole-in-the-ground hearth is identical with that of the bottom of a bowl. This shape of slag results from the refining process, which uses a hole-in-the-ground hearth. However, if slag is made by the refining process, material of decarburisation such as iron sand and iron ore can be traced in the micro-structure of the slag.

4-8 Conclusion

If the smelting process is not familiar to a society and raw material is not available in society, as in the case of Ainu society, then iron materials are obtained through a distribution network.

In the above discussion, I have considered four ways of distributing iron to consumers: [1] A cast iron product such as an iron pan is produced and distributed to a market. [2] It is possible to distribute a lump or a bar of *sentetsu* to a market. [3] Steel iron bars or a mass of steel can be distributed to a market. [4] Forged iron products can be distributed to a market. Therefore, there are four roots of distribution can be considered to Ainu society. These include iron products such as completed objects and basic material in the form of bars, ingots, etc. A reconstruction of the Ainu iron technology is offered in Chapter 5.

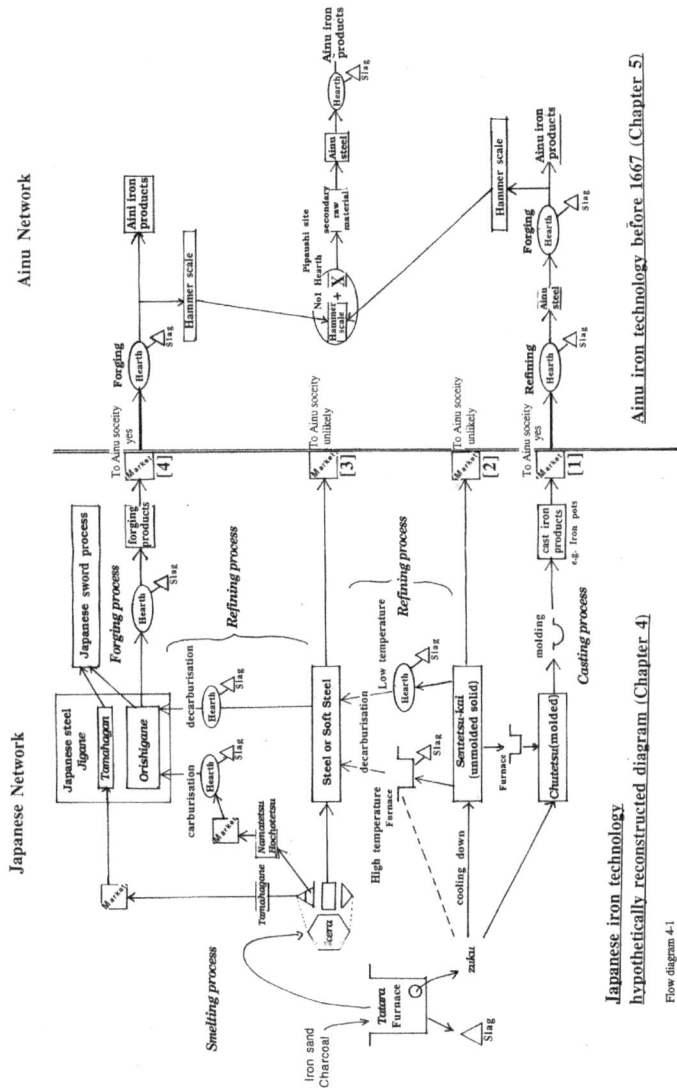

Pg 49

Please note that a full-size version of this page is available to download from www.barpublishing.com/additional-downloads.html
The original foldout has been reduced in size to match the A4 format of this book, the image is therefore not as clear as the original foldout. Please refer to the original foldout via the download for the original content.

Chapter 5

Iron technology and the steel production process of the Saru Ainu, Hokkaido in the 17th century

5-1 Introduction

In this chapter, I shall discuss the Ainu sites where artifacts relating to iron metallurgy and iron artifacts dating from before 1667 were found. I shall try to interpret Ainu iron technology based on the archaeological and ethnographical evidence, and upon the results of metallurgical analysis. I shall attempt to reconstruct the process by which iron came into and passed out of the Ainu culture within the Ainu network and how it related to the Japanese network.

5-1-1 The Ainu sites in Nibutani, Biratori-cho

The present Nibutani village was formed sometime between 1877 and 1888 and consists of old Nibutani (Niputani) *kotan*, Pipaushi-*kotan*, and Kankan-*kotan* (*kotan* usually means village; however, it does not correspond precisely to our concept of a village because even a single house standing by itself can be termed a *kotan*). The Ainu population of this village at the present is still large.

These three *kotan* are all situated along the lower reaches of the Saru River, which is located in south-west Hokkaido, running from the Hidaka mountains towards the south-west until it reaches the Pacific Ocean. The Ainu who lived along the Saru River were called the Saru Ainu (see Fig. 5-1).

According to a historical document (Matsuura 1858), the Honkankan Stream was on the flat east terrace of the Saru River, and there were 3 houses on the terrace; because of the height of the terrace, they were safe from flooding. Matsuura also mentions the origin of the place name Nifutani (Nibutani), which means 'the place where long ago someone had dedicated a wooden sword which had been decorated with metal'. There is another interpretation of this place name is given by Yamada (Yamada 1984). He divides Nibutani into three parts: Nipu-Ta-I, which means 'the place where handles were made'. The meaning of the name is still debatable. I mention particularly, Matsuura's interpretation because it refers to the use of metals.

There is a stream called Furenai in Nibutani: *fure* in the Ainu language means 'red'. Matsuura mentions that the name refers to the colour of the stream, which is iron red, and means water containing iron. There is an other place called Furenai, 10 km upstream from Nibutani on the Saru River. This was a mining village between 1817 and 1944. A total of 200,000 tons of chromium was mined there at that time according to the records (Biratori-cho 1974). Chromium here means chromium iron, therefore iron was also obtained as a by-product. There are places called Furenai which are linked to some kind of iron mining, not only in Biratori-cho but also in many places in Hokkaido. Sulphide ore was also mined by open-cast mining at Furenai in Abuta-cho, Hokkaido.

The geological composition of this area (the Hidaka district) is a Tertiary formation. The existence of well-formed chromium iron deposits on the upper reaches of the Saru River indicates that iron sand is obtainable in the middle reaches of the river. There is also evidence in an old geological record that deposits of the old type of iron sand have been mined in Hobetsu in the Mukawa River valley which is parallel to the Saru River valley. The iron sand is normally found as lens-shaped deposits; one edge of the deposits might have been exposed in the Saru River valley.

The area of my fieldwork is located along the Saru River in Hidaka. The Ainu sites which have been excavated in the present Nibutani village are the Yuoichashi, Poromoichashi, and Nibutani site at Niputani-kotan. The Nibutani site is a settlement site, including two burials, which is located between Yuoi and Poromoi-chashi (a *chashi* is a place which is enclosed by a man-made structure such as a ditch or conveniently located on a higher geological level. Its functions are still debatable but were certainly multiple), both of which have ditches. It is thought that chashi always have such ditches. Within 1 km of these sites, up the Saru River, the Pipaushi site at Pipaushi-kotan is located, and another 1 km further on, the Iruekashi site at Kankan-kotan is located at the junction of the Kankan River and the Saru River (Fig. 5-2).

Especially in the area of Chitose and Hidaka, deposits of volcanic ash which fell in 1667 and cover a fairly large area up the east side of Hokkaido are found. It is archaeologically significant that all the sites were found immediately under Tarumae b (Ta-b) volcanic ash (deposited in 1667), which makes it possible to correlate them within the same time range using Tarumae b as a key layer. At the Pipaushi site, it is very significant that the dating of the site was determinable from the fact that the structures are sandwiched between two layers of volcanic ash which derive from different volcanic explosions in 1663 and 1667, datable from records in historical documents (see Chapter 3).

Although the archaeological evidence from the Yuoichashi, Poromoichashi, and Nibutani sites does not relate directly to iron technological activity (i.e. through the existence of tuyeres, hearth, slag and hammer scale, such as were found at the Pipaushi and Iruekashi sites), a great variety and quantity of iron artifacts were discovered amounting to more than 200 items. These included agricultural tools, fishing tools, living tools, ornaments, arms and weapons, etc. It follows that in the interpretation and reconstruction of the iron technology of the Saru Ainu, all the sites in the area of Nibutani should be taken into account.

There is another area, the Yukanboshi site, in which archaeological evidence of iron technological activity in the Ainu context before 1667 was also found. It is located in Chitose-shi, and it is interesting to note that it is said among

Fig. 5-1   The location of the Saru River.

Fig. 5-2   The excavated Ainu sites along the Saru River.

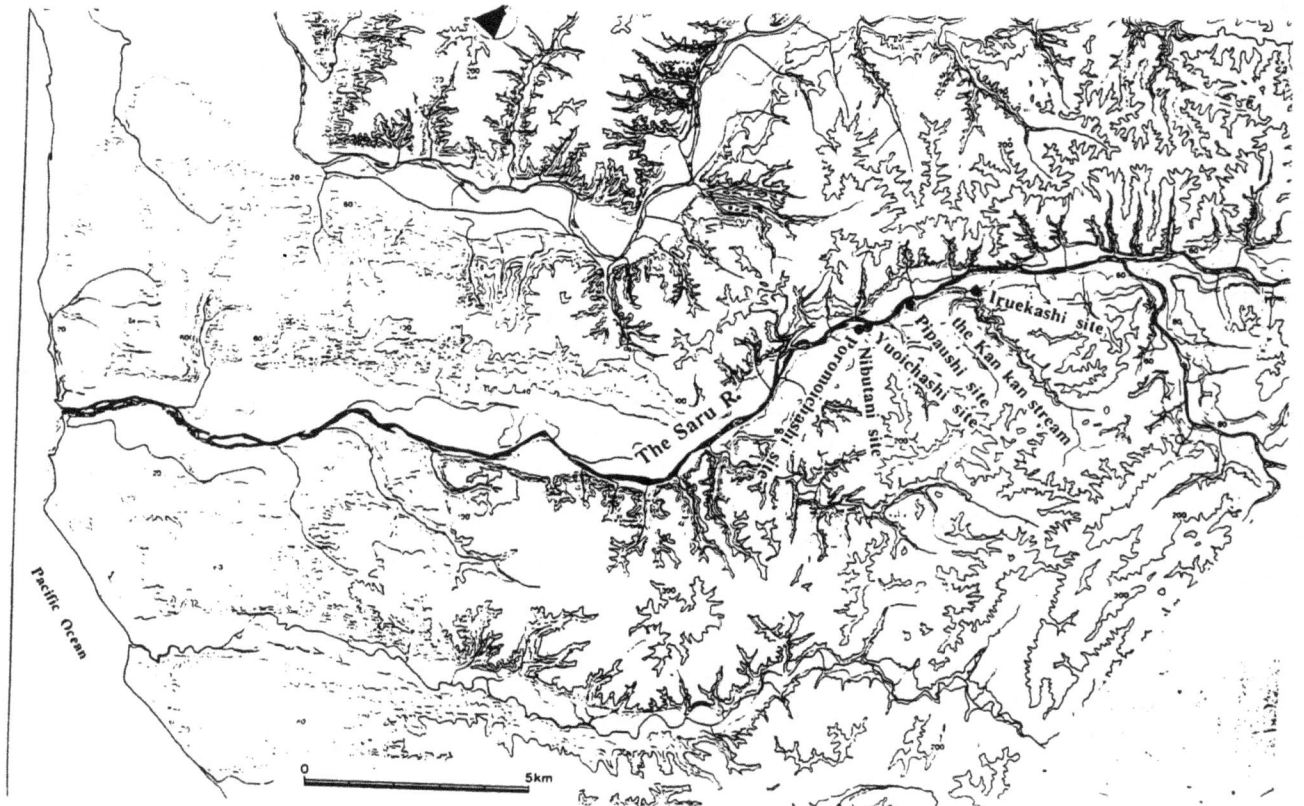

the Ainu people that the Saru Ainu and the Chitose Ainu had some kind of relationship in the past. The archaeological evidence of the burial structures and the burial goods which were found in both the Chitose area and at the Nibutani site have features in common too (Miura 1989).

Therefore, I would like to reconstruct the technological aspects of iron production, particularly in the area of the Saru Ainu, though considered within the wider context of Ainu culture as a whole during the 17th century.

5-2 How the Ainu obtained iron material: the distribution network

There is no historical, ethnographical or archaeological evidence, such as *tatara* furnace sites for the process of smelting iron in Ainu territories in Hokkaido, so it is unlikely that the Ainu produced iron from iron sand or iron ore by using smelting methods. However, according to Aida (Aida 1978), there was a *tatara* iron-smelting site operated by Wajin [Japanese] who were producing iron from iron sand by the *tatara* method in Hokkaido in the late 19th century (1860s) in the Wajin territory of Nakanosawa Valley in Kikyo-machi Hakodate-shi.

Previous to this, the ways in which the Ainu carried on iron production using material from outside their culture, need to be examined, including the way in which they gained iron products to furnish the basic raw material, both in the form of whole objects and unknown fragments of scrap iron. The four ways of distributing iron to the market within the Japanese network, discussed in Chapter 4, need to be taken into account in any consideration of exchange and/or trade or any kind of contact between the Ainu and outsiders (see Flow diagram 4-1 pp.49-50).

5-2-1 Voyage of Captain Maarten Gerritsz Vries to a Gold and Silver Island near Japan in 1643.

Before discussing of the technological interpretation of Saru Ainu iron metallurgy based on the results obtained from metallurgical analysis, I would like to examine a very important piece of ethnographic evidence from 1643 which was recorded by Europeans. This was published in 1858 by P.A. Leupe, a Dutch naval officer, who discovered this record in the Dutch National Archives (Leupe 1858, Kitagamae 1983). Although this ethnographic evidence does not relate directly to the area of the Saru Ainu, the date is very close to the pre-1667 date of the Saru Ainu sites. It is also useful in illuminating the Ainu iron distribution network and the way in which the Ainu obtained iron.

The document concerns the expedition of M. G. Vries, a Dutch captain who set off on a voyage on the 2nd of February 1643, from Batavia, Java, under the orders of Anthonio van Diemen, Head of the Dutch East Indian Company, which had been set up at Batavia in 1602. He was instructed to locate an island which was full of gold and silver.

The background to understanding this document is that

... a Spanish ship sailing from Manila to Mexico in 1582 was driven off course by a storm into the northern latitudes (F. A. Golder: Russian Expansion on the Pacific 1641-1850). An island was sighted, upon which lived a people possessing an infinite variety of gold utensils acquired from local resources. When the crew of this ship eventually reached Mexico, its members reported this experience with great enthusiasm. Ripples of interest aroused by these stories reached Spain and caused some Spanish atlases to depict an island to the north-east of Japan labelled 'Isla de Plate' island of gold (John 1969).

The King of Spain ordered an expedition to look for such an island in 1610, but it did not succeed. Captain Sebastian Vizcaino, a Spanish captain, also came to look for the island in 1611 (Kodama 1971). In 1639, Captain M. Cuast also tried to locate the island, but again the expedition did not succeed.

On this basis, the orders of Captain M. G. Vries were to find an island in the Pacific Ocean, which was thought to be located around latitude N 37.5 degrees, 343 Dutch miles east of Japan, and to make observations of the island and the habits of its people, who were said to be big, tall, and beautiful with white skin, and to be a highly civilised and friendly people. He was also ordered to establish friendly relations with them for future trade, as it was considered quite certain that the island was rich in gold and silver. In addition to this duty, Captain Vries was told that all islands and lands, wherever he stopped or stayed during his voyage, whether inhabited or not, should be claimed for the Dutch; if the land was already systematically ruled then it would take some time, but if it was an uninhabited land or without a ruler, then he was to leave a big memorial stone and put up the Dutch flag as evidence that the land had been occupied by the Dutch.

Because of this purpose of their expedition, Captain Vries and his crew paid particular attention to metals observed on the journey. The records of the voyage, which were written by Corneils Janzs. Coen, the first officer under Captain Vries, offer a tremendous opportunity for understanding the metallurgical aspects of the Ainu culture and the Ainu's situation at that time, as the records contain full descriptive details of his observations of metals in use among the Ainu. Captain Vries thought that the islands of Habomai, Kunashiri, and Urupu in the Kurile (Chishima) islands and Sakhalin (Karafuto) island near Hokkaido, where the Ainu lived, were the "islands of gold and silver", based on the observation that their inhabitants wore silver earrings and ornaments and possessed many silver decorated daggers. The people also showed an extensive knowledge of metal. These people were the Ainu.

This record has great value not only in respect of the metallurgical aspects of Ainu culture but also as a general ethnographic record of Ainu life and society on the east side of Hokkaido, including the north-east of the islands, in 1643. The record mentions that the Ainu were a friendly, jolly and generous people, for wherever Captain Vries and his crew landed, they were welcomed in a very polite way and received plenty of fresh fish to eat and to take away.

It is stated, for example, that ". . . the people gave us as many fresh fish as we wanted, so we gave them small gifts for their generosity" (Leupe 1858). On the 5th of July, (at Sapoi) it was noted (my translation from the Dutch and the Japanese):

> Landed by boat and launch. We brought a fishing net and some rice for the people as a gift. The people are eager for rice, and we have seen their poor way of life. As soon as we landed, they came to see us without any weapons, and expressed their friendliness to us as much as possible . When we gave them rice, they accepted it in the most polite way. They helped us to pull in our fishing net so that plentiful fish were caught, enough for all the crew to eat. In the afternoon, we landed again, this time, the launch was grounded due to the low tide. The people helped us anxiously and offered to let us stay at their house (Leupe 1858).

On July 17th, at Tamari (on Sakhalin island), Coen writes:

I, with two other crew members was invited to go into a hut which was built in a triangular shape. Inside the hut there was an iron pot with cooked fish and vegetables in it on the central hearth. We were served by women with salmon and green vegetables on a lacquer Japanese tray which has three legs, and is associated with chopsticks which are used for eating. One of the crew could not manage to use chopsticks so that he could not eat the salmon. All of us laughed together (Leupe 1858).

Noteworthy details of this record are that the Ainu were using an iron pot, a Japanese lacquer tray, and chopsticks in 1643; moreover, they ate salmon and green vegetables, which might have been wild vegetables, and rice, which the Ainu were very pleased to be given. In all these respects their lifestyle sounds almost the same as that of the Japanese. This may indicate that many Japanese goods had reached to the Ainu by exchange or trade at that time, though they seem to have had little rice, to judge from their pleasure at receiving it.

It would be fascinating to describe the whole of Ainu society based on this ethnographical material, including details of their houses, food, clothes, burials, behaviour, etc., but let us here focus on Ainu metallurgy, recorded only, in passing, are interesting detail noted by Coen: that Ainu dogs were trained to catch salmon.[1]

Captain Vries first met the Ainu at Tokachi on the southeast cost of Hokkaido on June 9th, before concluding that he had discovered the Gold and Silver Islands, when he saw that the Ainu possessed many silver objects around Tamari on July 16th. According to the record, there were holes in the ear lobes of the people, and strings hung from them. One had rings instead of strings made of an alloy of gold and copper. Daggers were hung on their hips and the hilts of these were decorated with silver. A golden sword appeared to be Japanese in style, but silver also could be seen upon it. These facts clearly indicate that the people were well acquainted with gold and silver (Leupe 1858). It is also recorded that the people wore big silver earrings, and that they knew a great deal about gold and silver, but they thought little of copper (Leupe 1858).

The record for July 4th states:

> the people here are the same as those whom we met before at Tokachi and Tamari. There were four men, two women, two girls and one young girl in all on this beach where we landed to enquire about gold and silver. One man possesses a sword of which the metallic part was inlaid with silver. I asked them with gestures how and where you obtain their silver. An old woman among them seemed to understand my question immediately, and she expressed by the action of inserting her hand into the sand and digging in it. Then she put some sand on her hand, making a sound like si! si! , and put it into a small pot which she then put onto a fire. Her action was quite clear so that we understood what she meant. "Kani" is their word for silver. I asked again with gestures where they find silver like this. They pointed to Anthony Peak as the place where they get it, then all agreed with each other (Leupe 1858).

I consider this record to be extremely important as corroboration of the fact that the Ainu already knew how to smelt silver, in the manner demonstrated by the Ainu woman. This is the first written evidence, to my knowledge, to discuss the Ainu's knowledge of silver. It is also possible to interpret it as indicating that they had an advanced knowledge of metal alloys, which implies an understanding of metal production as a process involving the transformation of silver from the solid state of silver as a raw material to the liquid state of silver in a pot, achieved by controlling the temperature with fire.

The Ainu and Captain Vries exchanged goods in a friendly manner; the Ainu offered many fish and animal skins. In return they received tabacco, rice, pieces of cloth, ribbon and glass beads. However, what the Ainu were eager to receive from them was iron. The record states:

---

[1] The report says that at Tamari (in Sakhalin), " When I was sitting in a hut, a surprising thing happened. It is that their dogs are trained to catch fish easily; the dogs wait along the river as if they were human, one of them keeping an eye on the river and the rest of them as a group running along the river. When the salmon come up the river, all of the dogs go into the water

making a formation like a semicircle and swimming in the water to create splashes so that the salmon jump up over the surface of the water into shallow places, then the dogs catch the heads of the salmon and bring them to their master in his hut, and go back to the river again".

an old man came towards me and gave me a nice sea-otter skin, so I gave him an iron axe used on the ship, which I found in the launch. He was extremely pleased so that his expression was more than full of joy (Leupe 1858).

The record also states:

we obtained fresh salmon, dry salmon and other fish, as much as we could carry by boat, exchanging an iron ring, rice, and also a piece of hempen cloth which we wear around the neck in our country. Women and children came towards us and brought many fish, making a heap of fish in front of us, as if they wanted to fill our boat with fish and each one of the crowd gave us their fish, saying "Takoi Kani", which sounded as if they are asking us "Friends, give us iron", so that we could not control our boat. When an old man in this village saw this, he stopped them coming along in such a crowd together. Then later 4-5 people in a small group came to us for exchange. However, our boat was so small that we had to leave it away from the land. When we returned to the main ship, almost 30 people came to send us off by singing a song as they had done when we landed. On the way back to the main ship until we reached it, they kept saying and shouting "Takoi, Tamari, Piruka, Kani", "Takoi, Tamari, Piruka, Kani" which sounded as if they were saying "Friends, come back again, when you come back next time, bring lots more iron". We went back to the main ship around 4:00 PM; it was raining hard (Leupe 1858).

It is clear from this description that the Ainu desperately wanted iron and got it by exchanging their goods such as fish and skins with whomever they could, whenever and wherever possible. The Ainu word *kani* here means iron; however, it also means silver as previously mentioned. The word *kani* refers to metal in general, but I shall discuss it in more detail in Chapter 6.

The report also mentioned that on July 19th:

A boat came to our ship from the land full of fish, and we started to exchange. We even obtained a live bear. A man showed a piece of mineral to Captain M. G. Vries apparently saying that it was silver and pointing to the mountain on the land from which it came. The mountain is in a south-south-east direction from us now, and is the same one that we saw on the 14th July. As we were sailing away from this bay, another boat full of skins and dried fish came towards us, rowing beside our ship. As we were sailing too fast, the boat could not catch us, and went back to the land with the others. -(omission)-
After we had been sailing for some time, I discovered that an official letter, which I had given to the people together with a Dutch flag

when we were on the land, had been left on the box of ammunition behind the cannons. I wonder what this means, and why they left the letter there; I am wondering the reason for this. There were many people here boarding our ship, they informed us that there is much silver in the mountain. The people here value iron more than silver (Leupe 1858).

As the record concluded, iron was clearly an important material for the Ainu people, at least by 1643. It is important to consider that there would have been no point in the Ainu asking for iron, if they had not known the value of iron, and had not known the ways in which iron can be used.

5-2-2 Archaeological evidence

The area described in these documents of 1643 is on the north and east side of Hokkaido. However, the archaeological evidence discussed here is concentrated in the south-west of Hokkaido, where the Saru Ainu live. The time range is sometime before 1667.

The archaeological evidence for iron products at Ainu sites comprises a wide range of material including Ainu daggers, knives, fishing hooks, harpoons, nails, iron arrowheads, drills, sickles, hoes, axes, points, iron pots, swords, and scraps of iron, including miscellaneous iron plates, iron rings, iron bars, and iron chains, etc. These iron products were potentially usable in two ways in Ainu society, either as iron objects in their own right or as a source of iron materials. Iron nails must have been brought onto the site as a result of trade, exchange, or collection — as the Ainu did not use nails for building their houses or ships or for any purpose other than recycling for the iron material.

It is possible to interpret such a variety of miscellaneous iron products as the result of Ainu attempts to obtain iron objects as a secondary raw material from which to make their own iron products. This also implies that the Ainu possessed some kind of iron technology. There would have been no point in obtaining miscellaneous iron objects without being equipped to transform them into useful objects using technology of their own.

Material modified by the Ainu which I have defined as "material of the Ainu's own processing" in Chapter 3, can be illustrated by the simple example of reuse of a broken sword that was found among these iron products (Miura 1989). Let us concentrate on the technological aspect and discuss iron objects which were used as a secondary raw material.

(1) Iron material

(a) Miscellaneous iron products

In view of the above comments, miscellaneous iron products furnish good evidence for the use of iron secondary raw material as a source for iron material. At the Iruekashi site (Biratori-cho Kyoiku-iinkai 1989), finds included nails, *kozane* (iron lamellae for armour) clamps, and miscellaneous pieces of iron shaped into bars and plates; the total weight of these was 413.2 g. These materials were not found near the forging hearth; therefore, an examination of the relationship between the area of distribution of these materials and the hearth is required.

According to the result of the metallurgical analysis of iron miscellaneous products at the Yukanboshi site (3) (see Table 5-1), the data indicate no common features in terms of proportion of chemical components which would facilitate tracing them back to their place of origin. This means that such miscellaneous iron products reached the site from various places. This is, on the other hand, not the case with iron pots, which share a diagnostic chemical characteristic, namely a high proportion of phosphorus (Akanuma 1989).

Among such miscellaneous iron products, there is evidence which may relate to trade to the north-east within the Ainu network, such as coil-like objects and coil-like rings found at the Nibutani site (Hokkaido Maizo Bunkazai Center 1986). Similar objects were found as burial goods at the Raitokoro-kawaguchi site (Tokyo University 1980), which is located along the Sea of Okhotsk — the area described in the ethnographic account discussed above.

Table 5-1   The chemical composition of miscellaneous iron products at the Yukanboshi site (3)

	T.Fe	Cu	Mn	P	Ni	Co	Ti	Si	Ca	Al
Arrow 4452	65.73	0.010	0.004	0.005	0.017	0.036	0.043	0.443	0.022	0.062
Chain 1084	62.61	0.004	0.012	0.096	0.014	0.012	0.017	0.443	0.077	0.098
Metal fitting 5580-126	59.26	0.022	0.002	0.079	0.037	0.059	0.026	0.220	0.018	0.029
Metal fitting 6078-68	88.09	0.002	0.029	0.083	0.010	0.009	0.030	0.079	0.016	0.033

(b) Iron pots

Iron pots and fragments of iron pots are also found on Ainu sites. These pieces of iron pots may have been used as a source of iron. 18 fragments of iron pots were found at Nibutani site (Hokkaido Maizo Bunkazai Center 1986), which is a large number considering the location and area of the site. 63 fragments of iron pots were found at the Iruekashi site, their average size being approximately 5 cm in diameter, and their total weight 748.5 g, while 37 iron pots were discovered at the Yukanboshi site (Chitose-shi Kyoiku-iinkai, forthcoming).

According to typological studies (Koshida 1984), they resemble Japanese iron pot types dating from the 12th century to the 17th-18th centuries. The iron pots are divided into two major types based on the type of hanging handle; one is an outer hanging handle type and other is an inner hanging handle type. The inner hanging handle type is considered to have appeared in the 15th century and is earlier than the outer hanging handle type, which was common in the 17th century. The outer hanging handle type has been found at the Iruekashi, Pipaushi, and Nibutani site. The inner hanging handle type was found at Poromoichashi. It is interesting to note that examples of the inner hanging handle type made in pottery (N.B. not an iron pot) were found among the Satsumon pottery at the Nishitsukigaoka site, Nemuro-shi, in Hokkaido and among Haji -ware pottery at the Yomogida-odate site in Aomori-ken, Tohoku.

According to the results of metallurgical analysis of the iron pots (see Table 5-2) from the sites of Iruekashi, Pipaushi, Nibutani, Poromoi and Yukanboshi, were all made of *chutetsu* (cast iron), as indicated by a carbon content of more than 1.7% and the evidence of ledebulite in the metallographic results. These pots also contain a high proportion of phosphorus.

Since casting sites are not found in Hokkaido, these iron pots must originally have been of external origin, and it must be assumed that the Ainu acquired them by exchange as a result of the trade. Judging from the typological and metallurgical studies, it is likely that these iron pots were produced in mainland Japan.

Table 5-2   The chemical composition of iron pots.
The following data are compiled from excavation reports, including forthcoming ones, listed in Appendix-1.

	Samples from sites	T.Fe	FeO	C%	SiO$_2$	Cu	CaO	TiO$_2$	Mn	P	S
1	Iruekashi I-35-18	87.06		4.48		0.008		0.002	0.006	0.092	0.055
1	Iruekashi K-35-10	86.54		4.36		0.013		0.012	0.003	0.150	0.036
1	Iruekashi J-34-1	82.08		4.22		0.0011		0.002	0.006	0.063	0.078
1	Iruekashi L-36-2	88.86		4.60		0.007		0.002	0.006	0.100	0.054
1	Iruekashi M-35-1	86.58		4.52		0.009		0.003	0.006	0.078	0.046
1	Iruekashi J-34-2	86.18		5.30		0.008		0.009	0.006	0.068	0.082
1	Iruekashi K-34-4	88.17		5.94		0.009		0.001	0.005	0.170	0.059
1	Iruekashi K-36-1	91.31		4.39		0.0018		0.009	0.007	0.120	0.036
2	Pipaushi G-11-68	85.00	12.70	4.83	1.19		0.085	0.019	0.033	0.280	0.065
2	Pipaushi G-11-69	77.00	<0.01	5.19	1.61		0.076	0.011	0.035	0.290	0.120
3	Yukanboshi 3761	85.43			0.396	0.012	0.044	0.014	0.010	0.174	0.156
	Poromoichashi	81.44				0.009			0.0016	0.173	
	Nibutani iseki	82.77				0.0073		0.0017		0.0505	
	Bibi 8	69.38				0.014			0.005	0.128	
	Bibi 8	78.16				0.034			0.009	0.220	
	Bibi 8	84.93				0.023			0.013	0.175	
5	Katsuyamadate	52.2				0.003		0.047	0.030	0.029	
	Ohamanaka	72.58				0.007			0.006	0.061	
	Yomogida odate	43.50				<0.001				0.112	
	Shoroyadate	59.10				0.0066		0.0133		0.3107	

5-3 Evidence of the forging process

It is clear from the archaeological evidence that the Ainu carried out forging prior to 1667. The evidence includes hearths, tuyeres, slag, hammer scale, and charcoal found at the Iruekashi (Biratori-cho Kyoiku-iinkai 1989), Pipaushi (Biratori-cho Kyoiku-iinkai, forthcoming) and Yukanboshi (Chitose-shi Kyoiku-iinkai, forthcoming) sites, which are within the Ainu cultural context. These finds definitely attest to a knowledge of the forging process of iron technology.

5-3-1 Hearths

Hearths were found outside the post holes of the houses at Iruekashi and Pipaushi; one was found within the post hole boundary of the house at Yukanboshi. These hearths contained slag and hammer scales, indicating their function as hearths where forging had taken place.

The structures of the hearths at these sites differ slightly in shape one from another, but, by and large, they constitute an oval shallow pit with burnt soil quite similar to standard forging hearths.

At the Iruekashi site, despite careful investigation around the hearth, no evidence, such as post holes, was found which would have indicated structures around the hearth; from this I assume that the hearth was situated outside and away from any structure.

The long axis of the hearth is 110 cm east-west and the short axis is 80 cm south-north. This area is divided into two parts. One is a cone-shaped hearth pit with dimensions of 15 cm in depth, 34 cm on the long axis, and 27 cm on the short axis. This is associated with a slag concentration. The other part is situated on the west side of the hearth pit, with dimensions of 13 cm in depth, 80 cm on the long axis, and 68 cm on the short axis; it is associated with burnt soil (see Fig. 5-3).

Fig. 5-3   Hearth at the Iruekashi site (1).

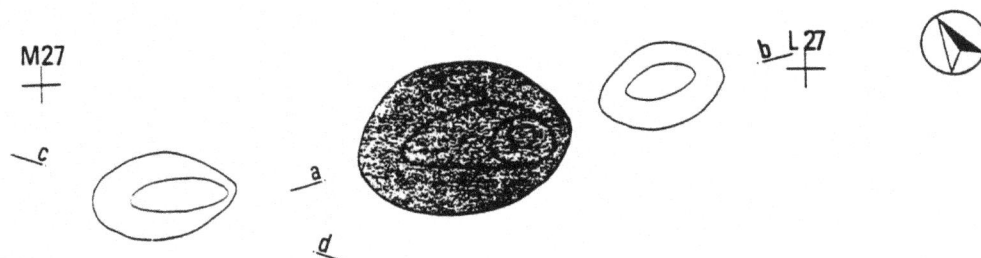

Fig. 5-4   Hearths at the Pipaushi site (2).
(see Photo. 5-5 for No. 1 hearth).

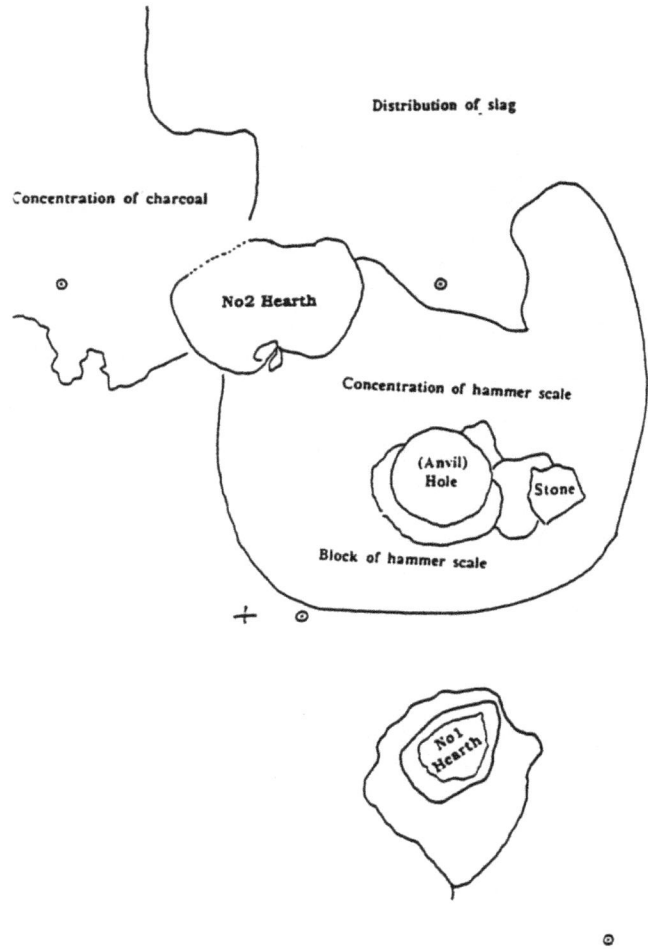

Distribution of slag

Concentration of charcoal

No2 Hearth

Concentration of hammer scale

(Anvil)
Hole

Stone

Block of hammer scale

No1
Hearth

Fig. 5-5   Hearth at the Yukanboshi site (3)
(see Table 5-3).

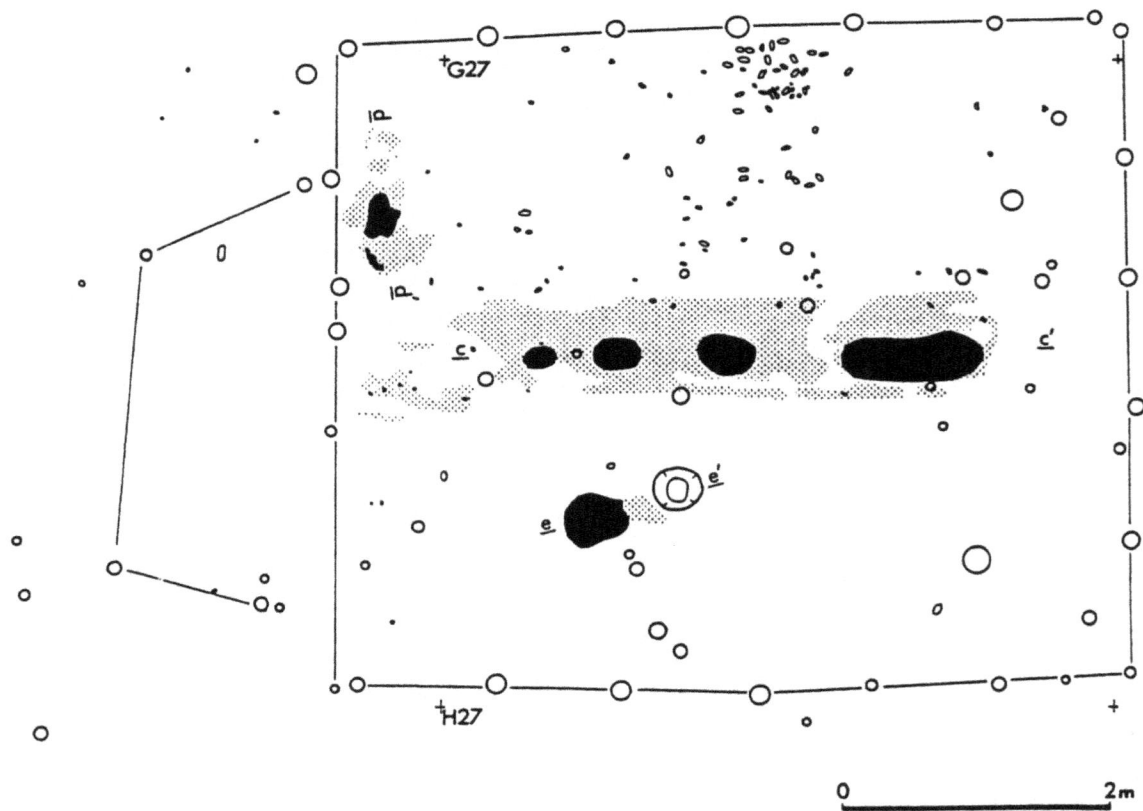

+G27

+H27

0   2m

However, two hearths found at the Pipaushi site exhibited totally different features even though they are located within 1m of each other within an area over which slag and hammer scale was spread. The initial appearance of hearth No. 1 was just a mound of yellowish clay associated with several orange blocks of burnt soil. It did not look like a hearth — in contrast to hearth No. 2 which was clearly a hearth relating to iron technology — but was identified as a hearth with some relation to iron technology because of the orange blocks of burnt soil.

No. 1 hearth (Photo. 5-5) consisted of a pit 20 cm x 15 cm in size, of oval shape and with a flat bottom, proving to be 6cm in depth after the excavation of a yellowish mound, and the removal of the yellowish clay until it disappeared at the bottom. Several pieces of hammer scale 1mm in size were found within this clay in the middle of the mound. No other material was mixed in it. However, there were several burned

orange blocks of soil on top of the mound and a piece of carbonised wood underneath it.

No. 2 hearth was 50 cm x 30 cm in area and oval in shape, although one quarter was destroyed by a later feature. It was surrounded by vivid orange burned soil associated with a considerable amount of slag and charcoal. This orange layer went below a black layer mixed with slag and charcoal in the centre. This hearth was clearly related to iron technology in view of the associated slag and burned soil (see Fig. 5-4).

It is thought-provoking to compare these Ainu forging hearths with the Satsumon forging hearths in the pre-Ainu period in order to identify any sequential features. The Satsumon forging hearth was normally situated inside the structure of the dwelling pit, but at the Ranshima site (9) (Otaru-shi Kyoiku-iinkai 1989), for example, one hearth was a hole-in-the-ground hearth (an open-field type), and at the Nishikicho 5 site (8) (Asahikawa-shi Kyoiku-iinkai 1984), one hearth was also located outside (see Table 5-3).

Table 5-3   The location of hearths.

	Inside	outside
The Ainu period	Yukanboshi site	Iruekashi & Pipaushi sites
The Satsumon period	most	Ranshima & Nishikicho 5 sites

In the Satsumon period, there are two examples of forging hearths which were divided into two parts: One contained slag and scale, indicating its function as a forging hearth, and the other one possibly contained an anvil at the Suehiro site (10) (Chitose-shi Kyoiku-iinkai 1981, 1982) and the Satsumae site (6) (Matsumae-cho Kyoiku-iinkai 1985) in Hokkaido respectively. Both sites are dated between the 8th and 10th centuries, and evidence of hammering techniques has been found associated with two pits in the centre of the dwelling pit. At the Satsumae site, in the hearth of the 21-H dwelling pit, the structure of the hearth consisted of two joined pits.

The number of craftspeople may be estimated by the size of the hearths, and by taking into account the frequency of use, specialisation, and character of the site. An illustration of the Sakhalin Ainu drawn in the 19th century (see Fig. 5-6, Mamiya 1808) exhibits three craftspeople working on the forging. In the case of the Iruekashi site, at least 2-3 people might have been required for the forging. The craftsperson who worked the bellows may have faced towards the west to take advantage of the prevailing wind direction, in which case the direction of the tuyeres may have been west-facing.

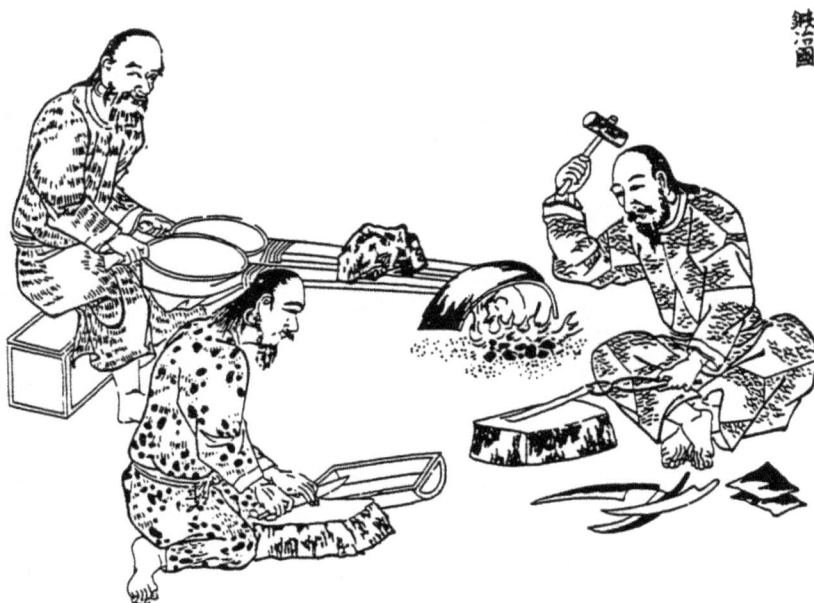

Fig. 5-6   Iron-working of the Sakhalin Ainu in the 19th century (Mamiya 1808)

5-3-2 Tuyeres

The thick walled type of tuyere from the Iruekashi and Pipaushi sites can indicate both the forging and the refining process.

At the Iruekashi site, the tuyeres are made of clay with some grass (scouring rush) mixed in as temper in order to make them stronger. The total weight of the tuyeres is 500g, which represents about 6 tuyeres; this estimate was made after refitting the pieces of tuyeres and counting the number of the diagnostic parts of the tuyeres.

At least three tuyeres were identified at Pipaushi site. This estimation was made by refitting the pieces of tuyeres and counting the numbers of the diagnostic parts of the tuyeres. Although it was not possible to reconstruct the complete shape of the tuyeres, it was possible to refit the pieces together. There were two spots, where the tuyere fragments were concentrated, which can be interpreted as indicating that the tuyeres were discarded and then broken into pieces. This thick type of tuyere is similar to the type from the Iruekashi site. The size of the tuyeres is 8-9cm in diameter, 3cm in thickness and 3cm in internal diameter. The Pipaushi tuyeres are made of clay without any temper, and are thus different from those at the Iruekashi site. The texture of the tuyeres is smooth, although they appear to be of a very coarse type.

5-3-3 Hammer scales

Pieces of scale approximately 5mm in diameter have been found by using sieves and magnets on the ash and the deposits from and around the hearth at the Pipaushi site. The total weight of the scale recovered is 540g.

Scale at the Pipaushi site was scattered in tremendously large quantities over an area 2m long axis, and 2cm in thickness; the area of greatest concentration occurred around a pit 30cm in diameter and 30cm in depth. Because of the exposed condition, considering the concentration of scale, the pit was identified as a hole in which an anvil had been inserted.

The pit was found associated with full of Tarumae B volcanic ash, which implies that the pit was empty when the ash fell in 1667, or that during the disaster, or immediately after the disaster, the area was cleared in order to move elsewhere. A mass of hammer scale was found around this pit indicating hammering activity. It is only the east edge of the pit which exhibits hammer scale tightly packed to a depth of 10cm below the surface.

The ground surface in this area was dark blue, because of the colour of hammer scale and brightly reflective. Most of the pieces of scale were still magnetised, so it was easy to collect them with magnets. The total weight of hammer scale was 3278.9g. Two different types of scale can be seen: one was thin and square in shape, 2 mm~10 mm, and the other was of spherical shape 2 mm~5 mm in diameter. A piece of silver 2 mm in length was also found.

Hammer scale has been interpreted as a decarburising agency at the Yukanboshi site (3) based on the analysis of scale size (Sato and Amano forthcoming).

Within the Satsumon context, hammer scale has been found at the Suehiro site (10) and the Nishikicho site (8), providing evidence of the hammering process associated with slag and scale.

Table 5-4   The chemical composition of hammer scale from the Pipaushi (2) and the Yukanboshi (3) sites. Shadowing indicates data analysed specially for my book by a metallurgical analyst K. Ito.

Site name	Sample no	T.Fe	FeO	Fe2O3	SiO2	Al2O3	CaO	TiO2	MnO	P	*
2	Pipaushi 1	71.2	61.0	32.8	2.53	0.70	0.46	0.12	0.20		3.89
2	Pipaushi 2	67.1	59.7	28.1	5.35	1.39	0.77	0.27	0.35		7.86
2	Pipaushi 3	51.3	11.8	59.6	7.84	2.51	0.68	0.13	0.73		11.76
2	Pipaushi 4	62.8	52.8	29.4	7.63	2.24	1.00	0.20	0.44		11.31
3	Yukanboshi 1	68.04	46.82	45.28				0.028			2.42
3	Yukanboshi 3	67.98	42.60	49.88				0.021			1.33
3	Yukanboshi 4	69.93	63.26	29.75				0.033			1.66
3	Yukanboshi 5	66.60	61.91	26.45				0.100			8.87
3	Yukanboshi 6	64.20	57.52	27.89				0.071			4.91
3	Yukanboshi 8	65.56	59.0	28.12				0.048			4.38
3	Yukanboshi 9	66.20	64.88	22.58				0.067			5.30

* = Si+Al+Ca+Mn

5-3-4 Slag

According to the results of the chemical composition of the slag found at the Iruekashi, Pipaushi, Yukanboshi sites, forging slag as well as refining slag was present (Table 4-3 in Chapter 4).

There was a slag concentration beside the hearth on the east side at the Iruekashi site. It lay in a shallow pit, as if it had been gathered from the hearth and collected into a heap. The total weight of the slag was 2.427kg. Metallurgical analyses of the slag residue indicate the process of forging, the raw materials used, and the scale of the forging. Morphological classification of the slag was carried out, using Kubota's method (Kubota 1983), which distinguishes 4 types; these are: 1) Slag that looks like solid thick malt syrup and appears to have just run out of the hearth. 2) Slag that is irregularly shaped, spongy with bubbles, and black in colour. 3) Slag that is brownish red and is assumed to contain lots of iron oxide. 4) Slag of low specific-gravity which had probably become attached to the wall or floor of the hearth. Among the materials excavated, I was able to classify the following quantities of each of Kubota's four types of slag: 1) 416g, 2) 231g, 3) 1595g, 4) 186g (Fukasawa 1989).

A small pile of slag was found at 1 m distance from the No. 1 hearth at the Pipaushi site. It lay on the volcanic ash of Usu (Us-b2), which indicates that it was discarded after 1663 but before 1667 (see Chapter 3). The area of the heap is 40cm x 30cm, and it is 5cm in thickness. The heap includes various sizes of dark brownish slag together with pieces of charcoal, pieces of tuyeres, and interestingly, pieces of burned deer bones which might indicate that the craftspeople ate deer meat during this work.

5-3-5 Charcoal

A concentration of charcoal was found at Pipaushi site (2) measuring 1.5m x 1.1m, and 10cm in thickness. It consisted of pieces of charcoal 1-3cm in diameter tightly packed together. It looks as if it was fuel and either had not been used or had been extinguished when in use. An attempt at identification using EMR indicated that the charcoal had been made from trees of the following species: Alnus, Magnolia, Fraxinus, and Fugas.

From all the above evidence there is no doubt that the Saru Ainu engaged in forging activities.

According to Rinzo Mamiya (Mamiya 1808), who reported forging among the Sakhalin Ainu in the early 19th century, accompanied by an illustration, mentioned previously (cf. Fig. 5-6):

> forging was usually carried out under the eaves of a house; a hammer could be anything suitable for pounding; iron was used not steel; they usually used iron objects like nails from old boats; they used any kind of iron which was available. Iron objects were obtained by trade at Shiranushi. The forging technique was the same as on the mainland of Japan; when an iron bar was to be extended they pounded it, and when an iron bar was to be joined, they threw ash and mud into the fire. When a blade was made, they put it into water for quenching. The process of producing iron objects was exactly the same as in Japan; however, the tools which they had were very primitive, so they could not make satisfactory products (Mamiya 1808).

Although the above evidence dated from the 19th century and the observation was made among the Sakhalin Ainu, it is clear that forging was practised outside but near the house, and that the Ainu obtained the raw material by trade. In Fig. 5-6, there is a cover over the hearth which might be a heat reflector; and the method of forging mentioned, using ash and mud, indicates that the iron was hot forged with a hearth of the same type as in Japan.

If this illustration is compared with the photograph of forging among the present-day Evenki, reindeer herders (see Photo. 5-1), one can find similarities between them. The area of forging among the Evenki is 2 x 2m; the ground is shallowly dug and the hearth is located in the centre of the area. Two tuyeres are set on the ground and are blown alternately. The Evenki collect and keep suitable iron objects, such as iron nails, lying nearby for use as a supply of iron materials. When a man decides to do some forging, on that day he starts to make a container from the bark of a white birch for the water used in quenching. The forging involves very hard work even to make only one knife. He is usually supported by a young man of his family or relations so that the young man can learn how to forge as he helps and can become his successor (Otsuka 1987).

5-4 Evidence of the refining process

The purpose of the refining process in iron technology is to produce finer quality iron or even steel from which the sharpest of iron tools can be produced. The steel is produced by refining the *sentetsu* by reducing the proportion of carbon content of the iron and removing inclusions from the iron. This process requires knowledge of how to control the proportion of carbon content of the iron, either from experience or through scientific knowledge. In the case under discussion, it was surely done by experience alone, as there were no written documents. In this process, certain additives, such as additional iron ore, iron sand, and ash, are required for controlling the carbon content. Thus, evidence of this refining process indicates advanced knowledge on the part of the craftsperson, and their intention to produce steel for finer iron and the sharpest of iron tools.

The slag which was found at the Iruekashi site (1) is a bottom slag (see Photo. 5-2). This type of slag is interpreted as the remains left at the bottom of the hearth, the shape of which it preserves, as a by-product of the refining process. This implies that the refining process can be carried out using a forging hearth as well as by using a furnace. In other words, a furnace is not necessary for the refining process, which is also dependent upon the temperature. This implies that the use or not of a furnace might also depend on the scale of the refining process: if it was only small-scale refining, it could have been carried out using a forging hearth.

According to the results of metallurgical analyses of slag at the Iruekashi site, a high proportion of iron oxide was also indicated (see Table 4-3 in Chapter 4), and iron sand particles were present. The question is at what stage was the iron sand utilised and how was it added. It needs to be determined whether or not it formed impurities in the iron products used as raw material. Iron sand particles may indicate that decarburisation had been carried out by the addition of iron sand during the melting process (see Chapter 4). If this interpretation can be applied to this material, then iron sand must have been added at an advanced stage of decarburisation.

The results of metallurgical analyses of slag from the Ainu site can be compared with those from a Satsumon example. According to the results at the Satsumae site (6) (see Table 4-3 in Chapter 4), iron sand particles were also found in the slag. This is interpreted as evidence for the refining of iron, as a decarburisation of *chutetsu* (cast iron) in the liquid state to produce steel (Osawa 1985). In this method the metal is heated, oxidised, and stirred in a furnace to reduce the carbon content. However, no furnace has been found at the Satsumae site. Therefore the existence of the refining process which was carried out by using a furnace has not been demonstrated as yet. However, a fireplace used as an oven, associated with a dwelling pit in Satsumon culture, might also have been used as a hearth for small-scale refining.

If this interpretation that the use of iron sand as an additive indicates decarburisation is correct, then it seems that several kilograms of iron sand would have been required, depending on the scale of activity. Taking as an example the blacksmiths (Fig. 5-6) among the Sakhalin Ainu in the early 19th century (Mamiya 1808, see above), I suggest that a handful of iron sand may have been thrown into the fire in the forging hearth several times. One who has knowledge of forging techniques can judge whether or not iron sand is obtainable from a river; presumably, that knowledge could have been shared among craftspeople. It is possible that iron sand was obtained locally from the Saru River. Even at present, iron sand can be obtained at approximately 50-60g per 1kg of river deposits, as can be demonstrated by geological experiment (Matsubara, personal comm.). The estimated date of the Iruekashi site is the 17th century, 300 years ago. At that time the proportion of iron sand obtainable from the river might have been much greater than 50-60g/kg, due to the fact that a chromium mining company was operating at the beginning of 20th century on the upper reaches of the Saru River and that it mined all the chromium iron deposits (Biratori cho shi 1974). In the 17th century, the technique for separating chromium and iron had not been discovered. Therefore, iron sand containing chromium might have used at that time.

An alternative interpretation is that hammer scale could have been used as a decarburising additive material at the Yukanboshi site (Amano, forthcoming).

It is possible that in an area where it was difficult to obtain refined products locally, pieces of iron pots could have played a very important role as a source of material. In this process, pieces of iron pot probably 5-10cm2 would have been heated in the hearth. Two methods of decarburisation are possible. Using a lot of air is one way; another is to use an additive which facilitates the decarburisation reaction, such as iron sand, iron ore, and hammering scale, and this may have been attached to such pieces of iron pot. Conjectural reconstruction of the method by which the process might have been carried out needs to take into account the temperature reached. In other words, it depends on the melting point of the pieces of iron pot.

Evidence from the Iruekashi and Pipaushi sites, and also from the Nibutani, Yuoi, and Poromoi sites, indicates that many iron pots existed in the Ainu culture as a result of trade with the mainland of Japan. Therefore, iron pots constitute a very likely source of iron material in Ainu iron technology. Taking this into account, a piece of iron pot which was made of *chutetsu* (cast iron) would require refining by heating and decarburising in a hearth in order to produce steel.

The role of iron pots found at Ainu sites is paralleled at Satsumon and Japanese sites. At the Satsumae site (6) (Osawa 1985), only a single piece of iron pot has been found, making it difficult to conclude that old pots were a major source of iron for re-use; however, the report mentions that the possibility of material reworked from pieces of iron pot is high because of the evidence of iron sand in the slag, as mentioned above. On the other hand, at the Kaminokuni-Katsuyamadate site (5) (Osawa 1985) many pieces of iron pots have been found. Bottom slag was also found. From this evidence, it is believed that iron pots were decarburised. They are believed to have been made into small iron products such as knives and fishhooks. However, examination of this lump of soft steel could lead us to an alternative interpretation. This find suggests that such small iron implements were made of soft steel, which might have been brought onto the site as discussed in Chapter 4.

There is no trace at the Ainu sites of lumps of refined iron such as ingot-shaped pieces of iron or *sentetsu*, or a semi-circular form of *sentetsu*, as the raw material for refining. Those iron products which have been found probably represent sources of iron as a raw material and would have been reworked into iron products such as *makiri* (the Ainu knife), daggers, *kite* (the Ainu harpoon), and fish hooks. According to the metallurgical analyses, the *makiri* at Iruekashi site (1) contains 1.17% carbon, which means it is steel (see Table 5-5). It cannot be determined whether iron was made from iron ore or iron sand on account of the lack of appropriate slag, although the proportion of phosphorus in the slag found was high (see Table 4-3 in Chapter 4).

Table 5-5   The chemical composition of *makiri* (small daggers) (from Iruekashi site report)

		T.Fe	FeO	C%	SiO2	Cu	CaO	TiO	Mn	P	S
1	Iruekashi F-12-2	93.92		1.17		0.011		0.023	0.003	0.062	0.120

According to the 18th-century historical document (Furukawa 1788) which I quoted in Chapter 2 indicating the iron prohibition policy adopted by the Matsumae-Han, it was said that many iron products, including carpenters' tools, had been passing to the Ainu for a long time. Such products were always of low quality, but when the Ainu received them, they transformed them into objects of higher quality. The writer continues by saying that he found it difficult to believe this story, but that he had heard it from the people who lived in the Matsumae territory so he recorded this fact. I interpret the sentence "when the Ainu received them they transformed them into objects of higher quality" as meaning that the Ainu knew how to make steel by the refining process. The Ainu could have had the technology to transform dull, blunt, and low-quality iron into higher-quality iron, such as steel by the time this document was written.

Furukawa did not know about iron technological processes, and he did not believe this story that he had heard in Matsumae. However, he honestly recorded the story as it was, even mentioning that he, as a representative of the Japanese at that time, did not believe the story. If the iron products made by the Ainu had been of low quality, as the Japanese expected, then no one would have talked about the quality of the iron material made by the Ainu. It is logical to suppose that the only reason this story became rumour among the people in Matsumae is that the Ainu genuinely were able to transform poor iron into higher-quality material. To someone equipped with a knowledge of metallurgy, this obviously implies that a refining process was being used to produce steel, thereby transforming low-quality iron material into iron of higher quality.

A historical document indicates that iron products were manufactured by the *tatara* process in a field, using iron sand at Usori beach in the Tsugaru area on the Shimokita peninsula in Tohoku, which was controlled by the Ando family in the 14th century. It is said that iron bars, harpoons, anchors, chains, wires, and iron pots were produced on a large scale and were distributed by the fleet of the Ando family. The Ainu may have obtained such iron pots as iron products and objects, both for use and as a source of raw iron material by trade and contact with the Japanese.

5-4-1 A different social context

The points which I have discussed above show that the Ainu wanted to obtain steel and that they had a knowledge of refining techniques sufficient to produce it.

Although the nature of steel is admirable, so that the demand for it is very high, it is not easy to produce steel directly. For example, the production process of *tamahagane* (the best Japanese steel) by the *tatara* smelting method, particularly the *keraoshi* method (one of the traditional production methods for Japanese steel) was perfected only in the 18th century. Steel was previously produced by different kinds of decarburisation methods, such as the ones which I have mentioned above. Another strategy is to use objects made of soft steel hammering them into shape, and then attach a piece of *sentetsu* to the part of the objects which is required to be of steel, such as the edges of tools, blades, and swords, etc. This is done in a hearth in order to get the metal into a half-molten state and by repeatedly hammering in order to normalise it (i.e. the impurities in the iron become distributed uniformly by the force of hammering). It is very hard work.

This implies that in areas where steel was not obtainable, steel could have been produced from low-quality iron products such as dull, blunt, iron material and scrap. In other words, the Ainu could not easily have obtained soft steel as a form of iron raw material, so the Ainu relied on iron pots made of *chutetsu* (cast iron).

On the other hand, for example at the Katsuyamadate site (5) in Hokkaido, a Japanese site of the 15-16th century discussed in Chapter 4, a semicircular shaped lump of steel (soft steel) was found, and fish hooks were probably made from it. Moreover, at the Namiokajo site (34) and other sites in Tohoku which I also discussed in Chapter 4, dating to the 15th-16th century, iron bars of steel (soft steel) were also found. This can be seen as a reflection of a different trade/exchange network which also reflects a different social context. A society which could not get steel easily within its distribution network and needed to produce it by refining scrap metal and a society in which steel could be distributed within the network so that steel itself was obtainable constitute very different social contexts.

5-4-2 An example of the Japanese swordcraft technique

As an aid to understanding the Ainu attempts to produce steel in order to resolve a situation in which steel was difficult to obtain, it is useful to explain the method of making Japanese swords used at the present time. The problem which Japanese craft swordsmiths face nowadays is a lack of the old type of steel which they obtained in the past from the traditional *tatara* production. Such steel is no longer obtainable due to the fact that traditional *tatara* production has been totally replaced by modern steel-production methods.[2] Therefore, Japanese craft swordsmiths have problems in finding the appropriate steel for the Japanese sword. In other words, they have difficulties in obtaining steel.

After 1876, when the wearing of swords was prohibited by the Meiji Government, the Japanese sword lost its function as a weapon and become only an object of artistic admiration. There are still some swordsmiths working today, but they make swords for collectors and as a hobby. They attempt to make swords as shapely and beautiful as possible, in traditional styles. The society of the Japanese swordsmiths in the past was very closed. They were a guild who guarded their secrets closely. Nowadays the younger generation treats making swords as an art, holding competitions and training themselves as Japanese swordcraft artists — that is, as Japanese craft swordsmiths.

The emergence of the Japanese sword dates from about the 12th century, although there was, of course, an earlier prototype of the Japanese sword. Japanese swords were divided into two types: an old type and a new type based on the period in which they were made and on their appearance, which probably derives from the different production method of the raw material.

The old type was made during the Kamakura period (1192-1333) from the 12th to the 14th century. However, the technique used to make this old type is extinct, so that the present-day swordsmith cannot reconstruct the process to produce them as they were. These early swords are considered the finest ever made, and it is the dream of smiths at present to match them for excellence. This old type of sword is

---

2 A pseudo-traditional method is practised as cultural heritage rather than commercial production.

called a *tachi* and was worn suspended from the hip with tied cords. The edge of the sword faces downwards.

The new type of sword was made during the Muromachi period (1392-1573), when *zuku* (see Glossary) was produced by a different process using the *tatara* in the fields in the late 14th century and the early 15th century. This new type of sword is called a *dato* and was worn on the hip. One edge of the sword faces upwards. During the Muromachi period, Japanese swords were the most important goods exported to China, almost 1,130,000 being sent there during the century after 1450. *Tian gong kai wu* (1637), a Chinese technical book of the Ming period, states that the Japanese sword was the most excellent sword and that its production techniques were not known in China. However, Japanese documents say that the swords exported were made only for that purpose and were mass-produced low-quality products (Hara 1988:100).

The Japanese sword was made from Japanese steel (*wahagane*), and this provides the distinctive texture of the sword; smiths describe such steel as having 'contractile power' and flexibility suitable for folding many times during the forging process. Because it is an adhesive iron — adhesiveness being a property of Japanese iron — it is easy to obtain good contact between the layers when the surface is folded during the course of forging. It is a very important point that this texture cannot be obtained using foreign steel. Therefore, Japanese steel (*wahagane*) which was produced by the traditional method is absolutely necessary in order to retain the distinctive features of the Japanese sword.

The process from raw material to sword consists of seven steps (Ono 1978):
1, *shitagitae* (lower forging): this step consists of the selection of raw material through to forging and folding of the first stage of steel.
2, *agekitae* (upper forging): fine forging in order to get rid of impurities and inclusions within the steel.
3, *kumiawase* (combination): the combining of different types of iron in order to make the blade functional as well as beautiful.
4, *seikei* (sword forming): the process of making the basic body of the blade.
5, *yakibatsuchi* (preparation for quenching): making the special soil to cover different parts of the blade during quenching. This gives the various parts of the blade different qualities and is a very secret part of the process.
6, *yakiire* (quenching): heat treatment.
7, *shiage* (finishing): sharpening and signing.

I will concentrate on steps 1 and 2, which relate to my discussion of the raw material for sword-making. The rest of the steps relate more specifically to the making of the Japanese sword itself, which I do not intend to discuss here.

The most important technique for making swords by this method is dependent upon obtaining the best type of *jigane* (raw material). *Jigane* includes: 1) *tamahagane* (the best steel), which does not need the *oroshi* process (refining) but can be used directly for making swords due to the fact that it is already high-quality steel, and 2) *oroshigane* which has already been through the *oroshi* process (refining). The *oroshi* process is one which adjusts the carbon content of the

iron either by carburisation (*shintan*) or decarburisation (*zuku oroshi* or *dattan*). It is equivalent to refining in the forging process.

The *zuku oroshi* method involves carrying out decarburisation on *zuku* (equivalent to the process of refining pig iron into steel) in order to obtain the most suitable *oroshigane* for the Japanese sword, which requires sharpness, beauty, and perfect clearness. The finest Japanese swords, by the name of Kunihiro or Kiyomaro, exhibit sharpness, beauty, and a perfect sheen, as well as being functional. For this reason, the decarburisation method is highly developed in association with a wide range of techniques among Japanese swordsmiths in order to produce the required colour and texture in terms of shininess, hardness or softness, and flexibility, although carburisation was also carried out on *hochotetsu* (or *namatetsu*) (see Glossary). These processes depend entirely on the judgement of the swordsmith and have a fundamental effect on the function and the artistic worth of the sword. The swordsmiths learn through the accumulation of experience, so that techniques are kept secret. Among those techniques, the *oroshi* process (refining) is a very crucial and sensitive one in the process of Japanese sword-making.

The *jigane* (raw material), is still in the form of a lump at the start of the process and requires *wakashi* (melting steel by fire) in order to produce steel in the right condition to be forged into a rectangular plate or bar shape.

The rectangular plate or bar of steel needs further forging in order to remove impurities or inclusions to turn it into pure steel. At this stage, layers of steel are piled up on top of each other and folded over again and again. This process of forging and folding is repeated from 14 to 20 times, depending on the quality of the steel. Although this process depends on the abilities and skill of the smith, the previous process, namely the preparation of the *oroshigane*, is the most important and is a very delicate process.

The problem which Japanese craft swordsmiths face nowadays is the lack of *jigane* (raw material) which they obtained in the past through traditional *tatara* production. It is no longer obtainable, owing to the fact that traditional *tatara* production is extinct as I have mentioned earlier. Therefore, Japanese craft swordsmiths have problems finding appropriate raw material for making the Japanese sword. In other words, they have difficulties in obtaining the Japanese steel (*wahagane*).

Although the quantity is now very limited, some Japanese craft swordsmiths collect used material which was made of *zuku*, such as old iron pots, and old objects made of Japanese steel (*wahagane*), such as used nails and old agricultural tools, and so on; anything made of *zuku* or *wahagane* (Japanese steel) in the past is collected in order to obtain raw material to be decarburised to make Japanese steel.

Some of them try to produce their own Japanese steel (*wahagane*) from iron sand which they buy and smelt in small home-made furnaces, reconstructing them so as to be similar to the traditional *tatara* furnace, in order to obtain and decarburise Japanese steel (*wahagane*) by themselves. This approach has two purposes: one is to solve the problem of the lack of Japanese steel (*wahagane*) at present, and the other is to take up the challenge of reconstructing the process of making the old type of Japanese sword, current in the Kamakura period, when the finest of all Japanese swords were made. The methods are now extinct, however, and have not been fully reconstructed by any modern Japanese craft swordsmiths.

As I explained earlier in this chapter, the Ainu also collected used iron products, normally old nails and iron pots, acquired through cultural contacts, in order to process them and to make their tools by refining such scrap iron. In this respect, Japanese craft swordsmiths at present have a problem strikingly analogous to that which Ainu society faced in the past in terms of a lack of raw material for steel.

An awareness of how Japanese craft swordsmiths at present try to solve this problem helps us to understand the archaeological evidence from the Pipaushi site and to discuss how the Ainu might have tried to solve the problem of a lack of steel. In this way, it is possible to obtain an understanding of the level of their technology at that time. It is also important to bear in mind that the origins of the technique of Japanese sword-making must have derived from and relate to techniques used in the production of raw material developed before the 12th century. The reason for pointing this out is that Ainu iron techniques may have been derived from those of the Satsumon culture, themselves probably a result of cultural contact between the Satsumon and Japanese cultures in Tohoku during the 8th-10th centuries (see Chapters 3 and 4).

An example is provided by a Japanese swordsmith, Toshimitsu Imaizumi, born in 1898, who is a Living National Cultural Asset because of his skill as a maker of traditional Japanese swords (Ono 1978). He explains the importance of obtaining *zuku oroshigane* by the *zuku oroshi* method (decarburisation). He has devised a method of obtaining *zuku oroshigane* under the current difficult conditions.

His method is to collect hammer scale (iron oxide) from the floor; hammer scale is a by-product of the forging process when the sword is hammered. He removes the dust and soil from the collected hammer scale and grinds the selected fine scale using a grinding stone. He then passes the ground material through a sieve. Thus, powdered scale (iron oxide) is made. A piece of *zuku* is taken and mixed with wheat flour glue, and any extra wheat flour glue is shaken off. This is also mixed with the iron oxide powder made by the above process in order to make it stick together. It is left out naturally in the sun to dry. The processing of this piece by the *zuku oroshi* method (decarburisation) takes place, and thus *zuku oroshigane* is obtained.

From this description, it is clear that hammer scale need not be only a by-product but can be recycled, making it a potential resource for some purposes.

Having understood the above craft swordsmith's awareness that hammer scale is not only a waste by-product but can also play an important role in the iron-technological process of producing decarburised material, the rectangular-shaped iron material from the Pipaushi site may be interpreted as reflecting a similar awareness on the part of an Ainu craftsperson that hammer scale can be used for steel production.

5-5 The evidence for the possibility of secondary raw material

The evidence which was found at the Pipaushi site (2) requires further discussion.

Metallographic analysis of iron material in a rectangular shape (see Photo. 5-3) from the Pipaushi site, shows that it consists of hammer scale and some kind of glue. In fact, it is not just hammer scale; the metallographic analysis reveals that it is scale reduced to micro-fine powderish scale (see Photo 5-4).

The micro-structure consists of wustite in the middle next to a zone of magnetite and hematite on the outside. The result of the chemical composition of the rectangular-shaped iron material is shown in Table 5-6. DIGH speed qualitative analysis (see Graph 5-1 and Table 5-7) indicates that it consists mainly of iron (60.497%) and carbon (24.823%), the latter possibly interpretable as glue or some kind of organic material such as starch, farinaceous material or dung. The rest of the components are 10.588% oxygen, 3.305% silica, and 0.786% aluminium. It is formed into an ingot shape, so it is possible to regard it as having been made intentionally for some purpose.

Table 5-6 The chemical composition of the rectangular-shaped iron material from Pipaushi (see Table 4-6 in Chapter 4).

	T.Fe	FeO	Fe2O3	SiO2	Al2O	CaO	TiO	MnP	P	C%
Pipaushi	65.90	<0.01		4.83	1.48	0.400	0.068	0.04	0.06	

Table 5-7   The chemical composition of the rectangular-shaped iron material from the Pipaushi site.

RATIO

NO.	ELE.		XTAL	W.L.	PKI-BGI	STD(I)	I-RATIO	WT(%)	ELE.
1	FE	Ka	LIF1	1.9373	986.3	373.2	2.6426	60.497	FE
2	C	Ka	LSA4	44.7000	5783.3	5333.5	1.0843	24.823	C
3	O	Ka	LSA5	23.6500	1480.0	3199.9	0.4625	10.588	O
4	SI	Ka	PET2	7.1260	81.3	563.2	0.1444	3.305	SI
5	AL	Ka	RAP	8.3390	80.5	2343.6	0.0343	0.786	AL
TOTAL								100.000	

RATIO

NO.	ELE.		XTAL	W.L.	PKI-BGI	STD(I)	I-RATIO	WT(%)	ELE.
1	FE	Ka	LIF1	1.9373	1620.2	373.2	4.3412	66.079	FE
2	C	Ka	LSA4	44.7000	4365.0	5333.5	0.8184	12.457	C
3	O	Ka	LSA5	23.6500	2354.3	3199.9	0.7357	11.199	O
4	AU	Ma	PET2	5.8400	62.1	138.5	0.4486	6.829	AU
5	SI	Ka	PET2	7.1260	62.7	563.2	0.1113	1.695	SI
6	AL	Ka	RAP	8.3390	186.6	2343.6	0.0796	1.212	AL
7	CA	Ka	PET2	3.3600	72.5	2085.7	0.0347	0.529	CA
TOTAL								100.000	

The rectangular-shaped iron material from the Pipaushi site explained above can, as we have seen, be interpreted as secondary raw material for further production of steel. If this interpretation is correct, this material would have undergone further processing. In such a case, it would have to undergo reduction in order to obtain a high concentration of carbon and oxygen, using something like charcoal, under the conditions of relatively low temperature in order not to accelerate the reduction process. Steel can be produced with this process by controlling reduction additives and the temperature.

To do this, a hearth structure would be required which satisfies the condition that it excludes most of the air. In other words, a hearth covered by clay or something similar would be needed in order to roast this material while controlling reduction and maintaining a low temperature.

This interpretation would explain the existence at Pipaushi of the hearth nearby which exhibits very different features from the hearth as a-hole-in-a-hearth for forging or refining at the Pipaushi site, which I have mentioned previously (Photo. 5-5). The No. 1 hearth consists of a pit, 20cm x 15cm in size of oval shape and with a flat bottom 6cm in depth — after excavation of a yellowish mound, and removing the yellowish clay until it disappeared at the bottom. Several pieces of hammer micro-scale 1mm in size were found within this clay in the middle of the mound. There was no other material mixed in with it, except that there were several orange blocks of burnt soil on top of the mound and a piece of carbonised wood underneath the mound. Several pieces of hammer micro-scale were found within the clay which had been packed into the middle of the hearth —

which is very unusual for a forging hearth. Thus it is possible to consider that this hearth was designed for making iron products rather than the material for decarburisation.

Based on both the evidence of the hearth and the rectangular shaped ingot-like iron material, it may therefore be suggested that already in the 17th century the production of secondary raw material was being undertaken by Ainu themselves, although I have discussed how the Ainu iron technology was based on the iron which the Ainu obtained from outside their culture.

The production of secondary raw material by the Ainu themselves was presumably a desperate measure taken under the pressure of necessity, due to the fact that steel bars and lumps of iron such as those found at the Katsuyamadate site (5) would have been very unlikely to have been distributed to the Ainu.

5-6 Conclusion

To conclude this chapter, together with Chapter 4, I will summarise the iron technology of the Ainu in so far as it is possible to reconstruct it.

Ainu iron technology in the 17th century was based on the iron material which they acquired from outside by exchange and trade. However, the Ainu practised iron technology, including the forging and refining processes; moreover, the evidence suggests that they may have been capable of producing steel by recycling scale, using unique techniques of their own devising. Thus it may be said that the Ainu technology involved not only processing but also producing their own iron.

The purpose of developing these techniques was to produce steel, from which they produced their *makiri* knives, using the decarburising method of refining process. In this way, the Ainu could have transformed low-quality iron into higher-quality iron.

Before the iron prohibition was forced upon the Ainu by the Matsumae in 1669, Ainu society must have reached a level at which they were reliant upon the use of iron products and were engaged in the production of iron objects based on the iron techniques which they possessed. Thus, the iron prohibition must have affected strongly the everyday life of the Ainu at that time; after the prohibition policy, iron technology must have fallen into a decline in Ainu society as it became harder to obtain the iron materials required.

A report written in the early 19th century (Mamiya 1808) stated:

> in those days only the Sakhalin Ainu practise smithing but the Hokkaido Ainu do not. There was an old man near Soya in Hokkaido who was the only one who knew how to practise smithing. A reason for this may be that in the past, when iron products were not widely available in Ezo [Hokkaido], they practised smithing in order to supply iron products for their own needs; but nowadays iron products are easily imported from the mainland so they have ceased smithing (Mamiya 1808).

In the light of this statement, Ishizuki points out that "this tells us that in places that were nearer to the mainland, which was a source of iron products, it was easy for the practise of smithing to be forgotten" (Ishizuki 1983).

I question the logic of this statement, however. It is difficult to imagine that if smithing techniques were already known as a method of producing iron materials in the Ainu culture, it would not be easy to forget how to forge even if iron products were flooding in from outside. For example, in Japan during the Edo period (the 17th-19th centuries), and in Edo itself (Tokyo before 1868) where iron products were especially abundant, the smith existed as a craftsperson.

There were two kinds of smiths at that time in Japan: one was the *kakeya* (wandering tinker) who travelled from village to village in order to mend iron pots; the other was the *imonoshi* (workshop founder), who had his own small workshop and waited for customers to come to him (Kubota 1980b). Therefore, small-scale smithing techniques were required not simply in relation to supply and demand, but in connection with maintenance and repair, mending, and reproduction of all sorts of work related to iron.

One can wonder why Ainu iron technology apparently disappeared from the Japanese historical record, as in Mamiya's statement (1808) which was only 20 years after Furukawa's account (1788). Furukawa, however, already found it hard to credit the story of Ainu iron-working skill which he had heard in Matsumae. This may imply that the Ainu practised iron-technology out of sight of the Japanese because of the iron prohibition. In other words, the Ainu may have practised iron-working secretly. A tong found at the Setanaichashi site (4) (Kitahiyama-cho 1980) in an Ainu context dated to around 1724, although unaccompanied by any other evidence of iron processing at the site, and in spite of an abundance of iron products, suggests that Ainu smiths must still have existed.

There are also some indications of the existence of Ainu smiths in historical documents of the later 19th century, which include such comments as "the blade was made by the Ainu themselves; it is sharp enough for shaving hair and is similar to Japanese blades" (Matsumae 1863); and "In Furebetsu village, the chief of the Ainu is called Seiji. He is well informed about forging and all the knives which cut salmon are made by him" (Amari 1877); or "A dagger made by Daisaku who is an Atsukeshi Ainu" (Sato 1975). Thus it may be said that Ainu iron technology survived in some measure into the 20th century. This was clearly the case in Sakhalin, as Pilsudski took a photograph of the Sakhalin Ainu blacksmith (Photo. 5-6), between 1896 and 1905, when he was staying.

An archaeological and archaeometallurgical approach can not be ignored in developing an understanding of the technological aspects, indeed merits very serious attention. In the present study, in which my discussion is based on the results of such analysis, I have tried make full use of its potential.

Graph 5-1   The result of the DIGH speed qualitative analysis carried out specially for this book by K. Ito.

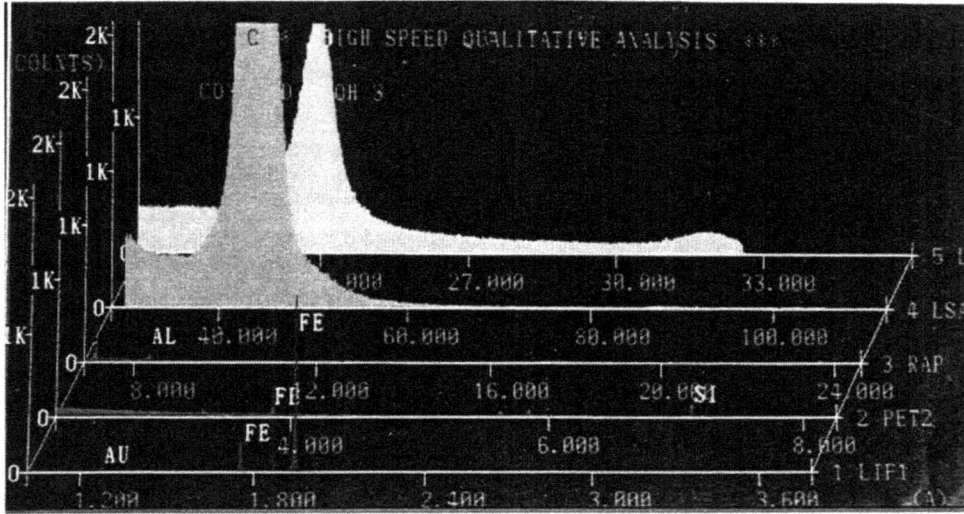

Photograph 5-1   Forging among the present-day Evenki in northern China
(Reproduced with the kind permission of Professor K. Otsuka).

Photograph 5-2   Bottom slag from the Iruekashi site (1).

Photograph 5-3   Iron material in a rectangular shape from the Pipaushi site.

Photograph 5-4 Micro-structure of iron material in a rectangular shape from the Pipaushi site.

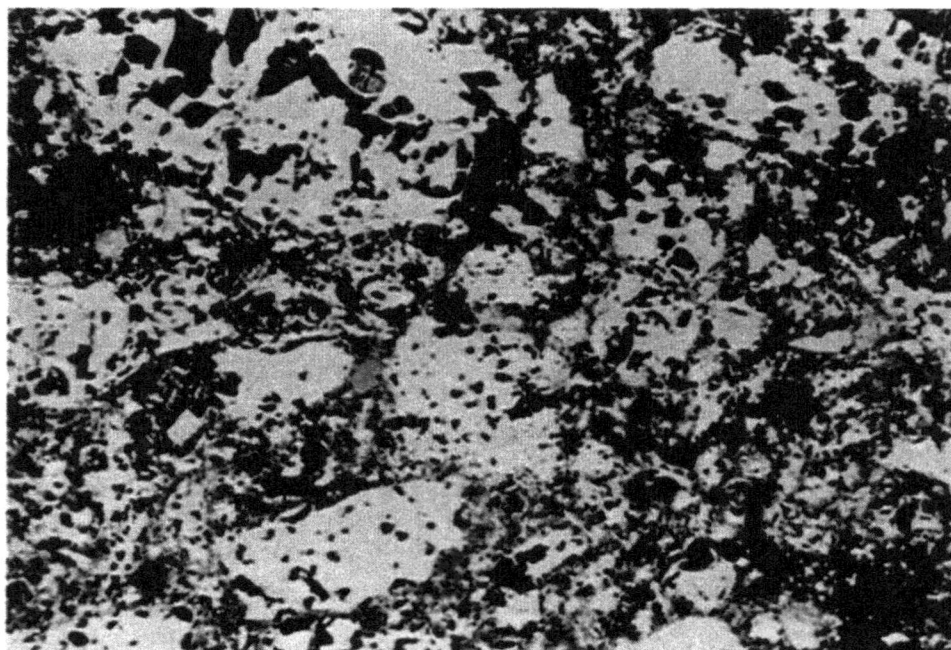

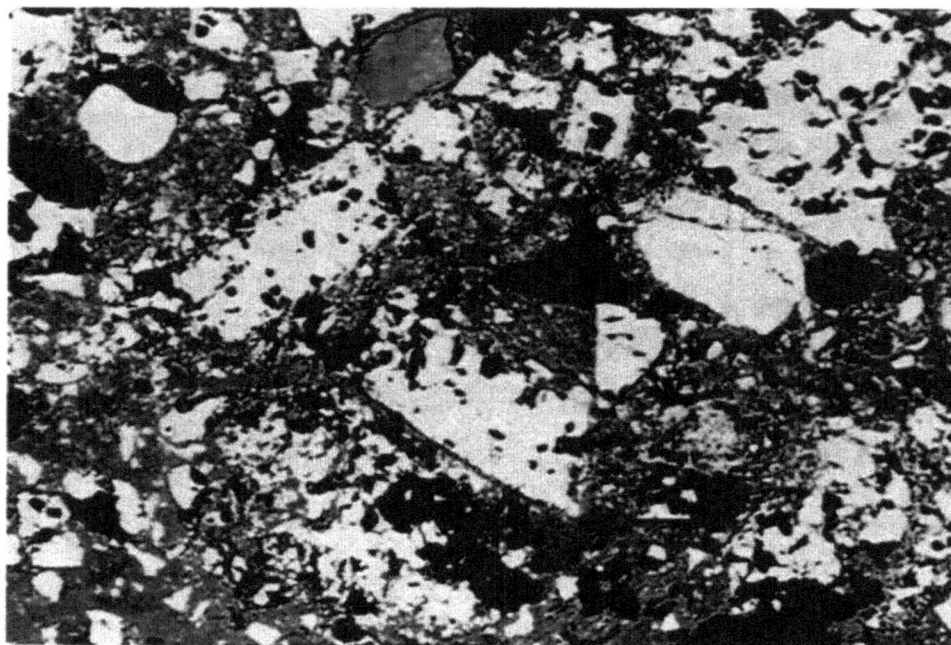

Photograph 5-5 (a) Initial exposure of No. 1 hearth at the Pipaushi site.

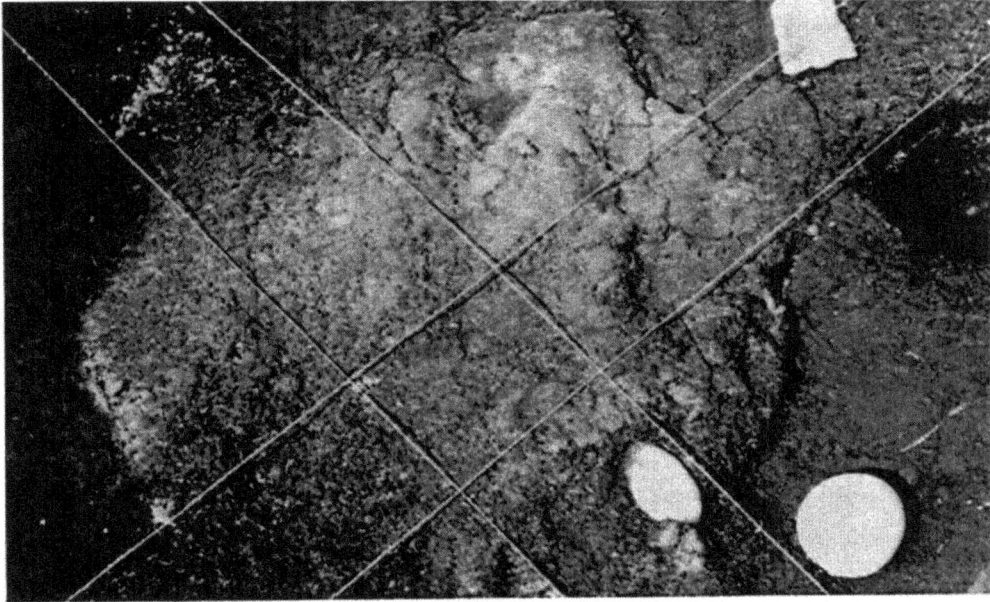

Photograph 5-5 (b) Plan of No. 1 hearth at the Pipaushi site with one quarter excavated.

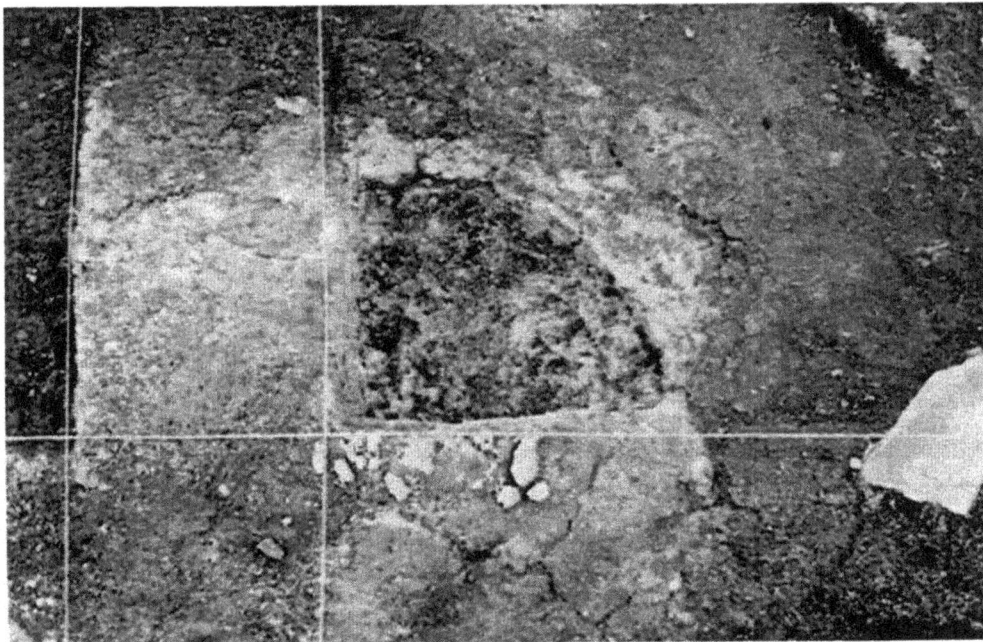

Photograph 5-5 (c) Section of No. 1 hearth at the Pipaushi site. The markers indicate the position of micro-scales.

Photograph 5-6 A Sakhalin Ainu blacksmith at the beginning of 20th century.
(Reproduced from the collection of the Museum of Archaeology and Anthropology, University of Cambridge. The registration number is P.6092.ACH1.)

Chapter 6

The examination of words for materials and other things in order to understand the Ainu cultural context

6-1 Introduction

In Chapters 4 and 5 I have examined iron-working technology in Ainu society from the material point of view. In this chapter and the succeeding Chapter 7 my approach shifts to identifying the meanings of words in the Ainu language for materials and things and investigating them, in the context of the Ainu oral tradition, for material culture within the Ainu social context. I propose to approach the subject by attempting to gain an insight into the Ainu view of their own internal culture.

The Ainu language and their oral tradition is a rich field as an information source for understanding their material culture and should not be ignored. It is a useful aid to understanding the context of archaeological material. An approach which combines investigations from both material cultural and linguistic points of view may be useful for both fields of study. This kind of approach has not been adopted by any Ainu linguistic scholars, as they are usually keen to concentrate on the language structure and its linguistic affiliation.

To recognise things in a society, in the same way that a person has a name in a society so that people can identify who you are, so things have names to aid us in expressing what they are. There is no society in which materials and things exist without a name by which they are called within that society. A name may simply give a thing a label, or it may express its attributes, such as its function or its morphological features. What these things and materials are called in a society is very important. For example, there is no English word for 'cicada' because cicadas are not found in England. The word 'cicada' originated in the Mediterranean area where cicadas live, and it was then introduced to and established itself within the English-speaking world. As a matter of course, there is no name to refer to things which do not exist in a society. When a thing enters a society, it frequently bears the name by which it was known in the original society, and this then establishes itself in the recipient society. Thus, it is very significant for the study of material culture in a society to examine the relationship between things which existed in that society and the names by which they are called, in order to understand their social context in that society. A study which considers material culture from the point of view of the relationship between things and their names has been carried out in Japan by Minao Hayashi, who directed the projects which examined the material culture of the Han dynasty, China. His method has been established in the book entitled *Kandai no bunbutsu* (Things and Words in the Han period) (M. Hayashi 1976). Thus this kind of approach can be useful for understanding the material culture.

6-2 The Ainu language

The Ainu did not have written language, thus the Ainu language here referred to is only the spoken language and records of it written in romanised letters or Japanese *kana* syllabary. Some records were written by outsiders, including the Japanese, and some were written down by the Ainu themselves.

The Ainu language is no longer spoken by the Ainu in everyday life. Although the Meiji government did not prohibit the use of the Ainu language, it declined within Ainu society during the Meiji period (1868-1912).

It is difficult to generalise about how the Ainu language declined within Ainu society. However, it can be said that the generational differences clearly reflect the attitude to the Ainu language. The generation born at the beginning of the Meiji period, around 1868, had the Ainu language as their mother tongue. Although they may have understood simple Japanese conversation, they could not speak —or did not want to speak — Japanese. It is interesting to note that, prior to Meiji, speaking Japanese was prohibited under the Matsumae. The increasing number of Japanese-speakers among the Ainu went against the monopolistic policy of the Matsumae (Sato 1786). Among the generation born around 1880, bilingual speakers appeared, due to the fact that they worked among the Japanese. By the time of the generation born around 1900, their mother tongue had became Japanese, due to the fact that the Japanese educational system became common among the Ainu people, under the direction of the Japanese government. In other words, Ainu children went to a school where the Japanese language was taught. However, they understood the Ainu language without any difficulty. As regards the generation born around 1910, their mother tongue was Japanese, their everyday conversation was conducted in Japanese, and they could not speak the Ainu language since they had not been trained to use it, although they could understand it when they heard it (for more detail, see Fukasawa 1993).

6-2-1 A brief history of Ainu linguistic studies

(1) Ainu language studies from the 18th to the mid-19th century (the Edo period)

Explorers and travellers collected some examples of the Ainu language and recorded them in their diaries and reports. These are, of course, not systematic, especially in terms of writing the language in the *kana* letters of the Japanese phonetic syllabary. Among these documents, the most remarkable is called *Moshihogusa*: it was made phonetically accurate by inventing new phonetic signs and was written by Kumajiro Uehara in 1792. Documents which were written after *Moshihogusa* recorded a more extensive vocabulary. It also mentions regional differences within Ezo [Hokkaido].

An epic type of oral tradition was also mentioned in another travel dairy called *Ezo Joruri, joruri* being a term for narrative stories in Edo-period Japan.

There are some articles on the Ainu language written in European languages, especially German and French, by people who travelled through out the Russian continent and went to Sakhalin Island (cf. Le Perouse 1797). These documents describe the Sakhalin Ainu, who, I assume, were already by that time very different from the Hokkaido Ainu, showing regional variations in their culture and language.

(2) Ainu language studies from the mid-19th to the early 20th century

John Batchelor (1845-1944), an English missionary who lived in Hokkaido, collected Ainu vocabularies and oral traditions. He also established the framework of Ainu grammar, based on the principles of English grammar (Batchelor 1889). Although this was later criticised by Chiri (Chiri 1942, 1974) for its failure to take account of Ainu philosophy and cosmology, it was the first Ainu Dictionary and Grammar, published in 1887 and 1889 (1890 transactions of the Asiatic Society of Japan). Batchelor thought that the Ainu language was the original language of the Japanese, and also that the Ainu were the native people of Japan.

However, the notion of a relationship between the Ainu and the Japanese was a hypothesis rejected by Basil Hall Chamberlain (1850-1935), who was a Japanese linguist and made comparative studies of Japanese and other Oriental languages. He concluded that the Ainu language must be considered an isolated language, as it is related to neither Japanese nor any of the Altaic languages (Chamberlain 1887).

Pilsudski (1866-1918), a Polish anthropologist, went to Siberia as a political prisoner. He married a Sakhalin Ainu woman and had two children. He made sound-recordings of the Ainu oral tradition not only amongst the Ainu of Sakhalin, but also the Hokkaido Ainu of the Saru area, using wax cylinders. His works were discovered in Poland in the 1980s, and are currently being studied by linguists (Kokuritsu Minzokugaku Hakubutsukan 1987).

(3) Ainu language studies at the beginning of the 20th century

Study of the Ainu oral tradition was started in earnest by Kyosuke Kindaichi at the end of the 19th century. Meeting competent Ainu speakers was important for the collection of oral tradition at that time, since they were decreasing in numbers as they grew older. Most of Kindaichi's work relied upon encounters with great Ainu speakers and informants such as Yukie Chiri (1902-1922), Matsu Kannari (1875-1961), Wakarupa (1863-1913), and so on, and he is the foremost of the Ainu linguists who has collected and analysed data. He concentrated on the collection, transcription and translation of Yukara and on writing about their grammar. His first published book was *Ainu Seiten* (Kindaichi 1923), a study of Yukara. His major work was *Yukarashu* (published between 1959 and 1964), a collection of Yukara compiled in collaboration with an Ainu speaker and accomplished Yukara reciter, Matsu Kannari, along with his grammar of Ainu, included in his volume in 1960. Kindaichi's work can be said to be the most comprehensive and accessible material on the Hokkaido Ainu. Yukie Chiri was a sister of Mashiho Chiri and niece of Matsu Kannari. Although she died at the early age of 19, she wrote an important book called *Kamui Yukara* in romanised Ainu, with a Japanese translation (Chiri 1922, 1978). She also left several notes about Ainu stories.

Chiri Mashiho (1902-1961) was a student of Kindaichi. He was an Ainu himself, but his first language was Japanese and he learned the Ainu language as a foreign language. However, his insights into the Ainu culture were profound. Most of the more recent work in this field depends heavily on the works of Kindaichi and Chiri. Chiri's contribution includes not only grammatical work but also a study of Ainu lexicography and an etymological study of Ainu place names (Chiri 1973). Kindaichi taught the Ainu language at the University of Tokyo for 40 years and Chiri was his first student.

Kubodera was also a student of Kindaichi; his contribution to this field is the collection and translation of the Kamui Yukara of the Saru area (Kubodera 1977).

In this period, the Ainu language, originally only a spoken language, was given a written form using the roman alphabet, although it has to some extent still not been systematically worked out. There are now two ways of writing the Ainu language: one, following Yukie Chiri and Matsu Kannari, uses roman alphabets, while the other like the Japanese language, employs the Japanese syllabary *hiragana*.

(4) Ainu language studies after the 1960s

This period is characterised by the development of studies of regional differences in the Ainu language. Ainu linguistic studies were initially based mainly on research in the Saru and Horobetsu areas, since it was in these areas that the seminal studies by Kindaichi, Chiri, and Kubodera were carried out.

After the publication of work by Shiro Hattori (Hattori 1964), linguists became more aware of regional differences. Hattori's research on Ainu dialects is a pioneering study. He provided the basic lexicographic materials.

Suzuko Tamura's work was carried out especially in the Saru area (Tamura 1960, 1961, 1964). It covers a substantial portion of the grammar of this dialect, which is a main dialect of the Hidaka region and a direct descendant of Classical Ainu as represented by the version of the yukara "Itadorimaru" ("Kutune Shirka") described by Kindaichi (Kindaichi 1961).

Kyoko Murasaki's contribution to this field is the Ainu language of Sakhalin. Her work was done with the co-operation of an Ainu woman, Haru Fujiyama, one of the last fluent speakers of Sakhalin Ainu. She has recorded data for a grammar of Sakhalin Ainu, the Raychishka dialect, and has provided a sizeable body of data in the form of tape recordings and texts (Murasaki 1978). Toru Asai's work on the Ishikari area (Asai 1970), undertaken with the co-operation of an Ainu woman, Kura Sunazawa, was also carried out in this period.

Although data concerning dialects increased, the work has frequently been the result of a close relationship between the researcher and the informants who provided the dialect information. As a result, it is not always clear whether the dialect spoken was individual or social. In a way, this kind of dialectical study is not the same as those normally associated with linguistic studies. However, it is now very difficult to trace back Ainu dialects within a social context.

(5) Ainu language studies after the 1980s

Recent Ainu language studies in different areas indicate that the framework of yukara studies which has already been established may not be adopted in other regions, since transmission is rather idiosyncratic and personal in character. It has been realised that yukara especially would have been changed very slightly from reciter to reciter. As time goes by such differences gradually increase, although it had been thought that yukara preserved their original form and had never changed. Regional context and the process of transmission both need to be considered in the study of yukara.

Osami Okuda is researching data from an informant and reciter called Suteno Orita (1901-1993); he is collaborating with Toshihiko Kohara, who is trained as an archaeologist. Their research has led to a new aspect of yukara studies which emphasises the channel of transmission (Okuda 1991, Kohara 1991). The nature of the channel may relate to the transformation of the yukara in the process of transmission.

Okuda and Kirsten Refsing work in the Shizunai area. Refsing's work (Refsing 1986) on a grammar of the Shizunai dialect contributes to dialect studies of the Ainu language in English, although her interpretation of Chiri's criticism of Batchelor (ibid.) seems to me to indicate that she does not wholly understand Chiri's work.

Mie Haginaka's gender interpretation of yukara was also carried out in this period (Haginaka 1982). This offers unique and important aspects of study for understanding and reconstructing Ainu society, the potential of which has not been fully developed as yet in the linguistic field.

Hiroshi Nakagawa plays a leading role in Ainu linguistic studies at present. He is the only person teaching the Ainu language at one of the National Universities. He works on the Chitose area.

Yuko Yoneta is an Ainu language teacher of children at Nibutani in the Saru area and is an assistant to Shigeru Kayano, who is himself an Ainu, and who teaches the Saru dialect. Kayano is not only a linguist but also teaches about Ainu life in general. He collects folktales of the Ainu Uepekere and has published them (Kayano 1974).

6-3 The Ainu words for metals

Ainu words were collected by Japanese travellers, inspectors, and interpreters who belonged to the Shogunal government in the 18-19th centuries. The Ainu words which were collected make it possible to understand what kind of vocabulary existed in Ainu society at that time. This is useful in so far as it helps us to understand the material culture of Ainu society. It also reveals the extent to which those words were collected by the Japanese and thus sheds light upon the degree of Japanese knowledge of Ainu society. It is possible to perceive a relationship of correspondence between Japanese terms for things at that time and the Ainu words for them. Since my purpose is to investigate the meanings of metalwork within the Ainu cultural context, I shall examine the words for metal in Ainu society.

The oldest record of Ainu words is *Matsumaeno koto*, in which 117 Ainu words were collected in the early 17th century [the exact date is not known, but was probably between 1630 and 1640] (Narita 1977). There are no words which suggest or relate to metal. The word *piruka*, mentioned in Chapter 5, is described as meaning 'good' or 'well'. *Moshihokusa*, written by Uehara in 1792, records 2740 Ainu words. These words were collected through direct contact with the Ainu people, and the words were classified into 10 categories, comprising the first dictionary of Ainu and Japanese. Kindaichi mentioned that the orthography used in this publication was advanced for its time (Kindaichi 1925). In 1850, Takeshiro Matuura published *Ezogo* which collected 1850 Ainu words (Narita 1986). In 1855, he also published *Shiribeshi oroshi*, which forms a collection of 1048 Ainu words (Narita 1991). Jiro Yoda recorded 838 Ainu words in *Ezo tsushikan* in 1854 (Narita 1988). There are detailed Ainu words for metal in these four records, which provide us with very useful evidence. Table 6-1 indicates that there were different names for different kinds of metal, and it is possible to compare the words.

Although Captain Vries's record of 1643 mentioned *kani* as the word for both silver and iron, in the broad sense of 'metal', around the Sakhalin area (see Chapter 5), by the 19th century, there were names for each specific metal, such as *konkane* (yellow metal) for gold, *shirokane* (white metal) for silver, and *kupuka* or *kuuka* for iron. It is interesting to note that there are two forms of the word for metal — that is, *kane* or *kani* — so that both *yai-kane* or *yaya-kani* are found. According to the linguist Okuda, who specialised in the Shizunai dialect, there are two ways of saying metal in different areas (personal communication). *Kane* was used particularly in the Saru area, and *kani* was used in the Shizunai area and the rest of the east part of Hokkaido. This may reflect different cultural contact within different regions.

Table 6-1   A comparative table of the words for metal.

English	Japanese	Ainu *Moshihokusa* (1792)	Ainu *Ezogo* (1850)
gold	kin or kane	konkane	konkane
silver	gin	shirokane	shirokane
copper	do	furekane	furekane
iron	tetsu	kupuka	kuuka
tin	suzu	yaikane or yayakani	yaikane or yayakani
Chinese copper	karadou	karankani	karnakani
red copper	sekidou		shakunndo
purple copper	shidou		abeshakundo
mercury	suigin	shirokanewakka	shirokanewakka
gold leaf	kinnpaku	konkanewakka	konkanewakka
silver leaf	ginpaku	shirokanewakka	shirokanewakka
money	sen or zeni		shamotakara or isen
nail	kugi		shikae
felling axe	masakari	mukkari	mukkari
hoe	kuwa	shakushi	shakushi
copper pot	donabe	kabarushu or fureshu	
		sayatsura	sayatsura
		ishika	ishika
		yu-paka	yu-paka

It is also interesting to note here that iron is written neither as *kani* , as in Sakhalin in 1643, nor as *kane*, but as *kupuka* (Uehara 1792), (Matsuura 1855) or *kuuka* (Matsuura 1850). Moreover, other records mentioned the words *kubuka* (Yoda 1854), and *kufuka* (Notoya 1864) in the 19th century. Although it is not known exactly where these words were collected in Hokkaido, it was presumably somewhere near the Matsumae domain in the south of Hokkaido, as the words were recorded by Japanese. According to Kindaichi (Kindaichi 1960), there were two different cultivating tools, called *kukka* and *kupuka*, which functioned like hoes. The former, the older type, was made of wood or antler, and the latter was made of iron in the same way as an iron hoe. Takakura's interpretation is that cultivation tools made of wood or antler were normally called *shitappu* in Ainu society; they were also called *kukka* based on Kindaichi's distinction. However, Chiri is against Kindaichi's idea that there is no material distinction between *kukka* and *kupuka*; he believes that cultivation tools made of wood and antler were called *shitapu* as was the case recently.

My interpretation of all this is that an iron hoe, called *kuwa* in Japanese society, entered Ainu society as the material of iron itself as well as in the form of a cultivation tool. Thus, the Ainu words *kukka* or *kupuka* were used both for the material of iron and the cultivation tool. This interpretation may be supported by the examination of the word for iron in the languages of surrounding ethnic groups which, with the exception of the Japanese, do not exhibit a strong correlation with the Ainu language as regards their words for iron.

In Japan, iron is called *tetsu* or *kurogane*, *kurokane* (black metal); *tetsu* can be traced back to *ti*, used in the Han dynasty in China. *Ti* is thought to be transformed from *temur* in Mongolian (Torii 1925). However, in ancient Japanese chronicles, such as the *Hitachi-Fudoki* and *Kojikiden*, there are the words *mara*, *maura*, and *maro* which indicate people or a family, called in full 'Ama-tsu-Mara', who worked as *kannuchi* who dealt with iron (i.e. blacksmiths) and were particularly associated with iron sand. These words are also thought to be derived from the Mongolian word *temur* (ibid.).

On the other hand, iron is called *soe* or *chol* in Korean (Korean-English Dictionary); these words are similar to the word for iron in Manchurian, which belongs to the Tungusic language family. In Manchurian, iron is called *selā*. Table 6-2 shows the words for iron in the surrounding areas and languages, which show little resemblance to the Mongolian *temur*.

In addition, the Uilter in Sakhalin also refer to iron as *sələ* (Hokkaido 1981). Since the Uilter, who are the northern neighbours of the Ainu, use the word *sələ* for iron, *kane* or *kani* clearly relates to Japanese alone. To summarise, it seems that there are two different roots of the words used to designate iron in East Asia. In the Ainu case, derivation from Japanese seems the most reasonable scenario, given the verbal similarities noted.

Table 6-2   Words for iron in north-east Asian languages (based on Torii 1925).

the word for iron	language	area
sele	Orucha	inner Mongolia
`sala	Orucha	inner Mongolia
sëllä	Manchuria	Manchuria
sèh-lèh	Jürchin	Manchuria
sélö	Koldogil Tungus	
sälä	Tungus	
sölö	Ramuto (Lamut)	
sélé or sêl'ó	Daunren	
sölö or sälö	Tungus	along Lake Baikal
sêla	Amur Tungus	along the Amur
séle	NeruchisTungus	
sele	Angara Tungus	along the Angara
selle	Enise Tungus	along the Enise
söllo	Manguzea Tungus	
zölla	Tunguska Tungus	along the Tunguska
cil	OkotsukuTungus	along Sea of Okhotsk
hölö	Wirui Tungus	along the Amur
ersele	Soron	

There are other words related to iron technology. The Ainu vocabulary is shown in Table 6-3.

Table 6-3   The Ainu word for 'to melt'.

English	Japanese	Ainu Moshihokusa (1792)	Ainu Ezogo (1850)
to melt	torokasu	rure	
to cast	tokeru	rurekaru	rurekare
melt	you	ruwo	ruwo
melt	you	ruwokere	ruwokere

These words might imply the smelting of silver, as recorded by Captain Vries (see Chapter 5). Although it is difficult to explain in English due to the fact that the Chinese ideograms cannot be described, *tokeru* in Japanese means 'to melt'. Written with Chinese characters suggesting different kinds of melting, it can be used to express different kinds of melting in terms of purpose or function. The word is used to designate casting, which implies a transformation from the solid state of metal to the liquid state of metal.

Although the word *ru kani* can then be translated literally as 'to melt metal' or 'molten metal', it was used to mean 'melting silver' or 'water silver', indicating mercury. This term was frequently used in yukara (which I discuss in Chapter 7). Taking account of the fact that a vein of mercury is sometimes located at the end of a vein of silver (Shepherd 1993), then it might be possible to say that the Ainu in a certain region (i.e. wherever a vein of silver exists) had knowledge of mercury because of its association with smelting silver. However, the word *ru kani* still needs to be examined due to the fact that the word *shirokani wakka*,

which literally translated into English means white metal (or silver) water (or perhaps liquid) is also used for mercury.

The existence of the following vocabulary in the Ainu language also indicates activity which relates to iron-working. The words for charcoal (*sumi* in Japanese) used for fuel are as follows:

hashi hashi	(Uehara 1792)
hashi	(Takaya 1808)
usatsu	(Matsuura 1850)
hashibashi	(Yoda 1854)
hashisuke	(Notoya 1864)

The word for 'a tong' (*hibashi* in Japanese) is *aihashu* in Ainu (Notoya 1864). The words also reflect grinding stone and grinding (*toishi* [noun] and *togu* [verb] in Japanese) is *rui* (Uehara 1792), (Matsuura 1850, 1855), *furima* or *rui* (Yoda 1854), and *rue* (Notoya 1864).

Furthermore, even the word *kaneuchi* (Matsuura 1850), which means 'forging', existed in Ainu society. The word *kaneuchi* sounds Japanese, as in *kane* (metal) and *uchi* (pounding). This means *kaji* (forging) in modern Japanese, since the word *ka-ji* in modern Japanese may be traced from *ka-n-uchi* or *ka-n-nuchi*, in ancient Japanese, to *ka-chi* then *ka-ji* on phonemic grounds (Nakagawa, personal communication). According to Batchelor's *Ainu-English-Japanese Dictionary and Grammar* (Batchelor 1889), *kane kik guru*, designates a blacksmith in Ainu. *Kane* means metal, *kik* means pounding, and *guru* means a human or man. Thus the entire word means 'metal pounding man'. Although pounding in the Ainu language is *kik*, *uchi* (pounding) in Japanese is also used, as mentioned above. Thus there are two versions of the expression for pounding: *uchi*, which sounds Japanese, and *kik*, which sounds Ainu. It would then be possible to think that the word pounding as verb can be translated into the Ainu words easily from Japanese *uchi* to *kik*, if the word *kik* had already existed in Ainu society when the word was borrowed from the Japanese. It seems very reasonable to me that the word *kaneuchi* for forging was borrowed from ancient Japanese.

Among the Uilter in Sakhalin, forging is *tapici* (Hokkaido Kyoiku-iinkai 1981), and pounding iron is *taaltau* (forging) (Hokkaido Kyoiku-iinkai 1990), which are also different

from the Ainu *kik*. This implies that the act of forging itself had existed in Ainu society for a long time.

6-4 Conclusion

The existence in the Ainu language of the words for metals and iron technology which are different from modern Japanese words and do not correlate with them indicates that concepts, such as 'to melt metal', already existed in Ainu society long ago and had established themselves. It therefore seems that they did not come from Japan in recent times (i.e. the 18-19th centuries), as these are not loan words or words borrowed in recent times from Japan. It seems that they were passed down from ancient Japanese (i.e. around the 10th century), although it is not quite clear whether the words originated in Ainu society or entered from outside Japan. It can be said, at least, that a society which admitted the use of such words existed. This suggests that iron technology in Ainu society was not something special or unknown to them but an ordinary accepted everyday activity up to the 19th century.

In the next chapter, I expand my review of yukara, a specific type of Ainu oral tradition, in order to contextualise the word 'iron'.

Chapter 7

The anatomy of yukara

7-1 Introduction

In this chapter, I discuss the applicability of yukara, an epic form of oral tradition in the Ainu culture as evidence. In particular, the discussion considers to what extent we can extract the social context from the analyses of yukara to illuminate the Ainu social context. I also attempt to discuss the possibility of using the yukara to provide material useful for understanding the Ainu material culture.

7-1-1 What is yukara ?

The Ainu oral tradition is divided into two types according to linguistic studies: verse and prose. The verse type of oral tradition is the yukara. Yukara is an epic form of oral tradition which is/was transmitted by the Ainu recitors. It has rhythm and refrain and is an autobiographical story narrated in the first person by *kamui*. *Kamui* can be translated by such words as 'spirit' or 'god' and 'goddess' (cf. Philippi 1979). However, *kamui* in the Ainu world reflects a way of thinking that includes more than just gods or goddesses. The term sometimes refers to humans as well, such as Okikurumi *kamui*, and also to animals, plants, objects, and natural phenomena, which exist in an independent order in some relation with the Ainu. Although the gender of *kamui* can be identified according to the mode of expression of the yukara, the word *kamui* itself does not express gender, such as god or goddess. Thus, '*kamui*' is *kamui* and includes both sexes. For this reason, I use the word *kamui* which appears in yukara as they are part of the Ainu world.

The number of yukara in the Ainu culture is not known, as they have been transmitted from person to person in villages and local areas. In practice, there is no rule governing who becomes a yukara performer, although there might have been rules in the past for some reasons related to shamanism. Anyone who can remember upon hearing yukara at any occasion and can perform it on a subsequent occasion, can be a yukara performer, although not everybody does become a yukara performer. An ability to remember and perform is an obvious minimum requirement. People who are able to perform yukara are called *yukarakur*.

Yukara are performed when the Ainu have visitors and are talking and amusing themselves beside the fire in the evening; people ask a *yukarakur* to perform yukara. Then she or he can start. On such occasions, a *yukarakur* sometimes does not complete reciting a yukara to its end in order to sustain people's interest. However, in the case of funeral ceremonies, the yukara must always be recited to the end, and also performed perfectly because, if it is not, the dead person might come back in order to hear the end of the yukara, so it is very important that the recital of the yukara is completed (Haginaka, personal communication). Thus, among the Ainu, yukara is something to listen to again and again.

Yukara have been collected by Ainu linguists since the end of the 19th century: for example, by Batchelor and Kindaichi, who were leading scholars of Ainu linguistics. When Kindaichi first knew of the existence of yukara in the Ainu culture in 1906, he began a study of their structure. Kindaichi and his two students, Kubodera and Chiri, all agreed that yukara can broadly be categorised into two different groups determined by the nature of the narrator (Chiri 1973) (see Fig. 7-1 below): these are *kamui* yukara and human yukara, depending upon whether the narrator is *kamui* or human. Within *kamui* yukara, there are two further categories based on the type of *kamui*: *kamui* yukara and *oina*. If the narrator [i.e. the subject of the first person] is an animal, an object or any natural phenomenon, the epic is called a *kamui* yukara. On the other hand, if the narrator is *oina kamui*, i.e. a *kamui* of transmission or a *kamui* of creation, telling about the origin and creation of the Ainu world, then it is called an *oina*. If the narrator [i.e. subject of the first person] is an Ainu hero, Okikurumi, then it is called a human yukara or heroic yukara.

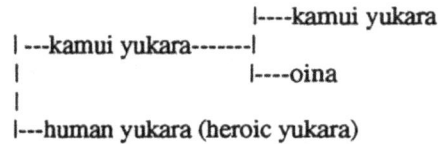

```
                              |----kamui yukara
        | ---kamui yukara-------|
        |                       |----oina
        |
        |---human yukara (heroic yukara)
```

Fig.   7-1   Category of yukara.

The name of Okikurumi is mentioned in Japanese historical documents. For example, *Ezo Danhitsuki* (Matsumiya 1629, cited in Kindaichi 1942), recorded that "the Ainu referred to Yoshitsune [i.e. a Japanese historical hero, who was a brother of Yoritomo Minamoto (Shogun of the Kamakura) in the 13th century] as Ukikurumi". The *Ezo Zuihitsu* (Anon. 1737, cited in Kindaichi 1942) said: "when the drinking feast reaches its height, the Ainu sing a song and narrate a *joruri* story [i.e. a ballad story in Japan in the 17th-19th centuries]". It also said:

> there is a story of Yoshitsune in a *joruri* story, that when Yoshitsune was young, he came to the Ezo land [Hokkaido] by ship and developed a close relationship with a daughter of Hachimen Daio. Yoshitsune stole a treasured article while Hachimen Daio was out hunting, and he escaped and returned to Japan by ship.

The account then says: "Yoshitsune in the Ainu language is Ukikurumi".

It is interesting that Okikurumi is mentioned in the 17th-18th centuries Japanese documents as Ukikurumi and also that he was referred to as Yoshitsune by the Ainu. Yukara in the Ainu culture at that time was interpreted by Japanese writers, as the equivalent of *joruri* in the Japanese culture, as is shown by the comment that "there is yukara in this country [i.e. the Ainu country], which are similar to the *joruri* in Japan" (*Ezo kenbunki*, cited in Kindaichi 1942).

This can be interpreted as indicating that the story of Yoshitsune, which was very popular in Japanese society during the 15th-17th centuries and was recited as a *joruri*, had already been diffused into the Ainu culture. Kindaichi considered that the role of Okikurumi in Ainu society, owing to his popularity among the Ainu, came to be identified with that of Yoshitsune, who was equally popular among the Japanese, and therefore Okikurumi came to be identified with Yoshitsune (Kindaichi 1942:349).

It is clear from the above discussion that yukara already existed in Ainu society in the 17th century. This implies that the style of yukara might have been formalised before the 17th century. Moreover, the existence of Ukikurumi in the heroic yukara indicates that the structure of yukara was already established in much the form in which it is categorised at present by Kindaichi and others. In other words, it is difficult to believe that the concept of the heroic yukara in Ainu society was formed after the 17th century, whether the idea derived entirely from the Ainu's own cultural experience or not.

It is thought that the yukara originated as a kind of divinely inspired monologue or divine message delivered through a shaman, since it is narrated in the first person (Kindaichi 1942). It has been noted that the yukara performer uses a bar, called a *repuni*, for keeping rhythm and hits something rhythmically. This activity is thought to have its origins in the practice of shamanistic drumming (Chiri 1973). The process of formation of more recent yukara derives from a transformation of a divine message; they developed initially as forms of *oina*, in which the origins of things in Ainu society are explained. Such forms further developed into autobiographical messages from *kamui* and stories like the heroic yukara narrated by Okikurumi (Kindaichi 1942).

7-1-2 Yukara in the historical context

There is debate about the historical interpretation of heroic yukara, centred upon whether or not the ideas in the heroic yukara are based on real historical fact. The main motif of the heroic yukara is the warfare between two groups: the *yaunkur* (land people) and the *repunkur* (offshore people, i.e. people from the sea). It is debated whether these two groups actually represent certain ethnic groups within the historical context. Those who support the idea that it is not necessary to consider yukara as historical fact and believe that such groups are fictional, existing only in the yukara's world, are Kindaichi (Kindaichi) and Kubodera (Kubodera 1969). Others, who support the idea that the heroic yukara are based on historical facts, so that it is possible to discuss a particular ethnic group in the historical context, include Chiri (Chiri 1953), Emori (Emori 1979), Kaiho (Kaiho 1979), and Obayashi (Obayashi 1991). However, within the latter group, there are two different interpretations of *repunkur* based on analyses of yukara and on historical evidence. The term might refer to the Okhotsk people in the 8th-10th centuries in the Okhotsk culture according to the interpretation of Chiri and Emori, or it might refer to the Japanese, and the warfare between the Ainu and the Matsumae in the 17th century, according to the interpretation of Kaiho; Obayashi supports only the formation of yukara in the 17th century.

It is difficult to believe that the yukara, including heroic yukara, are simply stories or fictional literature, as they represent an oral tradition which has been transmitted down

the ages within Ainu society. Rather, it would be natural to consider that the concept derives from or is based on historical events or the Ainu ethnic experience and that this accounts for the particular way in which the stories were made up (cf. Vansina 1985).

Although I accept yukara as an oral tradition which relates to historical facts within the Ainu cultural experience, there is still the big problem of how the experiences of the Ainu in their oral tradition can be identified with the known facts of the historical framework without knowing the actual dates of the yukara. This is a problem common to all kinds of oral tradition, not only yukara, but also the "Iliad" and "Odysseys" in classical archaeology (cf. Gray 1954, Morris 1986, Snodgrass 1989, Sherratt 1990). It is an inevitable difficulty in assessing such oral tradition within a historical framework.

As yukara have been collected in the 20th century, all the experiences of the whole Ainu culture before the 20th century can form the basis of the motifs in heroic stories. Therefore, it is important to understand both the value and the limitations of the yukara as oral tradition in order to apply them to the historical context. Taking as an example the term 'repunkur', this can refer to any ethnic group, notably the Okhotsk and the Japanese opposed to the Ainu, who were 'yaunkur' in historical times. There is no reason why the ethnic group opposing the Ainu in historical times should always be one and the same. In other words, any ethnic group around the Ainu can be regarded as *yaunkur*. For example, the continental people (including the Mongols) who several times attacked the Sakhalin Ainu in the 13th century (Emori 1989), or the Japanese in the Tohoku area, with whom they must have had many conflicts in the 8th-11th centuries could have been *yaunkur* at different times. Therefore, it is more appropriate to discuss the concept and meaning of 'yaunkur' in the Ainu culture, in order to understand how the Ainu themselves regarded and described other ethnic groups or opponent groups, than to find out which historically known ethnic group is being referred to as *yaunkur* within the historical framework. For this reason, it is essential to understand the Ainu social context of the yukara world, and it is not enough to consider only heroic yukara; other types of yukara should be taken into account.

7-1-3 The purpose of yukara anatomy

The purpose of yukara anatomy is to understand Ainu social meanings within the Ainu context. In considering yukara as a record of various social expressions, it is essential to understand the role oral tradition played in Ainu society, including the meaning of the oral tradition. By social expression, I mean something which expresses aspects of society — that is, expresses scenes of a society — and which describes a society — that is, describes what happens in a society in the words of a member of that society. Thus, a scene which was occurred and been enacted in a society is described as a social expression. A scene which existed and has been enacted in a society can be expressed in representative words and this can also be a social expression.

I consider it important to define yukara as an oral tradition and as a form of social expression. Therefore, it should be interpreted as a record of various aspects of Ainu society. Yukara itself has a yukara context which reflects a variety of different expressions in Ainu society. This can be seen as the result of the combination of the Ainu way of thinking and their sensitivity to the particular circumstances of their everyday life. Thus, social scenes typical of Ainu society can be seen in yukara. This I term 'the yukara world'.

After extracting social expressions and social meanings from yukara, it is possible to understand the Ainu context in terms of social practices and practical phenomena by the process of testing these within the Ainu social context again.

The relationship between 'oral tradition' and 'context' can be analysed structurally (see Fig. 7-2 below): particular kinds of oral tradition can be extracted from their context for analysis, but they must be related back to their context to be elevated to a higher structural level. Without this kind of process, it

will be difficult to understand fully the relationship between 'oral tradition' and 'context'.

At the level above the particular circumstances in which oral tradition was recited is the overall social context. The social context can be exemplified within the society by various social expressions such as drinking feast, religious practice, bear feast, trade activity, subsistence activity, social classes, gender, the role of smithing, etc. Society as a whole can be regarded as comprising sets of social expressions. Therefore, an analytical method needs to be created to read the Ainu social context, which is expressed as social expression in yukara for an understanding of the Ainu material culture. The anatomy of yukara can be used to test the degree to which oral tradition can be of importance in the archaeological method. Understanding from materials to the cultural entity through oral traditions can be expressed diagrammatically as in Fig. 7-2. Fig. 7-3 shows a reflection of the material world and the yukara world as seen through Alice's mirror.

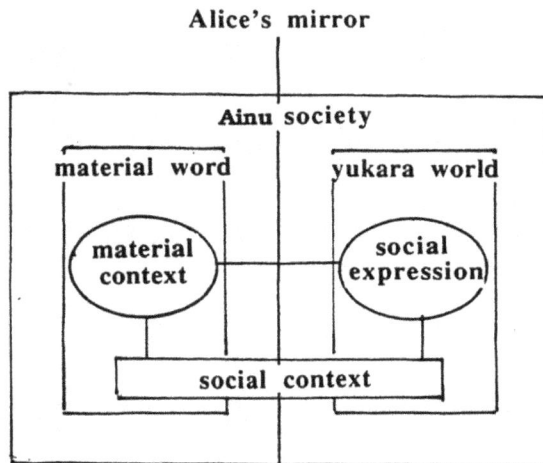

Fig. 7-2   From materials to the cultural entity through oral tradition.

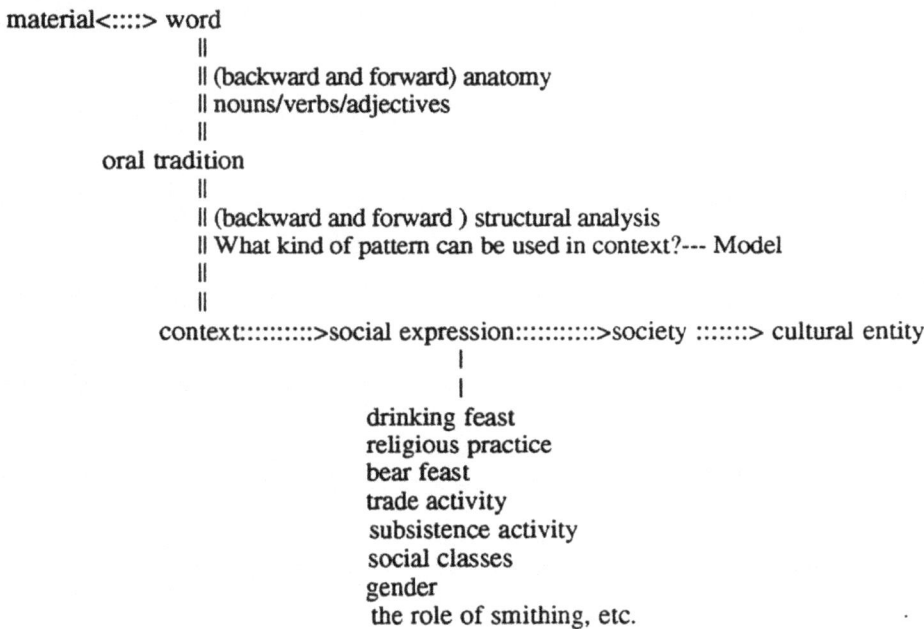

```
material<::::> word
            ‖
            ‖ (backward and forward) anatomy
            ‖ nouns/verbs/adjectives
            ‖
    oral tradition
            ‖
            ‖ (backward and forward ) structural analysis
            ‖ What kind of pattern can be used in context?--- Model
            ‖
            ‖
        context::::::::::>social expression::::::::::::>society ::::::::> cultural entity
                             |
                             |
                        drinking feast
                        religious practice
                        bear feast
                        trade activity
                         subsistence activity
                        social classes
                        gender
                         the role of smithing, etc.
```

Fig. 7-3   A reflection of the material world and the yukara world as seen through Alice's mirror

81

7-2 Analytical methods

7-2-1 Analysis of vocabulary

Analysis of the vocabulary used in yukara here means considering particular nouns in yukara in order to cross-check between words and material objects to discover precisely what they refer to. These words may or may not literally exist within Ainu society. The purpose of this kind of analysis is to find out the material context both in the yukara and in Ainu society. Metal objects and anything which relates to metal have been central to the discussion throughout this book, so I am particularly concerned with words for metal or words which relate to metal. It is important to know how words which are in any way related to metal are used in the yukara context, in order to understand the meaning of metal in Ainu society. Therefore, expressions containing words like *kani* will be checked to see whether the word is being used as a noun denoting metal, gold, and iron as the material of objects and/or whether it is being used as an adjective to describe something gold-like, or iron-like.

It is also important to identify the words imported from outside the Ainu culture, particularly Japanese words. The existence of Japanese loan words in the yukara implies that the objects did not exist originally in the Ainu culture and that the words are used as they were originally used in the culture from which they were borrowed. It is also evidence that the objects or things denoted by such words were in use among or familiar to the Ainu by the time the yukara were composed. This clearly indicates cultural contact and interaction between the Ainu and other cultures including the Japanese. Then the words can be compared with the material which existed in the other cultures relating to the chronological order within that historical context. In this way, it may be possible to trace the approximate date of the emergence of the word which can be identified in Ainu society.

7-2-2 Structural analysis

(A) Patterns of expression

In yukara, certain expressions are used as metaphors in order to express certain activities and behaviour, or things and subjects. These expressions which are used as metaphors occur within all categories of yukara and always refer to the same kinds of activity or behaviour. These set patterns of expression can be extracted and are useful features to notice as a key for understanding the use of metaphor in the structure of yukara as a whole.

For example, a pattern of expression which frequently appears in yukara is "I get along with concentrating on needlework". This is a female mode of expression, and implies that a woman is speaking. By the same taken, a pattern "I get along with concentration on a carving on a sheath" implies a male mode of expression, and that the speaker is a man. The *kamui* who narrates a yukara does not specifically mention whether the 'first person' is female or male but the kind of expression mentioned above is used to indicate its sex. This reveals whether the narrator [i.e. *kamui*], is female or male.

Another type of set expression is a certain phrase which does not explain things but is a symbolic metaphor: "Atsushi with a blaze, the end of the sheath is burned" implies the appearance of Aeoina *kamui*. This phrase is used as a metaphor for Aeoina *kamui* whenever he appears in yukara. The reason why is explained in *oina*, which tell about the origins of customs and the reasons for them in the Ainu culture. Therefore, every Ainu understands that the phrase expresses the costume and appearance of Aeoina *kamui* (Kindaichi 1942).

Contrasting with the above, certain set patterns of expression are used for certain activities, as a descriptive expression rather than a metaphor. They are clearly recognisable and evoke the process of an activity. For example, expressions like "put a pan on to the fire, put millet into the pan, stir with a spatula" and "thin-made bowl, thin-made tray, one upon another" are used to evoke the preparation of a meal in the yukara, and are understood to refer to the cooking process and how the food is served.

It is clear, as mentioned above, that certain set patterns of expression are used for the description of particular activities and things, so the same pattern of expression is retained, although the phrases are not necessarily exactly the same in all cases, as individual reciters have their own modes of expression. For example, the order of the words may be reversed so that "thin-made bowl, thin-made tray, one upon another", becomes "thin-made tray, thin-made bowl, one upon another".

Therefore, cross-checking patterns which are frequently recognised and used for certain expressions makes it possible to analyse the structure of yukara. Moreover, descriptive expressions which also explain certain activities and things make it possible to understand both the processes and the expressions which were used in Ainu society.

(B) Idiomatic expressions

There are also set expressions which create an antithesis in the yukara. These antitheses express the same meaning or say the same thing but use different phrases coupled together, or they express pairs of opposed elements, but the coupled juxtaposition is the same. For example, in the expression "Japanese land, *Repunkur* land", the word 'Japanese' and the word '*Repunkur*' are in apposition, which indicates they have the same meaning. In this case, *Repunkur* means Japanese. However, in another example '*Repunkur*' is used in this way: "the sea of the *Repunkur*, the sea of the Ainu, in the middle of the sea". Here *Repunkur* and Ainu are coupled as an antithetical expression, and are different in meaning. By analysing this kind of cross-checking, it is possible to understand the concept and the meaning of *repunkur* as referring to 'other people' in a broad sense, as opposed to 'our people' or 'ourselves', the members or the groups of Ainu society. Therefore, it is possible to understand which word was used with different meanings and it is possible to estimate the meanings of the word which is used differently.

7-3 Data

The data which are used in this analysis are 182 yukara, listed in Appendix - 2. These were collected by Kindaichi (Kindaichi 1959), Kubodera (Kubodera 1977), Chiri (Chiri and Pilsudski (Pilsudski: 1902 in National Ethnological Museum 1987). All of these have already been translated into Japanese by their collectors, except for Batchelor's contribution, which has been translated into English. The translations have mostly been published together with the Ainu original. Written transcriptions in roman letters of the original text in the Ainu language were made for Kindaichi's and Chiri's collection by the Ainu informants themselves, and for Kubodera's collection by Kubodera himself, as he was an Ainu linguist. Batchelor's collection is written in English, and Pilsudski's collection is in the form of wax cylinder records which were translated into Japanese both by an Ainu and by Japanese linguists. The details of the recording situation and the reciter's name at that time are not known.

For the purpose of yukara anatomy, I needed to examine exact original Ainu words in terms of the vocabulary and from the point of view of the material culture. Therefore, I have referred to the Ainu language text first and used the Japanese translations as a reference. I found it difficult to use the Japanese translations, because words are not translated consistently either by Kindaichi or by Kubodera. For example, in Kindaichi's case, the Ainu word *rukani* means 'to melt metal' and 'melted metal' or melted gold, melted silver, or melted iron; this word is translated as 'mercury' or 'poison' or 'water gold', appearing differently in one page although the original Ainu word keeps the same form and so on. Initially, I thought that the translation reflected the reciter's interpretation, and I assumed that the translators had asked the reciters what the words meant in an Ainu context. However, having studied the yukara, I came to the conclusion that this is just inconsistency in the translation. This kind of translation may not be a problem in the case of yukara treated as literature. However, from the material-cultural point of view and social context, it is necessary to consider exactly what the object or phenomenon referred to by the given word is, otherwise there could be serious misunderstandings in the context of an analysis of vocabulary for the purpose of this study. For this reason I have taken particular care to use and rely on the original Ainu vocabulary.

The reciters of these yukara are listed below (Table 7-1). It is important for this study to concentrate on yukara which were transmitted in the area of Saru, where the archaeological studies discussed in previous chapters were undertaken. 14 of the reciters were Saru Ainu, including two unknown reciters. In one version from an unknown reciter, the area of Shishirimuka, which is a word for the Saru River, is mentioned; thus it is clear that somehow this unknown reciter's yukara relates to the Saru Ainu. Another example, the reciter of which is unknown, was collected by Batchelor. Since Batchelor's field studies were mainly carried out in the Saru area, this may also relate to the Saru Ainu.

Table 7- 1 The list of reciters

Name of reciters	Sex	Dates	Area	Village	*
Utomuriuku	M	?	Saru	Siunkotsu	1
Takuuno Nabesawa	F	1860-1920	Saru	Siunkotsu	2
Kanumore Hiramura	F	1860-1951	Saru	Biratori	3
Wakarupa Nabesawa	M	1863-1913	Saru	Siunkotsu	3
Kotanpira Hiramura	F	1860-1941	Saru		1
Etenoa Hiraga	F	1880-1960	Saru	Shinpiraka	56
Karepia Hirame	F	1880-1947	Saru	Nina	49
Motozo Nabesawa	M	1886-1967	Saru	Siunkotsu	1
Kunimatsu Nitani	M	1888-1960	Saru	Nibutani	9
Sankirotte	M	1907-?	Saru	Nikappu	2
Tumonte Hiraga	F	?	Saru		2
Yayashi Hiraga	F	?	Saru		1
Matsu Kannari	F	1875-1961	Iburi	Horobetsu	29
Yukie Chiri	F	1902-1922	Iburi	Horobetsu	13
Shimukani Shikada	F	1887-1944	Asahikawa	Chikabumi	5
Yone Iwayama	F	?	Chitose	Rankoshi	2
Names not known					3

*: No. of epics recounted by each reciter.

7-4 Ainu society in the Yukara world: Discussions and interpretations.

(Numbers in parentheses refer to the numbers in the list of yukara in Appendix - 2)

Although my discussion through out this book focuses on iron, I have to discuss the other activities in Ainu society in order to show that iron activity is one part of society. I treat iron activity as equal to any other kind of activity in Ainu society. For this reason I have to balance iron activity against other aspects of society to show it as part of the same system.

7-4-1 Alcohol: *sake*

The thing most frequently described and the most frequently used word in yukara is alcoholic drink — *sake*. For instance:

> I visit the Ainu place/ and returned with *sake/ inau/* and *shito-mochi* as souvenir/ I invited the *kamui* which is near/ which is in distance/ (I hear) the *kamui* voices which sound merrily/ to my heart/ I enjoy/ the *kamui* entirely thank to me/ speak very highly/ my rank of the *kamui/* getting high rank/ I live (12).

In Ainu society as described in yukara *sake* and *inau* (whittled sticks) form an antithesis expressed in such phrases as "Ainu *sake/* Ainu *inau*" (6). It is easy to understand that *sake* and *inau* are very important in maintaining the relationship between the *kamui* and the Ainu. It is very important that the *kamui* should be presented with *sake* and *inau* offerings by the Ainu in order to become a higher *kamui* (i.e. a more important *kamui*) in the *kamui's* world.

When the Ainu drink *sake*, they invite many people for a drinking feast as is described in yukara lines such as the following: "brew *sake/* and invite one of you as my guest/ treat one of you as my master/ then we will have a drinking feast and a merry time together" (24), or "having a drinking feast/ having a dinner party/ it is ready/...to *kamui* which is near/ *kamui* which is in distance/ my foster brother/ send invitations" (62), and "Ishikari *kamui/* brew *sake/* good *kamui/* bad *kamui/* invite the same number of *kamui/* good *kamui* sit at high table in a line/ bad *kamui* sit at low table in a line/ facing each other/ for drinking feast" (80). This drinking feast is not just a party; it is also a ceremony at which to revere the *kamui*. Therefore, a seating plan involving a high table and a low table is decided upon. "The *kamui's* drinking feast/ from a high table to a low table/ all together/ all of them/ sit at table" can be visualised as a formal dinner party at which all the invited guests are seated at table together.

When a drinking feast takes place, preparations must be made by the host and the process of brewing *sake* is described: "brew *sake/* two or three days/ wait for *sake* ready/ ...then/ splendid drinking feast took place" (16), or "having passed/ two or three days/ *sake* has been brewed well/ drinking feast takes place" (51, 58, 81), and "having passed/ two or three days/ now/ *sake* being brewed well/ nice smell

of *sake/* in a house/ drifted all around" (62), also "I stand up/ a big bowl of *sake/* I received it/ six *sake* containers in line on one side/ a big bowl of *sake/* I received/ I poured *sake* into containers". Although such a drinking feast is organised by a host, preparation for it seems to be done by servants who belong to the host: "servants/ who make *inau/* use knives/ who filter *sake/* use spatulas/ for a drinking feast/ for a dining party/ it is ready" (59, 62, 110). The *inau* and *sake* are prepared by different servants, and it seems that the Ainu drank filtered *sake*.

At the drinking feast, *sake* is served to the guests, as in "I serve/ hold a cask/ walk along/ serving/ pour *sake*" (59, 62, 110). There is a certain manner of drinking *sake* which is described as "carrying myself on my knees/ receive a bowl of *sake/* present it on high/ present it lower/ drink it at one go/ return the bowl of *sake*" (106), or "a big bowl of *sake/* present it on high/ present it lower" (152).

The Ainu enjoy these drinking feasts and they like drinking *sake* : "when *sake* arrived/ I was invited/ I am able to join a drinking feast/ as I drink *sake* along/ my heart becomes soft with *sake/* my heart becomes merry with *sake*" (47), and "I hear the voice of a drinking feast and dining party joyfully...you join and make your heart happy" (28). At the climax of a drinking feast, songs and dances are performed, as in "dance a dance/ again and again/ *kamui* laugh loudly/ voices sound joyful" (74), "I insist on drinking *sake/* a deer *kamui* became completely drunk/ started to dance/ a stamp dance/ I help the deer *kamui/* dance together" (75), so "many kinds of dances are performed" (81). When the Ainu perform yukara, they use a bar called a *repuni*, as previously mentioned, in order to keep rhythm, as in "take a shamanistic bar from the breast/ start a song (i.e. yukara)" (152). These lines clearly indicate that the *repuni* was an implement used by a shaman.

Inau, whittled sticks, are as important as *sake* at the drinking feast, so that it can be said that a drinking feast is not only a party but also a ceremony. *Inau* are wooden sticks: the body of the wooden bar is shaved repeatedly thinner and thinner towards the end of the bar, which creates lots of wood shavings, still attached to the bar, which are used for the Ainu ceremonies. *Inau* must be produced by men, to judge from lines like "the thing which women should not do is producing *inau* for the *kamui*" (55). It is narrated as " *sake* was brewed/ *sake* and *inau* are presented to me/ words of thanks to me are given/ so I become a higher and higher *kamui/* I live" (50), while other lines: "*inau* made by humans (i.e. the Ainu)/ are what I want to have/ then if it is presented to me and prayed for me/ I go back the *kamui's* land with it" (104). As mentioned above, it is very important for *kamui* to have *inau*. If a *kamui* does not have the Ainu's *inau* when it goes back to the *kamui's* land, then the *kamui* feels shame. The rest of the *kamui* in the *kamui's* land look down on it. For the *kamui*, therefore, *inau* is an important material received from the Ainu. A yukara which is narrated by a *kamui* which did not bring Ainu *inau* to the *kamui's* land, but had instead the Japanese *inau*-like object, tells how shamed it was, as in: "*kamui* which was sent off by the Japanese under their custom/ with a branch of willow trees with pieces of paper attached/ ...climbing along up to the sky/ lots of pieces of paper around the *kamui*'s body/ pieces of paper swinging/ making an ugly noise/ what a shame such an ugly sight is" (45). It is very interesting that the Ainu knew that the Japanese have an *inau*-like object for Japanese gods, which the Shinto priests use in Japanese shrines and that some parts of those *inau*-like objects are made of paper. However, the Ainu clearly felt that the *kamui* should have the Ainu *inau* not the Japanese-style one as in: "Ainu's *inau* and Ainu's *sake* from the Ainu/ arrived for me/ ...I become a higher *kamui*" (108).

For the Ainu, the meaning of the drinking feast as a ceremony is that it involves sending *sake* and *inau* to the *kamui* in the *kamui*'s land: as these lines put it "Okikurumi *kamui*/ brew *sake*/ sake and *inau* for my wife/ arrived with prayer" (58). The drinking feast thus plays a very important role in Ainu society, so it should take place. On the other hand, from the *kamui*'s point of view, *kamui* go to the Ainu's land to visit and come back to the *kamui*'s land with lots of souvenirs such as *sake*, *inau* and shito-mochi from the Ainu. The *kamui* is therefore able to invite other *kamui* to a drinking feast to share the souvenirs, and then the rank of the *kamui* which is offering the souvenirs becomes higher in the *kamui*'s land. *Kamui* in the *kamui*'s land also receive gifts such as *sake*, *inau*, and *shito-mochi* (Ainu food, made of millet) from the Ainu and prayers through out the drinking feast, and the *kamui* recipient also shares the gifts among the other *kamui* so that its rank as *kamui* becomes higher. So, as mentioned earlier "I visit the Ainu place, and returned with *sake*, *inau*, and shito mochi as souvenir, I invited the *kamui* which is near, which is at a distance, (I hear) the *kamui* voices which sound merrily, to my heart, I enjoy, the *kamui* entirely thank me, speak very highly, my rank of the *kamui*, getting high rank, I live" (12). For the *kamui*, therefore, it is important to visit the Ainu in order to receive gifts/offerings, otherwise the *kamui* is not able to become a higher *kamui*. *Kamui* want to visit, to "make a fortune/ I go down to the Ainu's land" (45).

When famine occurred in Ainu society, "the last food which we have/ that is only cereals/ I brew *sake* from the last cereals/ and with this *sake* and *inau*/ I pray" (81). In other words, the last cereals are used for brewing *sake* for the *kamui* in order to pray for bringing food down from the *kamui*'s land. *sake* is used for prayers and to give thanks to the *kamui*, and also in memorial services.

It is clear that the relationship between the Ainu and the *kamui* is maintained through the agency of *sake* and *inau*, and the role *sake* plays is a very important one.

As mentioned above, *sake* is produced by the Ainu themselves and the last cereal is used for brewing *sake*, which means that Ainu cereals such as millet and barnyard millet were used for producing Ainu *sake*. However, another kind of *sake* is also mentioned in yukara, and that is Japanese *sake*, which is imported from Japan and called *uimam sake* or *tonoto*. The original Ainu *sake* is called *ainu sake* or *ashikoro*. It is narrated that "trade with the Japanese/ I go to/ trade *sake*/ bring/ bring back by ship" (7), or "I go to trade/ ingredients for *sake*/ I bring back" (8), and "trade *sake*/ trade Japans *sake*/ Ainu *sake*/ both together" (9). A bear-cub *kamui* describes how an Ainu said to it that he is

going to trade for the bear-cub *kamui* to give it a splendid sending-off feast. It is important to note that the purpose of Ainu trade with Japan is to get Japanese *sake* and ingredients for making *sake* for drinking feasts and any other sending-off feasts. This is because *sake*, according to the Ainu, is the most important thing for the *kamui*.

Poisoned *sake* is mentioned in yukara; for example, "my father was deceived and given poisoned *sake* by Ishikari" (152), and "bad Japanese interpreter/ poisoned the *sake*/ gave it to me to drink/ I was killed" (92). It is possible to speculate that similar things happened in Ainu society.

7-4-2 Expression of social classes

It is possible that the kind of drinking feasts mentioned above could only be offered by rich Ainu, based on the existence of the words *usshin utar* and *shukumi utar* or *ainu ewn kur*, which mean 'servants'. According to Batchelor's dictionary, these words mean 'slaves', while Kubodera's translation is 'servants'. What type of relationship was involved is not clearly identified, without knowing whether the 'servants' were paid or just given food. However, the behaviour of *usshin utar* and *shukumi utar* as expressed in yukara, seem to me to imply that they were not 'slaves', because they sometimes behave badly and are lazy, not working while the master is away. There are male and female members of this class: a man servant is *okkayo usshin* and a woman servant is *menoko usshin*. It seems that they were not temporarily employed.

The jobs which they do include "clearing on mat" (62) for women servants, "gathering wood for fuel / making fires" (62) and "everyday/ go hunting/ bring deer and bears back home" (62) for men servants. When a drinking feast is to take place, they produce *sake* and *inau*: "servants who make *inau*/ run knives each other/ servants who filter and squeeze *sake*/ run spatulas each other" (36, 59). They also build a house as in "beautiful hut/ was built" (106). There are also described as looking after a bear which is being kept, giving it food. However, according to one bear-cub *kamui*'s narration, servants did not feed it: "I was not fed at all" (8) while the master went to trade. In another case, when the master came back and saw a fireplace with almost no trace of fire, he kicked the servants who were sleeping and said: "as you are low-class people/ how dare you sleep" (62), then the servants got up one after another in surprise.

It can be seen that these servants live in two types of places: one is inside the master's house, and the other is outside the master's house. The former live in the lower position of the master's house: "a young woman servant who is in lower place" (107). The latter live outside the master's house, in which case they live in another house or even outside the *chashi* : "I order servants who live outside chashi to build a beautiful hut" (106).

There are words indicating high and low classes, such as *yai-utar-keshi*, which means 'low-class people in my village', or *yai-utar-pa*, which means 'high-class people in my village'. There are also expressions that reveal that rank was inherited such as "a woman servant whose nose shows low-class".

A category of classes distinguished by economic disparities is also indicated: there are terms for rich and poor. Words such as *nishipa-ne-kur* or *nishipane-kusu* are used for a rich Ainu, and his richness is described in terms of metaphor according to the same pattern: "what a rich man/ a line of treasure/ as if laid a cliff in low height/ laid a long line/ on them/ swords for a head/ many many heads of swords/ much much heads of swords/ overlapping one another/ tassels from swords/ swinging, moving/ bright treasure/ reflecting on the wall/ shining brilliantly/ reflecting shadow" (16, 60, 105, 107, 108, 110, 111, 113, 121). The above lines emphasise material wealth, which implies that the word rich refers to a man who possesses many fine goods. Wealth is also described as "game from offshore brought up to the land/ game from the mountain brought down to the land/ as this man is a true rich man (*nishipa*)" (101). Thus a man who brought back, and possessed plenty of game from hunting and fishing is also perceived as a rich Ainu.

On the other hand, the word *wen-kur-ne-kur* means a poor Ainu who is described as "a rich man in the past/ a poor man at the present" or "a poor man in the past/ a rich man at the present" (56). This indicates that status may not have been permanent. Moreover, it is said that "a child in poor status whose parents lived a good life/ after their premature deaths/ the child was brought up by its grandmother/ I know that is a poor child" (55).

However, this is an expression which may indicate that status was handed down from father to son: "a chief of this village/ as he was a child of/ surprisingly/ a master of this house is a rich man" (16). There are actions which are described as associated with degrees of status, as in "hide rich people's bodies/ go out and show poor people's bottom" (31, 49, 50). This is an example of an expression used frequently in yukara against unwelcome intruders, such as an epidemic-disease *kamui*, to prevent it from entering the Ainu village. According to Chiri (Chiri 1973), to display a private part of the body is an insult in Ainu society. The interpretation of the above sentence, then, may be that people of different rank in Ainu society played different social roles in keeping outsiders at bay.

7-4-3 Subsistence activity

(1) Cultivation

I have mentioned that Ainu *sake* is produced from cereals, and evidence for this has already been quoted: "the last food which we have/ that is only cereals/ I brew *sake* from the last cereals/ and with this *sake* and *inau*/ I pray" (81). The origins of *sake* in Ainu society must go back as far as their ceremony of the drinking feast which, according to their cosmology, could not be carried out without *sake*. The Ainu word for cereals is *amamu* and includes millet and barnyard millet. Therefore it seems likely that the Ainu must have started to cultivate *amamu* a long time ago in order to produce *sake*.

In one creation myth of the Ainu, the *kamui* which created the Ainu land used a hoe. The yukara narrates as "an elm tree/ made a handle of wooden hoe/ with the hoe/ land is created/ village is created/ after producing everything/ left the hoe on top of Oputateshike mountain/ from the hoe/ an elm tree grew" (109). In Chapter 6 I have discussed hoes called *kupuka* or *kutuka*. It was argued that they were an iron hoes but here *ni kupuk* refers to a wooden hoe made from an elm tree. There is another *oina* which relates that land was created by *kamui* using a wooden *shitapu* which is a different type of cultivation tool.

The activities of cultivation are clearly expressed in yukara. There is a description of "a land which is cultivated with hoes in the distance/ blackish black/ a land which is mown by sickles in the distance/ whitish white" (159, 160, 161, 162, 163). In the far distance, the land looks black where the soil has been laid bare by the hoe, while other areas where grasses have been mown by sickle shine whitish white. Fields, *toita* in Ainu, occur in yukara, as in "like digging up cultivated fields/ like more than digging up cultivated fields/ a turned over" (121, 122). This expresses the messy condition of the ground when the soil has been turned over after a field is cultivated. This image is used as a metaphor for disorder. There is also the passage in which a rabbit *kamui* narrates how it was asked "why do you eat such things/ and make a mess of the fields/ ... never make a mess of the fields/ probably cereal *kamui* get angry..." (30). "A big field/ a small field/ mowing" (152, 153) and also "a little field vegetable/ field tobacco" (33) are further references to cultivated land and cultivation narrated in the yukara.

When the Ainu harvest millet, they use tools made of shell, called *pipa*, in order to pick up the ears of millet. A yukara which is narrated by one of these *pipa* itself tells why Ainu women started to use *pipa* for picking up the ears of millet: "*pipa* made Samayukuru's millet field wither/ Okikurumi's millet fields rich/ knowing all that/ pick up the ears of millet with *pipa* shells/ then whenever Ainu women pick up the ears of millet use *pipa* shells" (137). After millet is harvested, the crop needs to dry outside, a process described in the following lines: "bring out dried things [i.e. millet] which is fully on a reed mat out/ bring out things which is fully on a winnowing basket". Then, the next stage, crops need threshing and pounding: "blow millet bran away" (126), and "pound millet with a pestle" (167), in a mortar. The cereal food *shito-mochi* is made by this process. When the Ainu make it "a group of men/ a group of women/ gathered together to make *shito-mochi*" (38). It is apparent from the reference in yukara narration to "mortar man and pestle man" (4, 5) that the pestle and mortar were widely known and used in Ainu society.

(2) Hunting

Although hunting activities do receive some attention in the yukara, the descriptions are by no means as full and detailed as those concerned with cultivation or the preparation of meals. Hunting in Ainu is *ekimme*, which really means 'to go to the mountains', to hunt, as in "go to the mountain to hunt/ an animal like a deer/ an animal like a bear/ bring it back to the house" (62, 105, 111). The hunting tool is a bow, which is made of the bark of cherry trees, as in "a bow which is wrapped in the bark of cherry trees" (65, 103, 111). When an animal is caught in the mountains, particularly a deer, it is cut into pieces, starting with its legs as in "the front leg of a deer/ the hind leg of a deer/ I thrust a knife/ I try skin scrape" (121). Other animals are brought home on the hunter's back. The animals are mainly deer and bears, as in "catch deer and bears/ for bringing up us" (88). A special metaphor to praise someone who is very good at hunting and catching game is to say of him that he brings the game of the sea to the land and the game of the mountain to the lowlands as in "game from offshore brought up to the land/ game of mountain brought down to the land" (100, 101, 103). Another hunting tool is a contrivance bow such as a trap in the form of an automatic bow for catching rabbits and small animals. In one yukara, a rabbit narrates how "my ancestor rabbits/ whenever you see a bow-trap/ dodge to one side to escape it" (29). The fox does not seem to be a favourite animal: "why should I set a bow trap for a despicable fox? never! " (24).

(3) Fishing

Fishing activity is described in yukara, especially catching salmon. The favoured technique among the Ainu was to hit the fish on the head with a wooden stick, described as in "although it would be better to kill salmon by hitting them on the head with a splendid stick made of willow" (81). An alternative method was to make a weir in the river, as in "put up posts for a fish trap made from the walnut tree" (134), and "a fish trap, eggs of salmon" (171). Sea fishing is described and includes an account of catching a spear fish and a swordfish. For this, harpoons are used. The harpoons are described in detail: the rope of the harpoon is made of nettle stems, the wooden handle of the harpoon is made of cherry, the head of harpoon is made of metal, and the shaft of harpoon is made of bone. The production process is also described, and will be discussed in the metal section.

(4) Meals

In the yukara, there are many narrations of meals and these include detailed accounts of the process of cooking and the manner of eating, which is expressed by the same descriptive patterns in the different yukara. First of all, fire is made, and a pot is set over the fire, as in "a chief of the Ainu/ make a fire rapidly/ wash a pot/ put a pot onto fire" (7), and "put a big pot onto the fire/ place the face under the pot [i.e. for blowing]/ make the fire rapidly" (11). The importance of having clean hands for cooking is stressed as in "wash your hands/ before cooking food" (105), "when you cook food/ wash from your arm to the tips of your fingers" (107, 108, 110), or "whenever you cook/ do it after washing your hands properly" (121). Then, the next stage is to wash *amamu* [i.e. millet or barnyard millet] and put it into a pot. Next the pot is put onto a fire, and then boiled millet is deliciously cooked, as in "two ladle water, three ladle water/ into a nice (or clean) small pot/ set on the fire place/ put washed millet into the pot/ sound of cooking, gutsu! gutsu!/ delicious boiled millet/ turn it over with a spatula/ mix it with a ladle/ take it off the fire place" (107, 108, 110), or "put a nice (or clean) small pot over the fire/ washed millet into the pot/ high-sound of dropping millet into the pot/ finished cooking by stirring the boiled millet with a spatula" (90). It is interesting to see the process described in such detail. This process of cooking is widely practised within the context of any rice-millet culture. Further, after the delicious boiled millet is ready, it is served into a bowl with a ladle, the

bowl must be filled up with boiled millet, then put on a tray for eating, as in "take a thin-made tray which is placing on the treasure place" (30), and "a thin-made bowl, a thin-made tray, one upon another" or "thin-made tray, thin-made bowl, one upon another" (90, 107, 108, 110, 121, 154). The meal is then served in a very polite way; serving a meal for a husband is described thus by the wife: "respectfully/ to the *kamui* whom I raise up/ to the living *kamui* whom I revere/ this is what I want" (121), while a *kamui* husband describes the serving process thus: "when ready is the bowl which is full of boiled millet/ puts her hands down/ carrying herself forwards on her knees/ presents it to me from below" (107, 108, 109, 110). Regarding the manner of eating, when a meal is received, the bowl is raised high in the air, and then lowered as in "presented highly/ presented lower" (90). Then the meal is eaten.

As mentioned above, the expression for preparing and serving meals appears many times and follows the same pattern. It is possible to consider that these formulae represent the social expression of the accumulated experience of daily life in Ainu society reflected in yukara.

7-4-4 Famine

Famine is a serious matter in any society. Narratives about famine are common in yukara: for example "in the Ainu land/ as if all fires (lights) go out/ because of famine occur" (75) and "made the Ainu land to be famine/ thus the Ainu land is gripped by famine" (74).

According to the Ainu, the reason why famine occurs is that the *kamui* in the land of *kamui* do not send food down to the Ainu's land for some reason; sometimes it is the Ainu's fault because the Ainu have treated the *kamui* carelessly, as the *kamui* relate, but, on other occasions, famine occurs both in the Ainu's land and in *kamui*'s land because a demon *kamui*, such as the Old Woman-Big Pot *kamui* appropriates all the food for itself, as in "big pot *kamui*/ demon *kamui*/ cause famine/ the Ainu's village/ gripped by famine/ the *kamui* too and the Ainu too/ are driven to extremity" (114) and "Old Woman-Big Pot *kamui* jealous too much/ prosperity of the Ainu village/ plunders spirit of food/ Shishirimuka.../ in the *kamui* village and the Ainu village/ famine occurs" (113), or "the Ainu village too/ *kamui* village too/ famine took place/ all are driven to extremity" (51).

To relieve the famine, the Ainu can only pray to the *kamui* to help them: "the Ainu village/ there is famine/ no food/ it becomes hard to pray to the higher *kamui*/ now there is no food/ driven into a tight corner/ only food (the last food) which we have/ by this / let the *kamui* know this fact" (74), and "the last food which we have/ that is only cereals/ I brew *sake* from the last cereals/ and with this *sake* and *inau*/ I pray" (81). When these circumstances are observed by the *kamui* with responsibility for caring for the Ainu land, the *kamui* says: "in the Ainu's land which I protect/ famine occurs/ the Ainu starve to death/ I am unable to go without leaving it" (131). The expression which particularly indicates that a famine is over always involves the affirmation that there are now many fish in the river, as in "a school of fish goes down deep rubbed the bottom stones of the stream/ a

school of fish which goes to upper level burn in the sun"
(75, 86, 113).

7-4-5 Trade

One of the reasons why the Ainu were eager to trade with the
Japanese was to obtain Japanese *sake* as I have already noted.
However, that it was not only for *sake*, but for other good
things which every Ainu wants to go trading is clear from:
"although good things what I want to do/ going to trade in
Japan" (92). Oina *kamui* goes to Japan to trade (143) and "to
go to Matsumae/ row the boat along" (150). Trade is
uimamu in Ainu, and *uimamu* particularly indicates going to
Japan, although there was trade also with the north and the
Asian continent. Receiving rice, tobacco, and swords as well
as *sake* from Japan, in return, the Ainu bring the skins of
bear and deer: "arrive in a Japanese town/ lots of *sake*/ lots of
tabacco/ lots of rice/ lots of treasure/ lots of treasure
swords... goods which the Japanese buy/ skin of deer/ skin
of bears" (69, 70, 71).

First of all, before going to trade, a ship is built from a
felled tree as narrated by a ship *kamui* : "a long long time a
ago/ when Ae Oina *kamui* intended to go to trade to Japan/
the *kamui* is going to built a ship" (102). Then the ship is
decorated with carving: "go to trade to Japan/ put goods on a
carve ship" ((102).

The type of trade which is described in the yukara is trade in
tribute to Japan. When the Ainu meet the Japanese, they
dressed in the Ainu costume which is embroidered and made
by Ainu women: "to meet the Japanese *tono*/ an embroidered
costume which I made/ a splendid costume/ my brothers/
changed cloth into formal dress" (102). They receive gifts
from the Japanese, in exchange for their goods. The gifts
which they receive differ according to the sex of the recipient
as in "gifts for women/ gifts for men/ difference from each
other/ take a sister to trade" (92) (in order to receive different
types of gifts). It is clear from this that the Ainu wish to
receive exotic goods and anything else which they do not
posses through trade with the Japanese. However, the results
of trade could be tragic. An Ainu woman narrated that she
met a big white bird on the way to trade by ship with her
brothers. It flew above their ship and told them through tears
"although I went to trade because that what I wanted/ a bad
Japanese interpreter/ poisoned *sake*/ gave it me to drink/ I
was killed/ I died/ now my dead body is on the way back to
my village/ do not go/ go back immediately/ return
immediately" (92). They went to trade in spite of the advice
of the big white bird, and then her brothers were killed with
poisoned *sake*. This implies that such a fate had befallen
certain Ainu and was known about in Ainu society.

7-4-6 The Japanese

As described above, whenever the Japanese are mentioned in
yukara, there is always accompanying tragedy: for example
the Ainu were killed by the Japanese. It can be said that
interaction between the Ainu and the Japanese is described.
Moreover, the sadness of the Ainu, and how they felt, was
surely most directly expressed in their own words and
through their own medium, the epic form that is yukara.
Thus, it is enough to say that yukara is a great form of

social expression among the Ainu, and is useful for
understanding the Ainu social context. This social
expression of interaction cannot be read out from data
provided by ethnography and historical documents, which are
based on outsiders' observations and are conducted within a
framework imposed by outsiders, rather than by the Ainu
themselves. It is also very difficult to recognise only from
material culture, which is mute testimony unless
accompanied by archaeological study and archaeologist's
interpretations.

An Ainu mother trying to stop her baby crying, tells how
the infant's father died before coming back to them after
being summoned by Japan and going unwillingly: "the rule
of the Japanese strict/ called up letter came from the Japanese
village" (96). He went to the Japanese village, saying:

> when there is an omen of calm from offshore/
> go out and look out to sea/ you will see a
> group of birds coming towards the land/ in the
> front of the group/ there is a bird *kamui*
> without a head among them/ it is I/ please
> cook any kind of vegetable (like stew)/ cook
> any kind of grasses/ and pray for me with food
> which you have cooked /I shall take the food
> and go to the *Kamui*'s land/ I shall live with
> *kamui* (96).

It is interesting to note the concept in Ainu cosmology that
birds symbolise the spirit of a dead person returning home,
as expressed also in yukara (92), mentioned above.
Moreover, the way in which the Ainu were summoned by
the Japanese is described: "long ago/ when your father was
still alive/ from the Japanese village/ from the *tono* village/
calling up again and again/ many times the summons/ again
and again" (97). There can be little doubt about the general
situation described by the yukara. It is a historical fact that
under the Basho-Ukeoi system (see Chapter 1), which was in
operation throughout the Matsumae's policy in the 18th-
19th centuries, the Ainu were called up for fishing labour.
These yukara describe the reality behind the history.

Furthermore, life for the Ainu in a Japanese village must
have seemed unfair in that, without knowing the reason
why, an Ainu was put to death:

> what was the reason/ be punished/ as I would
> be killed/ then/ would be struck down with a
> sword/ a mat was laid out/ I sat on it/ at the
> very point of being struck/ a Japanese master
> who was kind to me/ stooped to do so/ he said
> words of apology/ his apology was not
> accepted/ I was killed/ however/ do not feel so
> sad/ bring up my child/ that is all/ keep the
> ancestral feasts/ my lineage continues (97).

These are/were messages that the Ainu wanted to hand down
to posterity. In the relationship between the Ainu and the
Japanese, Japanese superiority was already expressed in such
a way that even the Ainu themselves endure to be the Ainu.

In contrast with the above, there are yukara describing the
relationship between the Ainu and the Japanese in which the

Ainu perceive themselves as being treated as equals. This equality is expressed in the form of an antithetical juxtaposition, as in "the Ainu's ..., the Japanese's..." (25, 65, 116, 124, 146). Ainu and Japanese made of grass are described thus: "the Ainu which are made of green grasses are at the stern/ in all sixty Ainu/ I made them by hand/ the Japanese which are made of green grasses at the prow/ in all sixty Japanese/ I made them by hand" (25). There are also lines relating that Japanese and Ainu sing songs to each other while rowing: "for the Ainu/ the Ainu boat song/ sing to each other/ carry on singing/ for the Japanese/ the Japanese boat song/sing to each other/ carry on singing" (25). The Ainu perceived that they and the Japanese were different societies but were close to each other as neighbours. When caught in a storm at sea, both, "whether Ainu or Japanese, ask Aeoina *kamui* for help". When cultural tradition and the origin of myths are recounted: "the song of the Ainu/ transmitted in the Ainu's land/ the song of the Japanese transmitted in the Japanese land" (124), or "the song of the Ainu/ to propagate it in the Ainu land/ the song of the Japanese/ to propagate it in the Japanese land" (146).

7-4-7 Disaster

There are description of phenomena which cause disasters, particularly related to the so-called *tsunami* which occur after an earthquake, when huge waves hit the land. This can create havoc, particularly in the coastal areas, destroying houses and deluging the land with salt water. A yukara describes how: "one day/ a terrible sea *tsunami*/ a surge hit the land/ a village was washed away/ the village people all died" (34). There is also a mountain *tsunami*, which may occur after very heavy rain, when the volume of water in the mountain streams becomes suddenly excessive and, sweeping down, pours along the river valley, carrying rocks and soil down from the mountains to the lowland, causing widespread devastation.

According to a crow *kamui*'s narration, a crow *kamui* gave warnings of a mountain *tsunami* as a metaphor to Samai-un-kur's village, as in "high mountains/ get wet, get wet/ low mountains/ not get wet, not get wet" (50). However, Samai-un-kur did not listen to the crow *kamui*; instead, Samai-un-kur said to the village people, "hide rich people's bodies/ go out and show poor people's bottoms" (31, 49, 50). As mentioned already, this expression is used in order to drive away someone/something as an unwelcome guest, so the crow *kamui* got angry. Then the crow *kamui* went to Okikurumi's village and said the same things. Okikurumi listened and believed the crow *kamui*'s warning, and then said to the village people: "rich people/ take out treasure/ poor people/ place *inau* outside" to provide offerings for the *kamui*. One day, in summer, after very heavy rain, a mountain tsunami suddenly happened and hit the villages. The people of Okikurumi's village all survived but those of Samai-un-kur village all died.

7-4-8 Warfare

In yukara, battles on various scales are described ranging from one-to-one confrontations to struggles between one village and another, and even wars between different ethnic groups. War between villages is described, as in "people in my village/ use swords violently/ people who kill Anrur-un *kamui*/ Anrur-un *kamui*'s treasure in his place/ when we plunder all of them to my village/ even those who were poor and low class in my village/ I will make such people rich" (62).

There is an expression which recurs in the final part of many yukara: "just now/ interval between wars/ we are resting/ I live". This expression is a pattern for ending a yukara. Moreover, the expression "interval between wars" is also frequently used as in: "for a long time/ one among wars/ always kept together with each other/ shared a tough time/ interval between wars/ took a rest/ thanking each other for fighting bravely/ exchanged our sisters" (151), or "one among wars/ supporting each other/ shared a tough time/ ties of relations/ placed upon/ the woman of Shintapuka/ went to Ponmoshiri village/ to marry/ origin of relations/ took place" (157), and " took a rest/ exchanged women" (155). This implies that Ainu life was characterised by many wars both within and outside Ainu society, so the lulls between these struggles were a time of rest when they could do something for their own society. This is also expressed in the following lines: "war breaks out/ in the land of Karafuto [Sakhalin]/ my father/ did not want to fight/ for who had not known the origin/ then he supported the *yaunkur* [land people, the people of the land i.e. our or us, his own people]" (157), thus the Ainu needed a good reason for supporting other people, such as a previous relationship, or a compatriot relationship.

7-4-9 Marriage and kinship

The expression which is used in yukara for transition from girlhood to womanhood is symbolised by wearing the *mour* (a piece of female underwear) and tying up a ribbon above the breasts, which have become well developed, as in "only now/ marriageable/ one can wrap yourself in a *mour*" (61), or "woman's ribbon/ I tie it in a high position round breasts" (105, 122), "a beautiful young girl/ only now/ a woman's ribbon/ tie it up in a high position round the breasts" (157). When a girl becomes of marriageable age, a house is built specially for her and she waits for a man who is suitable for her. This is narrated as "(my foster brother) built a splendid house and gave it me/ I live in the house/ I do only embroidery" (61) and "when woman reaches the right time/ woman's house (a house in which only a daughter lives)/ a separate house/ when it is built/ I live there" (106). When the right man appears, the woman prepares a meal and presents a bowl full of millet to the man, who receives and eats it. This process of preparation and serving has already been described in the meals section, and the same pattern of expressions is used in this context as well. Next, marriage is symbolised by the action in which the man eats half the bowlful and returns the rest to the woman; if the women receives it and eats it in the manner previously described, then the marriage is completed. It expresses the idea of sharing food together in life. The expression is described as "two water, three water...thin-made tray, thin-made bowl/ one upon another/ presented a bowl full of millet to Ponmoshirikur/ Ponmoshirikur bends the centre of his hip to receive it/ presented highly/ presented lower" (154).

From the above description it seems that a marriage partner can be decided upon entirely freely by a woman, as marriage does not happen if she does not accept the bowl returned to her by the man. However, there is a description which indicates that a marriage partner is decided on by the parents: "you two should become a couple/ ancestral words have been left/ it has been decided as a command" (105). These words were left by a father to a foster sister for his child. This is also indicated by the description of a young man who is very good at hunting, described as "game from offshore brought up to the land/ game of mountain brought down to the land", who turns up from somewhere and stays at the house of a rich village chief and then asks to marry the chief's daughter (100, 101).

Moreover, opportunities of marriage arose through wars, which enable people to get know each other while fighting on the same side, as narrated in "for a long time/ one of wars/ always kept together with each other/ shared a tough time/ interval of war/ took a rest/ thanking each other for fighting bravely/ exchanged our sisters" (151), or "one of wars/ supporting each other/ shared a tough time/ ties of relationship/ placed upon/ the woman of Shintapuka/ went to Ponmoshiri village/ to marry/ origin of relations/ took place" (157), and "took a rest/ exchanged women" (155). Theses narrations imply that regional relationships, union relationships, and friendly relationships were established by marriage alliances in Ainu society. Further, these kinds of relationship were strengthened in order to fight against a common enemy in war, and it can be said that this was a foundation of compatriot awareness within Ainu society.

My discussions are based on data collected mainly in the Saru area, in order to understand the Ainu social context of that area in relation to the archaeological data. In yukara, there is an indication of the relationship between the Saru area and the Sakhalin area, as narrated in "the war broke out/ in the land of Karafuto [Sakhalin]/...one of wars/ supporting each other/ shared a tough time/ ties of relations/ placed upon/ the woman of Shintapuka/ went to Ponmoshiri village/ to marry/ origin of relations/ took place"(157). There is also a yukara narrated by a close friend of wolf *kamui*: "I live in a village of the land of Karafuto/ ...one day/ suddenly/ in Shishirimuka [the Saru]/ ...my close friend/ I heard a scream of wolf *kamui*" (54), then the close friend of wolf *kamui* went to the Saru area to help the wolf *kamui*.

Although, interestingly, there are no description of any fights between wife and husband, there are expressions which describe fights over a wife and/or over a husband between members of the same sex, and also of unfaithful wives and husbands. There is an Ainu word, *tush*, for a mistress, and it is used in a yukara narrated by a first wife who won back her husband and lived happily again; the wife narrates: "that woman *kamui*/ I felt pity/ so I made her mistress" (48). There is also an expression "taking off six hoods", which is a metaphor indicating that a widow can marry after the six-year period of mourning expires, as in "six hoods/ when you take it off all/ a man will visit you" (90).

7-4-10 Gender

(1) Man

The expression "I get along with concentration on a carving on a sheath" implies a man in yukara, as already mentioned previously, and 'a carving on a sheath' is a symbolic phrase. The costumes which are described in yukara indicate the sexes as well. The splendid costume of a man is described as *kani kosode*; golden *kosode* (*kosode* is a word borrowed from Japanese, where it referred to a cloth *kimono*), as in "golden *kosode* / from the top of the *kosode*/ bells hanging down/ half way down/ a line is made by cutting/ from half of the *kosode*/ bells hanging down/ to the bottom/ a line is made by cutting/ because of this/ working along/ on the body/ ringing bells/ sound of bells, rin-rin" (60. 61), or "golden *kosode*/ pull on over my body / golden belt put on tightly/ thin-made small helmet/ tie strings of helmet tightly" or "received *kosode* from *kamui*/ pull up over my body/ golden armor/ in full armor" (107, 108, 113, 114), and "golden *kosode*/ pull on the layered/ surface of *kosode*/ along the back gold hanging down/ along the chest gold hanging down/ massive golden strings hanging down"(152). From this, it seems that 'golden *kosode*' indicates an armored costume. The word that I have translated as 'golden' — as did Kubodera — is the Ainu word *kani*, which, as we have seen, can also be translated as 'metal'. However it does not seem to me that the word as used here simply means the 'metal armor'.

(2) Woman

Women's costume is described as 'golden *kosode*' as well: for example, "golden *kosode*/ whip on/ six *kosode*/ on top of one another/ on top tie a belt/ and on top another six *kosode*" (16, 17, 53) It seems that this indicates the Japanese women's costume which was commonly called the '*kosode*', 'juni-hitoe' or 'the twelve-layered kimono' of the 17th century, since 12 layers are mentioned based on the calculation and it also says 'on top of one another'. The word *juni-hitoe* appears for the first time during the 13th century of Japanese history. It was a common rather than a formal designation, and it meant only a layered kimono at that time (Kawabata 1969). In yukara, a necklace (32), a ring (154), and earrings (106) are described, which normally did not form part of Japanese women's costume at that time since these were not worn by Japanese women from the 8th-10th centuries onwards. These ornaments are described as being passed on in the maternal line, as in "a bag which is transmitted in the maternal line/ necklaces (*kosode*, earring) which is transmitted in the maternal line" (106).

There is a further interesting description of the woman's costume used when a woman *kamui* is going out: "tie grass belt tightly around the waist/ do up hair in a knot high on the head/ to wear flying a pair of shoes/ to wear flying a pair of gloves/ to put a golden fan into a pocket" (1, 21, 48, 58), or reverse forms of the above (79, 80). However, the meaning of this is far from clear and cannot be interpreted.

(3) The role of gender

Expressions which describe gender roles or gender division are found in yukara. In the case of women, expressions of needlework or embroidery symbolise women's activities as in "being a woman/ is doing needlework/ do needlework" (105). On the other hand, "the thing which women should not do is produce *inau* for the *kamui*" (55), so that women are prohibited from making *inau*. The role of women is described. They undertake the weaving of matting: "my sister/ weaves a mat/ turns to the back of the room/ one layer/ turns to the front of the room / one layer" (18). They collect and bring in firewood, as in "one hold of firewood/ much firewood/ brought to the house". They prepare food with mortar and pestle: "outside house/ a woman/ pounding millet" (30). Moreover, there is an expression of an antithesis of man and woman as in "a group of men/ holding harpoons in hands/ for catching fishes/ a group for hunting deer/ bows in hand/ ...a group of women/ gathering lilies" (86), or "men go to mountains for hunting/ to get game/ our sisters go to a field/ working a field/ to fill many stores/ to fill many stores" (156), describing women's gathering and cultivating activities.

Further interesting expressions in yukara are descriptions of hunting and fishing activity by women, as in "my sister pulls a big whale to land by piercing it with a harpoon" (18), then "my foster sister cuts up and divides the meat of a whale into pieces" (18). This evokes the work which relates to whaling, and "whenever my sister goes to the mountains to hunt" (120) to hunting. There is a description of when she comes back from the mountains as in "meat covered in soil/ fish covered in soil/ coming back bearing it on her back" (120). A note by Kubodera on this expression states: "because she is a woman, she cannot hunt fish, and deer or bears. She picks up things on the ground which men have thrown away, that is why they are covered in soil" (Kubodera 1977: 556).

One role of men is to hunt and fish, described in "a group of men/ holding harpoons in hands/ for catching fish/ a group for hunting deer/ bows in hand" (86), and "men go to mountains for hunting/ to get game" (156). In addition, "an Ainu chief/ makes a fire rapidly/ washes a pot and puts onto a fire" (7), or "my father draws water/ cooks food/ brings me up" (87).

7-5 Conclusion: Metal and Yukara as a social expression

Two conclusions can be drawn. The second conclusion is derived from the first. The first conclusion is that, as I have shown above, for the Ainu yukara constitutes their view of things around them and familiar in their daily life expressed in their own words. Their accumulated experience based on their way of thinking and their lifestyle can be recognised in yukara, such as the *kamui*, the drinking feasts, trade, interaction with others, gender, marriage, and kinship. Therefore, yukara as a 'social expression' within the Ainu context can be understood by the study of yukara, and they can be used effectively in an archaeological study, as shown by the many examples of social expression that I have extracted from yukara in this Chapter.

Thus, the second conclusion is that it is possible to extract from yukara the social meaning of metal for the Ainu and to see its role as an expression of society.

The word *kani* appears in yukara very frequently: 85 of the 182 yukara in my data describe *kani*. Types of *kani* include *konkani*, *shirokani*, and *rukani*. They occur at least once and in some cases many times. This number of occurrences depends on the length of the text. For example, in yukara no. 150, which has 7080 lines, 46 lines describe *kani*, and this is not the longest passage. It is easy to get the impression that the Ainu liked *kani* very much. According to the linguist Chiri (Chiri 1955), the word *kani* can be interpreted as indicating that metal was a very precious material to the ancient Ainu; thus the word *kani* is used with the meaning of 'splendid' or 'magnificent', as in *kani chise* (gold house), which means 'splendid house' and not 'metal house'. There are many materials which support this interpretation. For example, house, hill fort, floor, arrow, fan, cloth, and 'bow' dance stick are described by adjectives such as 'golden', 'beautiful', 'nice', 'splendid', and 'magnificent'. This is particularly true in an example like *kani chise, poro chise* (gold house, big house), which creates an antithesis although there is the word *piruka* exists which means 'beautiful', 'nice', and 'splendid'. This appears in yukara in combinations such as *piruka chise*.

However, in Philippi's translation of yukara (142) collected by Batchelor, he translated *kani* as 'metal' in English, in such phrases as 'a metal-buckled belt' and 'a little metal helmet', although he suggested a confusion in this interpretation of the word in another place in the same yukara (Philippi 1979). These phrases commonly appeared in many yukara and are translated as 'gold-buckled belt' and 'a little gold helmet" in Japanese translations by linguists like Kubodera, Kindaichi, and Chiri. Thus the interpretation of the word *kani* needs to be considered in the context of yukara themselves.

In relation to metal objects like swords, which need to be sharpened, in the context of yukara the activity of sharpening on a whetstone is also described by the thunder *kamui* in an instructive example: "the village chief/ said to the village people/ a high *kamui*/ walking along/ so show respect/ do not sharpen/ do not weave" (77).

There are cases in which the word *kani* seems to imply merely that an object is made of metal, in the context of yukara. For example, an antithesis of *ni shintoko, kani shintoko* (55) implies 'wooden *shintoko*, metal *shintoko*' (*shintoko* is a word borrowed from Japanese and is the name of a round container with three legs, made of lacquered wood in Japan. It was used during the 16th-18th centuries). Although Kubodera interpreted this as 'gold' (Kubodera 1977:251), it may be right that there is no material evidence that such a metal *shintoko* itself existed in Japan or among the Ainu. However, it is interesting to note that *kani shintoko* means a wood-burning stove, made of metal according to an Ainu informant (1984). Moreover, an antithesis of *shirar suop* and *kane suop* (73), 'stone box and metal box', also implies material. Another example is *shirokane shutu* (silver club) (78), which implies that a wooden club made of silver appears in another part of this yukara. The comment made on *Kanepet* by Philippi is very interesting: it is "Metal River. The natives of Metal River wear metal armor, and the natives of Stone River wear stone armor" (142) (Philippi 1979:379). Here it is again part of an antithetical juxtaposition, 'people of *Kanepet*' and 'the natives of *Shirarpet*' as ' metal river' and 'stone river'. Thus it is possible to understand what *kani* or *kane* implies as a result of the context implied by yukara.

Furthermore, descriptions which indicate iron production and iron-working technology are described in yukara. There are five versions of the same kind of story, in all of which the refrain is "*tusunapanu*", recited by Kunimatsu Nitani, Utomuriuku, and Wakarupa, and performances by two unknown recitors were collected by Batchelor and Pilsudski. There is another version, in which the refrain is different, i.e. "*zussai-zori, zussai-matsu*" recited by Matsu Kannari. Although there are slightly different lines, which I assume are based on the capacity and circumstances of memory or different channels of transmission, the content of the story is the same, being narrated by a whale *kamui* or swordfish *kamui*, and the same patterns of expression describe the material of which harpoons are made and how they are made. Harpoons which were used for hunting whales or swordfish are made of bone and iron; therefore the head of the harpoons is made of metal, and thus you hear the sound of pounding metal; the shafts of the harpoons are made of bone and thus you hear the sound of shaving bones, as in:

> harpoon/ top of harpoon/ because it is metal/ to the inside of my stomach/ sounds of pounding metal/ inside of harpoon/ because it is bone/ to inside of my stomach/ sounds of shaving bone ...You came floating down the stream/ of Shishirimuka [the Saru River]/ to the mouth of the river/ be drifting ashore/ to my stomach/ pounding metal/ shaving bone ... (67, 68, 138, 139, 140, 141,168).

The word *kane kik hum* describes 'metal-pounding sounds', thus this implies that 'metal' here means 'iron' and also implies forging activity by an Ainu blacksmith in Ainu society in order to produce the metal head of a harpoon for hunting whales or swordfish. The use of the word 'Shishirimuka' for the Saru River clearly indicates the Saru River area.

From the above discussion, it can be seen that the forging process, at least, existed in Ainu society as a social practice and so is expressed in yukara. In other words, iron-working was a common part of Ainu daily life and experience in the Saru area.

Chapter 8

Conclusion: Ainu archaeology and ethnohistory

8-1 Introduction

In this chapter, I conclude this book by discussing how the meaning of iron technology functioned as a technological context in the Ainu culture and how the social context, which can be reflected in material culture, was understood within the Ainu cultural context. I also consider the meaning of history for the Ainu and the way in which it has been fashioned for them, and I discuss Ainu archaeology as ethnohistory from the point of view of contextual archaeology.

8-2 Iron technology of the Saru Ainu before the 17th century and its society.

Having examined Ainu iron technology in the 17th century, before the iron prohibition policy was adopted by the Matsumae, I can state that forging processes and refining processes were definitely practised in Ainu society. At the same time, customs of everyday life which needed access to iron products were being established. Moreover, production of iron itself, by a unique method, can be recognised. From all of this evidence, it is possible to determine clearly that the social demand for iron in Ainu society was very strong. At the same time, despite the demand, Ainu society was a society in which iron and particularly steel were difficult to obtain, or, rather, a society in which it was very difficult to obtain steel as a raw material because Ainu society was outside the distribution network for steel. Iron raw materials were obtained in the form of iron objects, such as iron pots and scrap iron, acquired by trade exchange. These iron products were processed and covered the demand for everyday necessities. The processing of these iron products on a hearth was already being practised at the end of the Satsumon period and had even reached the level of the refining process, as seen at the Satsumae sites. It is possible to argue that the social demand increased gradually in Ainu society and that the quantity of iron products imported increased in accordance with that demand. Thus, to judge from its technological aspect, iron processing technology was not derived directly from contemporary Japanese society. Rather, it is possible to consider that it derived from the Satsumon, who had already been influenced by Japanese iron technology at that time. The north of Tohoku in northern Honshu, probably the source of iron products for the Satsumon culture, increased production so as to increase the supply of such goods, a process that led to social change as a formation of Ainu society.

This interpretation can be taken further: there was a great technological difference between Katsuyamadate, a Japanese site of 15th-16th-century date, and Ainu sites of 17th-century date like the Iruekashi and Pipaushi sites. The former already possessed a lump of steel obtained within the Japanese network; on the other hand, the latter at an even later period than the former did not have steel. Instead a unique method was presumably invented to produce steel in order to meet the demand for it in Ainu society.

Thus, it can be assumed that iron technology was introduced into the Satsumon culture as a result of cultural contact with the Japanese, and that it was carried out continuously into the Ainu culture. The level of iron technology among the Ainu is very similar to that of the Satsumon. But it does not bear comparison with that of Japan, where iron technology had developed considerably, as the perfection of the *tatara* smelting method illustrates, and had reached a level of sophistication far beyond anything the Ainu could achieve.

On the other hand, in spite of some development of iron technology in Ainu society, it was adversely affected by the iron prohibition policy of the Matsumae. As a result, Ainu society faced conditions in which iron products as a raw material were difficult to obtain. However, as I have explained in Chapter 2, some iron products always managed to bypass the prohibition on iron exports. In Ainu society, it seems that Ainu blacksmiths continued processing iron products by small-scale forging. Supporting evidence for this persistence was found at the Setanaichashi site.

The social context can be examined from aspects of iron technology. It is possible to identify the different social contexts in Ainu society and Japanese society by considering the role of iron within each society, the distribution network, and the technology used.

After the breakdown of the Ritsu-Ryo system in the Japanese political framework, particularly in the Tohoku district around the 9th-10th centuries, there was increasing productivity and expansion of trade based on cultural contact without previous political borders. This increase in industry affected the Satsumon culture in the hinterland of north Tohoku and Hokkaido. Iron products were distributed by exchanging goods with people in Hokkaido. Material culture indicates many factors in the course of prolonged cultural contact with others and this cultural contact must have increased, owing to the expansion of productivity in Tohoku. Thus, iron as a component of material culture, which can be understood by archaeological study, needs to be tested within the Ainu cultural context.

The analysis of yukara was employed for understanding the Ainu cultural context. Ainu society, which can be seen through the anatomy of yukara is reflected in a wide range of Ainu activities, including widespread trade. The Ainu themselves realised that they were the Ainu; their identity was formed through their trade activity and gave their compatriot awareness. Group solidarity was reinforced by the warfare with outsiders. Yukara expressed their society, which was built on this awareness. The expression of *Yaunkur, and Repunkur* is a good example of it.

When and how the concept of a word like *kani chise* emerged, and whether or not the translation should be 'golden house' or 'splendid house', the meaning and concept expressed not only describe 'admirable' in a single adjective but also reflect the actual fact that someone had seen a real golden house, such as Chusonji Konjikido, (i.e. a real golden hall), which was built by the Fujiwara family in

1124 at Hiraizumi, in Tohoku. It seems that hearsay based on the experience of actually having seen such a house spread by word of mouth and was gradually transmuted into the symbolic image of the *kani chise*, or perhaps people heard at second-hand exaggerated Japanese descriptions that claimed "there is a splendid house, a golden house, in Japanese territory". Thus, yukara describe the society not only extensively, but also factually.

From the above, people of the Satsumon culture and people of the Ainu culture can be regarded as historically the same people, and can be interpreted as an evolving ethnic group. Thus, the Ainu are a group of people who formed through a process of cultural change from the people of the Satsumon. Their lifestyle was also transformed by the historical process of acculturation to the Japanese culture and included other influences.

8-3 What is ethnohistory to the Ainu?

By history, what I mean here is that diachronical process which can be set within a chronological order among things and objects. History through which the ethnic identity of a people who belong to a non-literate society is formed can be termed ethnohistory. The ethnic identity which is perceived by the Ainu ethnic group was formed through the ethnohistory of the Ainu. Ainu archaeology is considered, in this book, as an archaeological approach to the Ainu culture, which was created by the Ainu people, in order to establish its historical change and meaning. I have used several different modes of expression of history, depending on the nature of the data describing Ainu ethnohistory.

Data which are used for the investigation of ethnohistory can be divided into two different categories. One is data which describe the ethnic group on the bases of the observations and records from another culture, such as ethnographic data and historical documents. The other is data produced by members of the ethnic group itself, using their own mode of expression. This category includes archaeological data which reveal a component of their material culture, and also such evidence as the epic type of their oral tradition, yukara.

In this book, I have used the former categories, such as ethnographic and documentary historical data which were provided by other cultures in order to understand the substantive historical process of cultural change and to gain insight into Ainu social phenomena and to set up hypothetical models for archaeology. The latter categories of data were used to examine these hypothetical models and to test them in the light of archaeological data. The oral traditional epic type of data was used in order to understand the Ainu social context from within.

Although ethnographic, documentary, archaeological, and epic data individually express different modes of history and have different values for describing ethnohistory, these data make it possible to describe a more substantive ethnohistory by cross-checking between them, since they necessarily complement each other. In particular, this book confirms that the process of formation and the substantive reality of the existence of a non-literate ethnic society can be described by using data which the ethnic group itself possesses —

such as archaeological data, which consists of components of their material culture, and epic data, in which they express themselves in their own words. These data are most valuable for describing the ethnohistory of the ethnic group: at any rate, this is the result of my attempt to examine the technological context of iron technology in order to understand the Ainu social phenomena and the social meaning of iron technology in Ainu society.

Although historical documents are the most valuable data for describing history and are an important mode for expressing history, non-literate ethnic groups do not themselves possess historical documents to express their history. When historical documents, produced by another literate group with which they were confronted, are used to describe such an ethnic group, the information needs to be examined carefully to establish whether the documents are biased or not because of ethnic differences which might prejudice the literate ethnic group. It cannot be guaranteed that historical documents provide homogeneous information on all aspects of society. It might be said that the documents which were left by another society do not describe fully the society which was the object of study. Taking as an example Ainu iron technology, which is scarcely mentioned in Japanese historical documents, it is possible to claim that some practices in Ainu society have not been fully described in Japanese historical documents. Japanese historical documents which described the Ainu culture do not always agree with the archaeological data obtained from excavations. Archaeological data sometimes indicate something which does not appear in Japanese historical documents. Thus, these differences between the different modes of expression of history need to be examined, and explanations are required to fill the gaps. Acknowledging that there must be a gap between Ainu society itself and the image of it that emerges from Japanese historical documents, which are coloured by ethnic prejudice and distorted by ignorance, it is necessary to test these documents by using archaeological data. In other words, it is difficult to describe Ainu ethnohistory using only ethnographical and historical documents; it needs to be tested against the archaeological data.

Although the ethnographic present is clearly identified for ethnographic data, information which is transmitted by an informant is not clearly tied to a particular point in time. Information obtained from informants also needs to be examined within the social and historical context, and the informants who provide the information need to be placed within their specific conditions of life and the period in which they live.

However, ethnographic research carried out by ethnographers is already set within the framework of the researcher, so their questions cannot extend beyond their framework. It is thus very difficult for us to obtain information about phenomena which may have existed in a society but which no outsider ever considered. Such phenomena were never asked about by anyone or were kept secret within the society. There is a tendency for information from particular studies to be limited by the framework of the study. In the case of a study which is carried out for particular purposes, it would be difficult to expect to receive information relating to more than those purposes. Information obtained within the framework of ideas of the researchers themselves is limited to a specific area, at the level of sampling data, even before analysis. What is needed is not to discuss a research framework as used in ethnology, but to study ethnographic data, such as travel records or travel diaries which describe a society as an observed scene by the writer and which make it possible to understand social phenomena in their ethnic context. For example, as I have explained in the cultivation prohibition model, the reason why cultivation was carried out secretly is that "cultivation is wanted" but "it is prohibited", "if one is seen, the crops may be taken away", so they "must do it secretly". Where? "Deep in the forest" or "away from the home". Reasons of this kind, which derived from the Ainu themselves cannot be read unless people who shared the idea of 'cultivation prohibition' in a society. In other words, this phenomenon, practising cultivation secretly, can only be derived from the idea which only the Ainu can raise in order to compromise in their society. Ethnohistory, which is based on the characteristic ideas of an ethnic group, is difficult to establish from data supplied only by outside observations. What can be drawn by outside observations is the history of the society to which the observers belong or the history of ethnological thought. A framework which is based on ethnographic data needs to be tested against archaeological data. In other words, without the support of archaeological data, ethnohistory cannot be written (cf. Wilmsen 1989, Jonson et al. 1994).

8-4 Conclusion: Ainu archaeology and ethnohistory

Archaeological data used in this book, which are necessary to describe ethnohistory, are materials from excavations which make it possible to reconstruct iron technology by archaeometallurgical analyses. Further examination based on such data may help to illuminate the social context. From this examination, technological similarities can be identified with techniques employed in the Satsumon culture which preceded the Ainu culture. These similarities go beyond the immediate problem of iron technology and extend to other aspects of material culture as revealed by archaeology. Thus it can be argued that there was some continuity from one culture to the other.

Archaeologically, in general, it is difficult to perceive the process of the historical continuity of groups of people who exist at present and who came into existence through the archaeological process. Even within the same geographical area, historical continuity cannot be guaranteed, so it is not certain whether a present-day ethnic group is the same ethnic group as in the past in the same area.

In the case of the Ainu, it is possible to consider that the Satsumon and the Ainu are the same group of people in the historical sequence, since Japanese historical documents give no hint of ethnic replacement or ethnic movements or ethnic migrations between the 10th and 20th centuries. Therefore, the meaning of cultural change from the Satsumon to the Ainu needs to be questioned as culture change within the historical sequence.

However, in archaeology, 'archaeological culture' is defined by the characteristic features which appear in the material culture (Childe 1956), and the archaeologist tends to identify a group of people who have left a material culture as an ethnic group. As a result, arguments such as "the Ainu culture may be derived from the Satsumon culture, but the Satsumon people were not the same as the Ainu people due to the fact that pottery-making existed among the Satsumon" (Kaiho 1993) have became common knowledge among Hokkaido archaeologists and Japanese archaeologists. However, in these circumstances, only a historical change within the context of the same ethnic group of people can be extrapolated from such a limited aspect of material culture as pottery. If this a change in the ethnic character of the population is predicated only on the basis of the presence or absence of pottery, the logical conclusion drawn must be that the ethnic group who created the Satsumon culture was completely extinct before the Ainu ethnic group arrived, or that they were completely invaded by the Ainu ethnic group. It is necessary to examine how far an archaeologically defined culture can be regarded as synonymous with an ethnic group. It is a matter of how we interpret a group of peoples as an ethnic group which were defined by their 'archaeological culture'.

The way in which a group of people are recognised as an ethnic group based on ethnicity, needs to be examined. Is there ethnicity defined by common cultural factors? In other words, a cultural concept which has a structure — sharing a common code including language, though not necessarily only language, but a variety of cultural traits — needs to be recognised for a culture to be identified.

To interpret phenomena or things within the structure of culture is impossible without understanding the intentions or purposes of the people who acted to make these phenomena or things, because they are the product of the action as a result of the intentions and purposes of those people.

"How to recognise an 'archaeological culture' in archaeology" has been examined here because these has been a paradigm shift in archaeology (Hodder 1982): from a concept of culture in archaeology which was defined by phenomena and things as a result of action, to a concept of culture which includes a structure which has a commonly shared code, which makes it possible to read human ideas and intentions as a source of action.

Therefore, a group of people who shared a common code to communicate the intention of their actions as members of the structure of a culture, such as an ethnic group, needs to be examined archaeologically — as they are the same people in the concept of culture used in archaeology. At this point, Ainu archaeology, as examined in this book, has significant value in the context of reconsidering the methods of recognition and interpretation in archaeological cultures. People who left material culture, which archaeology interprets, and a group of people who are members of a culture as an ethnic group, i.e. the Ainu ethnic group, are possibly recognisable as the same people. Thus ethnohistory can be described as connecting the archaeological data and a group of people as an ethnic group.

Ainu culture includes a common code, which can be read as peoples' ideas and intentions of action. Those who belong to the Ainu ethnic group use this code as a source of action. A method of reading such a common code is needed.

Each phenomenon or thing or object, manifested according to people's ideas and intentions, have a role and meaning within each culture. Thus, it is difficult to read the ideas and intentions of people who carried out an action or use an object without understanding the role and meaning of those actions and objects within that culture. To understand the role and meaning of phenomena and things or objects is to understand their context within that culture. Things or objects are recognised from their surface appearance as being the same class of objects. However, if these things or objects enter a structure of cultural concepts which has a different common code, then the meaning and role of things and objects differ from other structures. Thus the meaning of things and objects is not one but includes many meanings according to different structures. To search for the common code which makes the same meaning within each context can be a method of contextual archaeology (Hodder 1986).

In Ainu archaeology, objects — e.g. iron pots, Japanese mirrors, swords, and coins — which are Japanese products acquire different meanings in the Ainu culture. If particular objects entering the Ainu culture change their original meaning, and other things or phenomena also change in the same manner on entering the Ainu culture, and if this manner can be recognised as the Ainu's inclination, then it is termed "the Ainu's inclination", as it is expressed in Japanese as "Ainu *gonomi*" in Japanese society, since Ainu taste differs from Japanese taste. The manner, which includes intended action as the result of their intention and meaning, is called "the Ainu's way" (i.e. expressed as *Ainupuri* and exists among the Ainu).

In this book, the desire for iron in Ainu society, the way in which iron entered Ainu society, the way in which iron was used, and the meaning of iron in Ainu society all indicate how the Ainu practice "the Ainu's way". Archaeological data within the Ainu cultural context and the people who left that material as a result of their action, i.e. members of the Ainu ethnic group, are connected with the same action through contextualising examination. If that is so, it is valid to record the names of artifacts from excavated sites and refers to them in publication reports, by using the names which the Ainu use in the Ainu culture as used among themselves — such as calling a small knife a *makiri*, or a harpoon a *kite*, and so on, which are called respectively *kogatana*, and *mori-gashira* in Japanese. By the same logic, iron pots, now called *tetsunabe* in Japanese can be called *kanishu*.

Further, in this book, it is considered that to search for the common code which bestows the same meaning and to understand iron and iron technology within the Ainu cultural

context requires the use data which can be expressed by the Ainu themselves. That is yukara, which is a message from the past as an epic type of oral tradition in Ainu society. Ethnohistory which seeks to describe an ethnic group in its own terms cannot ignore this epic type of data. This book has demonstrated that this kind of data is very significant and meaningful as a key to understanding not only how things were expressed but also a people's concept of their culture. Moreover, the expression used in the epic type of data is repeated in virtually the same pattern in a context in the society as a pattern of structure. So their expressions appear not to be dependent on a specific informant, which make them a very different mode of data from the ethnographic data: these expressions go beyond information based on the experience of an informant as an individual. Although it is true that it is difficult to locate in actual historical time the happenings narrated in the case of these epics, they are performed by people who themselves belong to Ainu society, so they are more reliable than ethnographic data written by outsiders, which depend on the framework of the researcher's ideas that inevitably interfere with the data. Thus, yukara are in a sense the most 'authentic' data for reconstructing Ainu society and for recognising the characteristics of the Ainu as an ethnic group. They are part of Ainu culture sharing the common code into which can be read the ideas and intentions of people who belong to the Ainu ethnic group.

From the above, the ethnohistory of the Ainu can be delineated using results from Ainu archaeology which are based on the substantive Ainu culture, approached through contextual archaeology. In this sense, Ainu archaeology as ethnohistory can be called the archaeology of *Ainupuri* (the Ainu's way) and can play a significant part in enhancing our understanding of Ainu culture. Furthermore, yukara, as messages from the past transmitted by the Ainu ethnic group, are significant for archaeological interpretation as one component of ethnohistorical data. In other words, in this book, the existence of yukara makes it possible for Ainu archaeology to become ethnohistory.

Therefore, Ainu archaeology which is further approached by contextual archaeology in order to examine some other aspects of the material culture of the Ainu, apart from iron and iron technology, will make it possible to understand the Ainu cultural context in more detail. In the future, it should be possible to achieve a more profound understanding of the Ainu culture as a total entity on the basis of this contextual approach. In this a case, yukara will play a more significant part in describing Ainu society, in order to provide further contexts supporting Ainu archaeology. Thus the ethnohistory of the Ainu will be delineated and defined more clearly.

Appendix - 1 List of data: sites

Introduction

From the following archaeological evidence at excavated sites, it is possible to interpret the existence of activities relating to iron technology. I shall summarise briefly the findings at each site as an introduction. The types of evidence referred to are those given in Table 4-1 in order to confirm the basic requirements of the evidence for iron technology.

The small numbers refer throughout to the site's number and refer to sites in Table 4-2.

The place names in parentheses are locations; ken = prefecture, shi= city, cho = township.

The site excavation reports are indicated within [ ] below each site name, thus they are not included in the **References** at the end of this book.

Numbers in parentheses refer to the numbers given to the basic requirements of the evidence, mentioned in Chapter 4. If the order of the numbers in the site description goes, for example, (2), (5), (6), (8), this means that evidence designated by the numbers (1), (3), (4), (7), (9) is not available at that site, so descriptions cannot be given.

A: Hokkaido

The following sites occur within the Ainu cultural context in the 17th century (before 1667)

1. Iruekashi site: (Nibutani, Biratori-cho),
[Biratori-cho iseki chosakai 1989 *Iruekashi site*]
The Iruekashi site is located on a terrace (60m above sea level) where the Kankan stream and Makaushi stream meet.

Until this site was excavated by the author in 1988, there was no archaeological evidence for whether or not iron technology existed in the Ainu culture, and it was thought that the Ainu did not practise iron-working. I would like to summarise the Iruekashi site from the archaeological remains only.

(2) Iron material
Many pieces of iron pots approximately 5cm in diameter, have been found at the site and their total weight is 748.5g. These pieces of iron pots might have been used as a source of iron material. There are some other iron materials, which may also have been used as a source of iron such as nails, scales, clamps, and miscellaneous pieces of iron which are shaped as bars and plates; the total weight of these is 413.2g. These materials were not found near the forging hearth; therefore, an examination of the relationship between the distribution of these materials and the hearth is required.

(4) Structure of hearth
Despite careful investigation around the hearth at the site, no evidence, such as post holes was found which would have indicated structures around the hearth; from this I assumed the hearth was situated outside a structure and away from it.

The long axis is 110cm east-west and the short axis is 80cm south-north. This area is divided into two parts. One is a reversed cone-shape hearth pit, dimensions 15cm in depth, 34cm on the long axis, and 27cm on the short axis. It is associated with a slag concentration. The other is situated on the west side of the hearth pit, dimensions 13cm in depth, 80cm on the long axis and 68cm on the short axis; this is associated with burnt soil.

(5) Tuyeres
At the Iruekashi site, tuyeres were made of clay mixed with some grass as temper (scouring rush) in order to make them stronger. The total weight of the tuyeres is 500g, and fragments of about 6 tuyeres were found; this estimate was also made by refitting the pieces of tuyeres and counting the number of the diagnostic parts of the tuyeres.

(7) Slag
There was a slag concentration beside the hearth on the east side. It lay in a shallow pit, as if it had been gathered from the hearth and collected in a heap. The total weight of the slag was 2.427kg. Metallurgical analyses of the slag residue indicate the process of smithing used, the raw materials used and the scale of the smithing. Morphological classification of the slag used Kubota's method (Kubota 1983), which identifies 4 types and different weights of each type. The following characteristics were identified: 1) Slag that looks like solid thick malt syrup and appears to have just run out of the hearth (416g). 2) Slag that was irregularly shaped, spongy with bubbles and black in colour (231g). 3) Slag that is brownish-red and assumed to contain lots of iron oxide (1595g). 4) Slag of low specific gravity which had probably become attached to the wall or floor of the hearth (186g).

(8) Hammer scale
Scales approximately 5mm in diameter have been found by using sieves and magnets on the ash and the deposits from the hearth and around the hearth. The total weight of the recovered scales is 540g.

2. Pipaushi site: (Nibutani, Biratori-cho)
[Forthcoming]
This site was excavated by the author in 1990. The site was situated on the terrace where the Pipaushi River meets the Saru River. The terrace is about 55m above sea level and forms an almost flat area. The site was divided into two areas by a small stream.

Two hearths, tuyeres, a pit which was considered to be an anvil hole, a charcoal concentration, a mass of hammer scale and a heap of slag were found after the removal of the volcanic ash of Ta-b, within four grids (8m x 8m) at the south-east corner of the terrace. The area was considered to be an iron-workshop area of the site. There were surface houses, stone heaps, iron materials such as daggers and iron pots, all within the context of Ainu material culture.

One of the hearths was located very near a line of post holes of house H-6. However, the hearth was not associated with this house. The overlapping of the house and the hearth was assessed by careful observation of the post holes and overlapping charcoal, which was associated with the hearth. In other words, the iron-workshop was located outside the house and was not covered by any kind of structure.

(2) Iron material (Photo. 5-3 in Chapter 5)
An iron bar, square in shape, was found in a pit which was considered to be an anvil hole associated with a rock of spherical shape. According to metallurgical analyses, it consists of scale with some kind of glue.

(3) Charcoal
A concentration of charcoal was found, forming an area 1.5m x 1.1m, and 10cm in thickness. It consists of charcoal pieces 1-3cm in diameter in a tightly packed condition. It looks as if they

were left to be used as fuel but had not been used or had been extinguished during use.

(4) Structure of hearth
Two different types of hearth were found. The initial appearance of No. 1 was just a mound of yellowish clay associated with several orange-burned blocks of soil (Photo. 5-5 in Chapter 5). Although it did not look like a hearth which one expected to see in contrast to hearth No. 2, which was evidently a hearth relating to iron technology; it was identified as a hearth which has some relation to iron technology by the evidence of the orange-burned block of soil. Therefore, it is called No. 1 hearth, and the other one is called No. 2 hearth.

No.1 hearth exhibits a pit 20cm x 15cm in size of oval shape and with a flat bottom 6cm in depth after excavation of a yellowish mound and removal of the yellowish clay until it disappeared at the bottom. Several pieces of micro-scale 1mm in size were found within this clay in the middle of the mound. There was no other material mixed into it; however, there were several orange-burned blocks of soil on top of the mound and a piece of carbonised wood underneath the mound.

No. 2 hearth is an oval 50 cm x 30 cm shape, although one quarter was destroyed by a later structure. It is surrounded by vivid orange-burned soil associated with slag and charcoal. This orange layer is beneath the black layer mixed with slag and charcoal in the centre. This hearth clearly indicates iron technology through the association of slag and burned soil.

(5) Tuyeres
At least three tuyeres have been identified. This estimate was made by refitting the pieces of the tuyeres and counting the numbers of the diagnostic parts of the tuyeres. From refitting pieces of tuyeres, it was almost possible to reconstruct all of them. There were two spots of concentration of the tuyere fragments which can be interpreted as indicating that tuyeres were discarded and then broken into pieces. This thick type of tuyere is similar to the type from the Iruekashi site. The size of tuyeres is 8-9cm in diameter, and 3cm in thickness and 3cm in internal diameter. The tuyeres are made of clay without any grass (scouring rush) mixed in. They are thus different from the ones from the Iruekashi site. The texture of the tuyeres is smooth, although they appear to be a very coarse type.

(6) Craft tools
A pit which was considered to be an anvil hole was found. A pit 30cm in diameter and 30cm in depth was found full of Tarumae B volcanic ash, which implies that the pit was empty when the ash fell in 1667. A mass of hammer scale was found around this pit, indicating that it was an anvil pit. The east edge of the pit was tightly packed with hammer scale extending 10cm below the surface.

(7) Slag
A small pile of slag was found at 1m distance from the No. 1 hearth. It lay on the volcanic ash of Usu, which indicates that it was discarded after 1663 but before 1667. The area of the heap is 40cm x 30cm and it is 5cm in thickness. The heap includes various sizes of dark brownish slag together with pieces of charcoal, pieces of tuyeres, and pieces of burned bones.

(8) Hammer scale
Scale at the Pipaushi site was scattered extensively and in tremendous quantity, the area of greatest concentration being around a hole, which was probably an anvil hole, 2m long and 2cm in thickness. It looked as if the ground surface was a brightly reflective dark blue. Most of the scales were still magnetic, so it was easy to collect them with magnets. The total

weight of the hammer scale is 3278.9g. Two different types of scale can be seen: one is thin and square in shape, $2mm_2 \sim 10mm_2$; and the other is spherical in shape, 2mm~5mm in diameter. A piece of silver 2mm in size was also found.

The following sites occur within the Ainu cultural context between the 17th and 18th centuries (before 1739)

3. Yukanboshi C2 site: (Chitose-shi)
[Forthcoming]
Two different types of hearth were found surrounded by the post holes of a ground-surface house at this site; the hearth in the centre of the house is a long axis hearth, and the other, which is located between the central hearth and the south side, was associated with fragments of tuyeres and slag. It indicates some kind of iron activity and is interpreted as a forging hearth. Unfortunately, half of the house had already been destroyed by cultivation when this was excavated. There is also a discard spot (approximately 5m in diameter and 0.7m in depth), 1-2m away from this house, which contained lots of slag (more than 1000g), hammer scale (500g), and fragments of tuyeres (31 pieces) and 6 iron tools. It is assumed that the spot is associated with the house.

(2) Iron material
Various types of iron pieces were found — including nails, needles, iron bars, iron plates and pieces of iron pot. Pieces of iron pot, particularly, had been found as if they were collected at one spot for some reason.

(4) Structure of hearth
The hearth exhibits a concave shape 40-50cm in diameter and 12cm in depth. One edge of this ovate shape is not clearly defined. This may indicate that tuyere(s) was (were) placed at this position.

(5) Tuyeres
44 fragments of tuyeres were found in all. These are not refittable into one, so the details of the tuyeres are not known. However, their thickness is ca. 2.4-2.6cm.

(6) Craft tools
A pit which was considered to be an anvil hole was found.

(7) Slag
Two thirds of the slag found at this site is from a discard spot and the rest is associated with the hearth. The total weight of the slag is 1841.4g.

(8) Hammer scale
The existence of hammer scale on the ground surface around the hearth definitely indicates forging activity. Total scale found at this site is 2900g, of which 2400g was found near the hearth within the house.

4. Setanai-Chashi site:
[Kitahiyama-cho Kyoiku-iinkai 1980, Setanai-chashi-ato iseki hakkutsu chosa hokokusho]
There is no evidence for a hearth or slag at this site.

(2) Iron materials
There are many miscellaneous iron products, including 410 nails and 304 pieces of iron pot.

(6) Craft tools
A pair of tongs was found, which might indicate iron activity.

The following site occurs within the Japanese cultural context in the 16th century

5. Kaminokuni-Katsuyamadate: (Kaminokuni Katsuyamadate) [Kaminokuni-cho Kyoiku-iinkai 1993, *Kaminokuni-Katsuyamadate ato* I-XIII]

According to Mineo Kaiho, an historian of the Middle and Modern Ages, almost 20 Wajin (Japanese) manor houses called *yakata, tate* or *date* in the south of Ezo (present Hokkaido) in the 14th century are mentioned in the historical documents of *Shinra-no-Kiroku*. Most of them had some kind of relationship to the Ando family, which originated around the coast of Mutsu and Nanbu (the present Aomori-ken).

These Wajin were growing in power, based on fishing and trade by which they exchanged northern goods for Japanese goods directly and indirectly via the Ainu.

These *yakata* were Shinori-date, Hako-date, Mobetsu-date, Nakano-data, Wakimoto-date, Onnai-date, Oyobe-date, Nebota-date, Haraguchi-date, Hiishi-date, Suzaki-date, Katsuyama-date, Yokurame-date, and Tomari-date. There were some others which may not be directly related to *Shinra-no-kiroku*: these were Yaemon-date, Kokubu-date, Hanamitai-date, and Toi-date.

These *yakata* had disappeared by the beginning of the Edo period due to the fact that the power of the Kakizaki increased and they were integrated into the holdings of the Kakizaki family at Matsumae.

Archaeological investigation has been carried out at these *yakata* since 1967 and has led to an understanding of the history of the area in the Middle Ages and an interpretation summarised as a view from the north.

According to historical documents, Katsuyama-date belonged to, and was probably used, in the period before the centre of power was moved to Matsumae.

The excavation of the site of Katsuyama-date started in 1979 as a part of a large-scale national heritage project over a long time span. The total excavation area by now is approximately 10,000 m2, and still is being worked at present. Excavation so far indicates a large complex settlement which was occupied for more than 100 years.

This site is significant for comparison with the Ainu sites and will be described in some detail. It is located on the whole mountain-side; the altitude of the slope is from 15m to 113m, immediately in front of a good port on the Japan Sea. The platform on the slope was made by two rivers, the Miyanosawa River and the Teranosawa River. The slope has three steps of flat terraces rising towards the top of the mountain. There are 2 V-shaped trenches at each side of the edge of the flat terrace. The inner is 8m in width and 2.5m in depth, and the outer is 4m in width and 1.8m deep. At the side of the second terrace, there are many post holes in a line, as if a fence had been set up. At the very top of the third terrace, there are post holes in a line, as if a fence was situated on top of the earthen wall which has a gate; outside the gate, there is a V-shaped trench. The line of post holes continues and is connected to the second terrace. Therefore, the site is surrounded by both natural river valleys and human-made trenches and fences, as if it were a type of mountain fort.

A main street and stairs approximately 3m wide connect the three stepped terraces, located at the middle of each terrace horizontally. At both sides of the main street — for example, on

the second terrace, which is the largest one at approximately 7000m2 — the area is divided into smaller units square in shape which are surrounded by ditches. Within these areas, there are both dwelling pits and surface houses. Therefore, it is like a small village or town.

A wide range and great variety of artifacts are found at the site, indicating a complex society and great variety in the everyday lifestyle. Most of the artifacts are porcelain and ceramics. These were Chinese, Korean, and Japanese ceramics which indicates that all of them were brought to the site. The existence of a tea ceremony set, *koro* (incense burner), *suzuri* (inkstone), and *goishi* (stones of the game *go*) indicate a high level of culture at that time.

The evidence for food was recovered mostly from the shell midden, located to the east side of the main plateau in the Teranosawa River valley; finds included rice, soba, millet, fish (including herring, salmon, trout, flatfish, mackerel, yellowtails, plaice, etc.), and shellfish. There are also faunal remains of deer, foxes, bears, wolves, dogs, and horses and also sea animals including whales, otters, fur seals, sea lions, etc.

Artifacts which were probably used as tools and made of iron include sickles, iron arrowheads, fish spearheads, fishing hooks, harpoons, nails, clamps, wedges, saws, and drills. More than 500 artifacts made of bone were also found, such as arrowheads and fish spearheads from the area of the shell midden. These indicate a social context interesting in terms of the relationship between the Ainu and the Japanese in the 16th century. Weapons such as swords, and parts of armour, such as *kozane* (iron lamellae for armour) and *kote* were found.

There is another flat plateau, approximately 3500m2, at the east side of the main plateau and at a lower location. In this area, 7 houses, 13 storehouses, and 3 miscellaneous buildings have been found. It is estimated that another 10 houses and 20 storehouses lie in an unexcavated area.

In this area, there are 3 areas of burned soil associated with hammer scale, and tuyeres were found in the area which is assumed to have been outside the houses. Artifacts which indicate some kind of activity related to iron technology are more than 600 pieces of slag amounting to 35kg in total weight, hammer scales, and tuyeres of a very large size made of stone and clay. A lump of iron, of semicircular shape was also found. From its context, this is very important for an understanding of iron technology.

The following sites are within the Satsumon cultural context between the 8th and the 10th century

6. Satsumae: (Matsumae-cho) [Matsumae-cho Kyoiku-iinkai 1985 *Satsumae iseki*] Out of 33 Satsumon dwelling pits discovered, 4 dwelling pits are identified as an iron-technology activity area through their association with tuyeres and slag at the Satsumae site.

These four dwelling pits, Nos. 11, 12, 15, and 21, are distributed randomly among the other dwelling pits. The shape of the pits is square, measuring 8m average on the long axis, associated with an oven on one side and with two central hearths at the centre. All of them indicate almost the same features as the rest of the dwelling pits at the Satsumae site. However, only No. 21 dwelling pit had a central hearth, exhibiting a gourd-shape as the result of the connection of two hearths. Along this hearth, a concentration of tuyeres and slag were found. Dwelling pits No. 6, 7, 8, and 9 also contain tuyeres and slag on the floor level.

Overall, Satsumon sites seem to have a strong relationship with activities of iron technology.

(4) A ground-shaped hearth which connects two oval shapes together was in the centre of a dwelling pit.

(5) Tuyeres were found on the floor level of the dwelling pits.

(7) Slag was found on the floor level of the dwelling pits.

7. Miyukicho: (Mori-cho)
[Mori-cho Kyoiku-iinkai 1985, *Miyukicho iseki*]
Although only one Satsumon dwelling pit was found at this site, it is estimated from the assessment of its situation that this was at one edge of a Satsumon settlement, of which the rest is still unexcavated.

The dwelling pit was square in shape, 3m on its long axis. There was no cooking oven, but a stretch of burned soil, 1.1m x 0.5m, in the corner of the pit, associated with slag, was identified as an iron-technological workshop. (5) Some tuyeres, (6) a grinding stone, (7) and some slag were found on the floor of this pit.

8. Nishikimachi 5: (Asahikawa-shi)
[Asahikawa-shi Kyoiku-iinkai 1984, 1985 *Nishikimachi*]
Three pits, SE-32, MK-20, and MX-12, were identified as belonging to an iron-technological workshop. These pits were situated at the edge of a settlement of Satsumon dwelling pits, in a somewhat separate area. However, the existence of the same kind of pottery indicates that they are almost contemporary with the main part of the settlement.

(4) The MX-12 pit was a shallow concave pit of oval shape, 5m in length. In it a hearth 1.2m x 0.6m was found, associated with slag. SE-32 pit had a large concave shape, 8m x 6m in area and 1.4m in depth. There was a flat area 1m x 1m in the middle of this pit. (4) A hearth was found on top of this flat area, and underneath the hearth a 15cm thick layer of gravel was found. This structure has been interpreted as protecting the hearth from the dampness of the ground. Stones were laid out on the side of the pit which were interpreted as intended to prevent the sides tumbling down. The hearth was associated with (8) slag and (5) tuyeres. The MK-20 pit was overlapped by SE-32 and slag was found in the concave shape, approximately 10m x 5m.

9. Ranshima: (Otaru-shi)
[Otaru-shi Kyoiku-iinkai 1989, *Ranshima iseki chipushitanai iseki*]
The site was excavated in 1988. According to a study of the Satsumon pottery typology, the site was associated with the early stage of the pottery around the later 8th century. (4) A hearth which was encircled by stones and clay in the middle was found on the ground surface, not within a dwelling pit. However, (8) hammer scale was found by sieving the burned soil in and around the hearth. (5) A flared tuyere (trumpet-shaped) was found in an isolated context.

10. Suehiro (multiple locations): (Chitose-shi)
[Chitose-shi Kyoiku-iinkai 1981, 1982, *Suehiro iseki ni okeru kokogaku chosa jo, ge, zoku*]
More than 100 dwelling pits were found on the river terrace of the Suehiro River in a series of excavations. (5) A trumpet-shaped tuyere and (6) an anvil stone with iron rust were found in the dwelling pit of IP-89, which had been half destroyed because it was at the edge of the terrace.

Dwelling pit IH-97 was square in shape, 5m long, and associated with an oven; it was identified as an iron technological workshop at the edge of a settlement of Satsumon dwelling pits.

This pit was a different feature from the other pits, as the depth of pit was deeper than the rest and it had a ditch around it. There were two areas oval in shape, 50cm in diameter, which were dug at the centre of the pits and connected to each other. At the north end of one, there was a burned ditch in which a tuyere might have been placed. According to the excavator, the other one might have been the position for the anvil. (8) Hammer scale, such as two sickles, an iron axe, iron arrowheads, a dagger and also slag, tuyeres, and a grindstone were found in this pit.

11. Nakajimamatsu 6 & 7: (Eniwa-shi)
[Eniwa-shi Kyoiku-iinkai 1988, *Nakajimamatsu 6 and 7 iseki*]
At the Nakajimamatsu 6 site, only (5) a piece of tuyere was found, and at the Nakajimamatsu 7 site, (8) hammer scale was found.

12. Sakushukotoni: (Sapporo-shi)
[Hokkaido Daigaku 1986, *Sakushukotoni iseki*]
(5) One tuyere was found. It is not fragmentary, although it is not complete.

(8) One piece of slag was found.

13. Okawa: (Yoichi-cho)
[Yoichi-cho Kyoiku-iinkai 1990, *Okawaiseki hakkutsu chosa gaiho*]
The site has been excavated since 1989 and the total area of excavation will be 20,000 m2. The site is situated on a bank of the mouth of the Okawa River, which runs into Yoichi Bay. Many results have come from this site including material from continental China. It covers the period from the 4th century to the 20th century, which includes the Zokujomon, the Satsumon, and the Ainu period of the Hokkaido chronological sequence. A significant find from this site was carbonised rice which was found by a method of flotation carried out on soil contained in Satsumon pottery. Millet and *Soba* were also found on the floor of the Satsumon dwelling pits.

(7)(5) Slag and tuyeres were found associated with material which is considered to have come from the Satsumon settlement and its 14 dwelling pits, burial pits, and pits.

14. Genwa: (Otobe-cho)
[Otobe-cho Kyoiku-iinkai 1977, *Genwa, zoku*]
(5) One tuyere was found.
(8) One piece of slag was found.

15. Aonae: (Okushiri-to island)
[Okushiri-cho Kyoiku-iinkai 1978, *Aonae iseki hakkutsu chosa gaiho*]
The site is associated with a shell mound of the Satsumon period. Almost 270 bases of Satsumon pottery, which had geometrical incised marks, were found. There were also bone tools, such as harpoons and (2) iron materials such as iron pans made of cast iron, and an iron ring, daggers, swords, sickles, hoes, axes, etc. However, these have not been examined to determine whether they were made of cast iron or steel.

According to the excavation in 1976, (7) almost 5kg of slag associated with (5) tuyeres were found, as well a block of white clay and burned soil. These finds indicate that the site was an iron-working site.

16. Atsusabukawaguchi: (Esashi-cho)
[surface collection, see Onuma and Sato 1976]

(8) One piece of slag was found at this site. However, this was not in situ.

17. Horonaipo: (Kitami Esashi-cho)
[Esashi-cho Kyoiku-iinkai 1980, *Horonaipo iseki*]
The site was excavated in 1978. This is the first site at which the existence of iron technology in the Satsumon culture was recognised due to the fact that there were (5) five tuyeres of which three were decorated with incised patterns which were exactly the same as the patterns on Satsumon pottery. Therefore, these tuyeres were clearly identified as belonging to the Satsumon culture.

The five tuyeres were found in two shallow pits which were concave in shape, 2m in diameter within the settlement of almost 25 dwelling pits at this site. It is significant that the tuyeres were decorated objects.

Although hearths were not found at this site, (7) a small amount of slag [2g] was found in the dwelling pit of D-83 and examined by a metallurgist.

18. Minami machi C: (Kitami-shi)
[see Utakawa 1981]
(5) One tuyere was found which is decorated in the same way as at the Horonaipo site, with a typical Satsumon pattern.

19. Kagawa-sansen: (Tomamae-cho)
[Tomamae-cho Kyoiku-iinkai 1988 *Kagawa sansen iseki, Kagawa 6 iseki*]
(5) One tuyere was found. It is not fragmentary although it is not complete.

(8) One piece of slag was found.

20. Takasago: (Obira-cho)
[Obira-cho Kyoiku-iinkai 1983 *Obiratakasaga*, 1985, *Takasago iseki dai 2 chiten hakkutsu chosa hokokusho*]
(5) One tuyere was found at location 2, within Satsumon dwelling pit No. 5, and another was found within Satsumon dwelling pit BH-54. It is not fragmentary although it is not complete.

(8) One piece of slag was found.

21. Higashihirosato: (Fukagawa-shi)
[Hokkaido Maizo Bunkazai Centre 1989, *Higashi hirosato iseki*]
(5) One tuyere was found. It is not fragmentary although it is not complete.
(8) One piece of slag was found.

22. Tanaka: (Chitose-shi)
[see Howard, J. A. 1960]
(8) One piece of slag was found.

23. Watenbetsu: (Shiranuka-cho)
[Shiranuka-cho Kyoiku-iinkai 1968, 1969, *Shiranuka-cho no senshi bunka*]
(8) One piece of slag was found.

24. Tapukopu: (Tomakomai-shi)
[Tomakomai-shi Kyoiku-iinkai, and Tomakomai-shi Maizo Bunkazai Centre 1984 *Tapukopu*]
(5) One piece of a tuyere was found.

25. Hokkema: (Otaru-shi)
[see Miya, H. 1982]
(5) One piece of a tuyere was found.

26. Tokachibuto-Furukawa: (Urahoro-cho)
[see Miya, H. 1982]
(5) There was a single find of a tuyere within the Satsumon dwelling pits.

27. Kawaguchi: (Teshio-cho)
[see Yoshizaki 1974]
(5) One piece of a tuyere was found.

28. Nishitsukigaoka: (Nemuro-shi)
[Nemuro-shi 1966, *Hokkaido Nemuro no senshi iseki*]
(5) There was a single find of a tuyere within the Satsumon dwelling pits.

29. Tokoro-chashi: (Tokoro-cho)
[Tokoro-cho Kyoiku-iinkai 1986, *Tokoro-chashi minami one iseki*]
(5) There was a single find of a tuyere within the Satsumon dwelling pits.

30. Sudo: (Shiyari-cho)
[Shari-cho Kyoiku-iinkai 1981 *Sudo iseki*]
(5) There was a single find of a tuyere within the Satsumon dwelling pits.

31. Gifu: (Tokoro-cho)
[Tokoro-cho Kyoiku-iinkai 1982 *Gifu dai 2 iseki*]
(5) There was a single find of a tuyere within the Satsumon dwelling pits.

32. Shintotsugawa: (Shintotsugawa-cho)
[see Takahata 1894]
(5) One piece of a tuyere was found.

The following site occurs within the Ohotsuku cultural context

33. Kabukai:
[Tokyo Daigaku Shuppankai 1976, 1981, *Kabukai iseki jo, ge*]
(4) A small tuyere was found (only 1.5cm in internal diameter). The inside surface of this is burnt and very badly damaged.

B: Tohoku

The following sites occur within the Japanese cultural context in the 15th-17th centuries

34. Namioka-jo: (Aomori-ken)
[Namioka-cho Kyoiku-iinkai 1984, *Namioka-jo ato VIII*]

(2) There are 30 iron bars which were tied up in a bundle as if they were distributed goods. There are also *kozane* (iron lamellae for armour).

35. Hamadoori: (Aomori-ken)
[Aomori-ken Maizo Bunkazai Centre 1983, vol. 80 *Hamadoori iseki*]
This site was dated based on the associated porcelain of the 16th-17th centuries, and also by association with a tobacco pipe which was introduced around the 16th century.
(2) There are iron nails.

(4) A hearth was found within a dwelling-type of structure, which is not exactly a dwelling pit, among 8 ground-surface houses. The hearth itself has a characteristic feature of being lined with clay in order to stop damp coming up from the ground.

(5) Fragments of tuyeres were found.

(8) Slag was found near the post holes of a structure with a hearth in it.

The following sites are located in the Tohoku district, dating between the 8th-10th centuries

36. Mokusawa: (Aomori-ken)
[Aomori-ken Maizo Bunkazai Centre 1990 *Mokusawa iseki*]
The Mokusawa site is situated in Ajigasawa at the foot of Mount Iwaki on the south-east edge of the Tsugaru Plain, not far from the Japan Sea.

Around Mount Iwaki, it is well known from local oral tradition that iron production was practised in the past, due to the fact that thousands of pieces of slag are scattered around everywhere, without it being known where they came from.

Archaeological investigation has been carried out since 1958. Settlement sites which are associated with iron craft tools such as tuyeres, hammers, chisels, and rasps have been found at the sites of Takadate, Furudate, and Chokaisan. Ion-production sites, which are indicated by the existence of hearths, having the function of either a furnace or a forge, have been found at the sites of Odatemoriyama, Mokusawa, and Yaegiku, on the Tsugaru Plain.

At the Mokusawa site, (4) 34 furnaces were found, together with 19 dwelling pits. According to the associated artifacts and the evidence of the volcanic ash, it is dated to the 10th and 11th centuries.

37. Kitsunemo: (Aomori-ken)
[*Aomori-ken kokogaku* 3 1986]
The site is dated to the 10th century (the Heian period) based on pottery such as Haji ware and Sue ware.
(4) A semi-underground shaft-furnace of oval shape was found at the surface, 69cm on the long axis and 67cm on the short axis.

(5) Fragments of tuyeres were found.

(7) Slag was found, containing a high proportion of titanium.

38. Furudate: (Aomori-ken)
[Aomori-ken Maizo Bunkazai Centre 1979, vol. 54 *Furudate iseki hakkutsu chosa hokokusho*]
The site is dated to around the 11th or 12th centuries. A forging place and (4) small-scale iron-working furnace were found.

(5) 168 pieces of tuyeres were found, of which 41 pieces were refitted. A cylinder-type and a trumpet-type of tuyere were found.

(6) Hammers and tongs were found.

39. Chokaisan: (Aomori-ken)
[Aomori-ken Maizo Bunkazai Centre 1977, vol. 32 *Chokaisan iseki hakkutsu chosa hokokusho*]
The site dates from around the 10th century. A forging place was found in a settlement. Iron products, such as iron agricultural tools and arms were found.

(5) Tuyeres were found
(6) A pair of tongs and chisels were found.
(7) Numerous pieces of slag were found within the dwelling pits.

40. Hagurodaira: (Aomori-ken)
[Aomori-ken Maizo Bunkazai Centre 1979, vol. 44, *Hagurodaira iseki*]
A forging place was found which had clay laid on the floor.

(4) Burned soil associated with slag and fragments of tuyeres were found, indicating hearths. The floor was plastered with silt soil.
(5) Large-scale tuyeres were found.
(7) Numerous pieces of slag were found

41. Uchiebisawa: (Aomori-ken)
[Tohoku-cho Maizo Bunkazai chosa hokokusho vol. 2 *Uchiebisawa emishi date*]
(5) Numerous tuyeres were found.
(7) Numerous pieces of slag were found.

42. Sumodaishimoyasuhara: (Aomori-ken)
[Aomori-ken Maizo Bunkazai Centre 1987, vol. 111 *Sumodaishimoyasuhara iseki hakkutsu chosa hokokusho*]
144 dwelling pits were found of which 84 were associated with ovens.
(5) Numerous pieces of tuyeres were found.
(7) 66 pieces of slag were found on a site assumed to have been a forging workshop.

43. Botandairaminami: (Aomori-ken)
[Aomori-ken Maizo Bunkazai centre 1975, vol. 26 *Botandairaminami iseki hakkutsu chosa hokokusho*]
14 dwelling pits dated to the 10th century were found.
(1) Iron sand which had been solid after heating was found in one oven and on the floor of a dwelling pit.
(5) Large type of tuyeres was found
(7) Slag.
(9) Limestone was found which was assumed to have been an additive.

44. Hachiazawa: (Aomori-ken)
[Aomori-ken Maizo Bunkazai Centre 1987, vol. 116 *Hachiazawa iseki hakkutsu chosa hokokusho*]
(2) An iron bar-like object was found.
(5) A piece of tuyere was found.
(7) Slag was found.

45. Odate: (Aomori-ken)
[see Kikuchi 1990 *Yomogida Odate site hakkutsu chosa hokokusho*]
Numerous iron objects were found.
(7) Slag was found.

46. Kodate: (Aomori-ken)
[see Kikuchi 1990]
(5) Pieces of tuyeres were found.
(7) Slag was found.

47. Asahiyama: (Aomori-ken)
[Aomori-ken Maizo Bunkazai Centre 1983, vol. 87 *Asahiyama site hakkutsu chosa hokokusho*]
(5) A piece of tuyere was found, 17.9cm long with melted iron attached.
(7) 19 pieces of slag were found, with a total weight of 1,163g.

48. Itadome 2: (Aomori-ken)
[Aomori-ken Maizo Bunkazai Centre 1979, vol. 59 *Itadome (2) iseki*]
(5) 10 pieces of tuyeres were found, some of them 33.9cm long.
(7) Several pieces of slag were found.

49. Shimoyachi: (Aomori-ken)
[Aomori-ken Maizo Bunkazai Centre 1987, vol. 109 *Shimoyachi iseki hakkutsu chosa hokokusho*]
(5) A piece of tuyere was found.
(7) 5 pieces of slag were found.

50. Takagi: (Aomori-ken)
[1980 excavation results not yet published]
(5) Pieces of tuyeres were found.
(7) Numerous pieces of slag were found.

51. Niwagamae: (Aomori-ken)
(5) Pieces of tuyeres were found.
(7) Slag was found.

52. Yaedaira: (Aomori-ken)
(5) Pieces of tuyeres were found.
(7) Slag was found.

53. Kamimura: (Iwate-ken)
[Forthcoming]
The site is dated to around the 8th century. There were also charcoal kilns nearby.
(1) Iron sand was found.
(4) 8 furnaces and 1 hearth were found.
(5) Tuyeres were found, some of which were still in situ and were complete in form.
(6) A pair of tongs was found.
(7) Numerous pieces of slag were found.
(8) Some pieces of hammer scale were found.
(9) Iron sand which may have been used as an additive was found.

54. Wandai: (Iwate-ken)
[Iwate-ken Maizo Bunkazai Centre 1993, vol. 186 *Wandai II & III iseki hakkutsu chosa hokokusho*]
The site is dated to around the 9th-10th centuries.
(4) The furnace was surrounded by large pieces of stone, which is unusual.
(5) Several pieces of tuyeres were found.
(7) Many pieces of slag were found.

55. Natsumoto: (Iwate-ken)
[Iwate-ken Maizo Bunkazai Centre vol. 134 *Natsumoto iseki hakkutsu chosa hokokusho*]
The site is dated to around the 9th century.
(4) 4 Hearths were found.
(5) Tuyeres were found.
(7) Numerous pieces of slag were found.
(8) Some hammer scale was found.

56. Rozawa: (Iwate-ken)
[see Sasaki, K. 1990]
The site is dated to around the 8th century.
(4) Fragment of tuyeres were found to which (7) slag was attached.

57. Kadowakizawa: (Iwate-ken)
[see Sasaki, K. 1990]
The site is dated to around the 8th century.
(1) 20kg of iron sand which might have been kept was found.

58. Shiwa-jo: (Iwate-ken)
[Morioka-shi Kyoiku iinkai series *Shiwa-jo iseki*]
The site is dated to around the 9th century.
(4) A fragment of a shaft furnace was found.

59. Shimouba: (Iwate-ken)
[see Sasaki, K.1990]
The site is dated to around the 9th century.
(4) A rectangular-shaped furnace was found. (7) A great volume of slag was found (more than 1 ton).

60. Osegawa A: (Iwate-ken)
[see Sasaki, K. 1990]
The site is dated to around the 9th century.

(4) A furnace was found.

61. Aozaru: (Iwate-ken)
[see Sasaki, K. 1990]
The site is dated to around the 9th century.
(4) A semi-underground shaft-furnace was found.

62. Asukadaichi: (Iwate-ken)
(see Sasaki, K. 1990]
The site is dated to around the 10th century
(4) (5) A hearth was found, associated with 59 pieces of tuyeres.

63. Sekisawaguchi: (Iwate-ken)
[see Sasaki, K. 1990]
The site is dated around the 10th century.
(4) A forging hearth was found.
(5) Pieces of tuyeres were found.

64. Komayakiba: (Iwate-ken)
[Iwate-ken Maizo Bunkazai Centre 1988, vol. 133 *Komayakiba iseki hakkutsu chosa hokokusho*]
(4) Hearth.
(6) Water stone.
(7) Total weight of slag was 1180g.
(8) Hammer scale was found within one of the dwelling pits.

65. Harimadate: (Akita-ken)
[Akita-ken Maizo Bunkazai Centre 1990, vol. 192 *Harimadate iseki hakkutsu chosa hokokusho*]
The site is dated to around the 10th-11th centuries and the 15th-16th centuries.
(2) 30 iron bars were found.
(4) 5 hearths were found.
(5) Tuyeres were long size in shape.
(7) Slag was found.
(8) Some hammer scale was found.

66. Uwano: (Akita-ken)
[Akita-ken Maizo Bunkazai Centre 1992 vol. 222 *Uwano iseki hakkutsu chosa hokokusho*]
The site is dated to around the 11th century.
(4) A forging hearth was found.
(5) Tuyeres were found around the hearth.

67. Samukawa II: (Akita-ken)
[Akita-ken Maizo Bunkazai Centre 1988 vol. 167 *Samukawa iseki hakkutsu chosa hokokusho*]
The site is dated to around the 9th-10th centuries.
(4) One rectangular shaft-furnace was found.

68. Kanninzawa: (Akita-ken)
[Akita-ken Maizo Bunkazai Centre
The site is dated to around the 10th century.
(1) Exposed iron sand mining was found near the furnaces.
(4) 13 rectangular-shaped shaft furnaces were found.
(5) Many tuyeres were found.

69. Ryugesawa: (Akita-ken)
[Akita-ken Maizo Bunkazai Centre 1990, vol. 188 *Ryugesawa iseki hakkutsu chosa hokokusho*]
The site is dated to around the 11th century.
(4) 2 semi-underground shaft-furnaces were found.

70. Odateno: (Akita-ken)
[Forthcoming]
(4) 3 semi-underground shaft-furnaces were found.

71. Junibayashi: (Akita-ken)
[Akita-ken Maizo Bunkazai Centre *Junibayashi iseki*]

The site is dated from the 11th century onwards.
(4) 2 round shaft-furnaces were found.

72. Sakanoue E & F: (Akita-ken)
[Akita-ken Maizo Bunkazai Centre *Sakanoue E iseki*]
The site is dated to the 10th-11th centuries.
(4) A furnace was found at the Sakanoue E site.
(3) A charcoal kiln was found at the Sakanoue F site.

73. Nakadai: (Akita-ken)
[Akita-ken Maizo Bunkazai Centre 1978 vol. 50 *Nakadai iseki chosa gaiho*]
The site is dated to the 10th-11th centuries.
(4) 2 round-shaped shaft-furnaces were found in a flat place.

74. Shironaganedate: (Akita-ken)
The site is dated to around the 10th-11th centuries.
(4) 3 round-shaped shaft-furnaces were found on a very gentle slope.

75. Kitazawa: (Nigata-ken)
[Niigata-ken Toyoura-cho Kyoiku-iinkai 1992 *Kitazawa iseki gun*]
The site is dated to around the 12th-13th centuries. It is very interesting that no tuyeres were found at this site.
(1) 600kg of iron sand was found.
(2) 6.5kg of *sentetsu* was found.
(3) Many charcoal kilns were associated within the area.
(4) 3 furnaces were found.

Appendix - 2 List of data: Yukara

[Ref. No.] refers to the following references, see
References at the end of this book.
[Ref. No. 1]: Kindaichi, K. 1959
[Ref. No. 2]: Kubodera, I. 1977
[Ref. No. 3]: Chiri, M. 1978
[Ref. No. 4]: Batchelor, J. 1890
[Ref. No. 5]: Chiri, Y. 1922
[Ref. No .6]: Pilsudski, B. 1987

Nos
Name of reciter:
Name of epic

1

Name of reciter: Etenoa Hiraga
Kamui huchi yaieyukare [Ref. No. 2]
The epic of a fire *kamui*

2

Name of reciter: Etenoa Hiraga
Isepo tono yaieyukare [Ref. No. 2]
The epic of a rabbit's chief

3

Name of reciter: Karepia Hirame
Isopo tono isoitak [Ref. No. 2]
The epic of a rabbit's chief

4

Name of reciter: Etenoa Hiraga
Nupuri kor kamui isoitak [Ref. No. 2]
The epic of a spider *kamui*

5

Name of reciter: Karepia Hirame
Name of the *kamui* is not known

6

Name of reciter: Etenoa Hiraga
Nupuri kor kamui isoitak [Ref. No. 2]
The epic of a bear *kamui*

7

Name of reciter: Etenoa Hiraga
Peurep kamui isoitak [Ref. No. 2]
The epic of a bear kid *kamui*

8

Name of reciter: Karepia Hirame
Peurep kamui isoitak [Ref. No. 2]
The epic of a bear kid *kamui*

9

Name of reciter: Etenoa Hiraga
Peurep kamui isoitak [Ref. No. 2]
The epic of a bear kid *kamui*

10

Name of reciter: Karepia Hirame
Nupuri kor kamui kor matnepo yaieyukar [Ref. No .2]
The epic of a daughter of a bear *kamui*

11

Name of reciter: Etenoa Hiraga
Nupuri kor kamui matnepoho yaieyukar [Ref. No. 2]
The epic of a daughter of a bear *kamui*

12

Name of reciter: Etenoa Hiraga
Nupuri kor kamui matnepoho yaieyukar [Ref. No 2]
The epic of a daughter of a bear *kamui*

13

Name of reciter: Etenoa Hiraga
Peurep Kamui isoitak [Ref. No 2]
The epic of a bear cub *kamui*

14

Name of reciter: Karepia Hirame
Wen ar sar ushi iisoitak [Ref. No 2]
The epic of a bad bear

15

Name of reciter: Karepia Hirame
Wen ar sarushi yaieyukar [Ref. No 2]
The epic of a bad bear

16

Name of reciter: Etenoa Hiraga
Pon moyuk isoitak [Ref. No 2]
The epic of a *tanuki* kid *kamui*

17

Name of reciter: Karepia Hirame
Apa samun kamui isoitak [Ref. No 2]
The epic of a *tanuki*

18

Name of reciter: Karepia Hirame
Pon moyuk isoitak [Ref. No 2]
The epic of a small killer whale

19

Name of reciter: Karepia Hirame
Pon repun kamui yaieyukar [Ref. No 2]
The epic of a small killer whale *kamui*

20

Name of reciter: Karepia Hirame
Pon repun kamui yaieyukar [Ref. No 2]
The epic of a small killer whale *kamui*

21

Name of reciter: Etenoa Hiraga
Repun menoko isoitak [Ref. No 2]
The epic of a female doliphin-like fish

22

Name of reciter: Etenoa Hiraga
Chironnup kamui isoitak [Ref. No 2]
The epic of a fox *kamui*

23

Name of reciter: Karepia Hirame
Chironnup kamui yaieyukar [Ref. No 2]
The epic of a fox *kamui*

24

Name of reciter: Karepia Hirame
Shik nak chironnup yaieyukar [Ref. No 2]
The epic of a blind fox

25
Name of reciter: Karepia Hirame
Chironnup kamui isoitak [Ref. No. 2]
The epic of a fox *kamui*

26
Name of reciter: Karepia Hirame
Esaman tono yaieyukar [Ref. No. 2]
The epic of a river otter

27
Name of reciter: Etenoa Hiraga
Horkeu kamui isoitak [Ref. No. 2]
The epic of a wolf *kamui*

28
Name of reciter: Kanunmore Hiramura
Isepo nitnehi yaieyukar [Ref. No. 2]
The epic of a monster rabbit *kamui*

29
Name of reciter: Etenoa Hiraga
Isepo tono isoitak [Ref. No. 2]
The epic of a rabbit's chief *kamui*

30
Name of reciter: Etenoa Hiraga
isepo tono isoitak [Ref. No. 2]
The epic of a rabbit lord

31
Name of reciter: Karepia Hirame
Isopo tono isoitak [Ref. No. 2]
The epic of a rabbit

32
Name of reciter: Karepia Hirame
Ninninkeppo yaieyukar [Ref. No. 2]
The epic of a firefly

33
Name of reciter: Yone Iwayama
Yaki yaieyukar [Ref. No. 2]
The epic of a cicada

34
Name of reciter: Yone Iwayama
Yaki yaieyukar [Ref. No. 2]
The epic of a cicada

35
Name of reciter: Kunimatsu Nitani
Yaki ikashpaotte [Ref. No. 2]
The epic of a cicada

36
Name of reciter: Etenoa Hiraga
Yaoshkep kamui yaieyukar [Ref. No. 2]
The epic of a spider *kamui*

37
Name of reciter: Karepia Hirame
Shak shomo ayep isoitak [Ref. No. 2]
The epic of a dragon

38
Name of reciter: Etenoa Hiraga
Shak shomo ayep isoitak [Ref. No. 2]
The epic of a dragon *kamui*

39
Name of reciter: Karepia Hirame
Shak shomo ayep isoitak [Ref. No. 2]
The epic of a dragon

40
Name of reciter: Karepia Hirame
Hure tokkoni yaieyukar [Ref. No. 2]
The epic of a red *mamushi*

41
Name of reciter: Karepia Hirame
Terkeipe tono isoitak [Ref. No. 2]
The epic of a frog

42
Name of reciter: Karepia Hirame
Tunin onnehi isoitak[Ref. No. 2]
The epic of an old earthworm

43
Name of reciter: Karepia Hirame
Enunnoya isoitak [Ref. No. 2]
The epic of a titmouse

44
Name of reciter: Karepia Hirame
Eyami isoitak [Ref. No. 2]
The epic of a jay

45
Name of reciter: Etenoa Hiraga
Kakkok tono isoitak [Ref. No. 2]
The epic of cuckoo *kamui*

46
Name of reciter: Etenoa Hiraga
Onne kapachir isoitak [Ref. No. 2]
The epic of an old eagle

47
Name of reciter: Etenoa Hiraga
Kararat tono isoitak [Ref. No. 2]
The epic of a carrion crow

48
Name of reciter: Karepia Hirame
Kararat kamui yaieyukar [Ref. No. 2]
The epic of a carrion crow *kamui*

49
Name of reciter: Karepia Hirame
Katken tono isoitak [Ref. No. 2]
The epic of a carrion crow

50
Name of reciter: Etenoa Hiraga
Katken tono isoitak [Ref. No. 2]
The epic of a carrion crow

51
Name of reciter: Etenoa Hiraga
Katken tono isoitak [Ref. No. 2]
The epic of a carrion crow

52
Name of reciter: Karepia Hirame
Kem chikappo (Menash un mat) isoitak [Ref. No. 2]
The epic of a red sparrow (woman of Menashi)

53
Name of reciter: Shimukani Shikada
Kikaoreu kamui isoitak [Ref. No. 2]
The epic of a female bird

54
Name of reciter: Etenoa Hiraga
Kesorap kamui yaieyukar [Ref. No. 2]
The epic of *a kesorap kamui*

55
Name of reciter: Kunimatsu Nitani
Kesorap kamui yaieyukar [Ref. No. 2]
The epic of a *kesorap kamui*

56
Name of reciter: Etenoa Hiraga
kesorap kamui isoitak [Ref. No. 2]
The epic of a *kesorap kamui*

57
Name of reciter: Karepia Hirame
Kesorap kamui isoitak [Ref. No. 2]
The epic of a *kesorap kamui*

58
Name of reciter: Etenoa Hiraga
Kesorap kamui yaieyukar [Ref. No. 2]
The epic of a *kesorap kamui*

59
Name of reciter: Etenoa Hiraga
Kotan kor kamui kot tureshi isoitak [Ref. No. 2]
The epic of an owl *kamui*

60
Name of reciter: Etenoa Hiraga
Kotan kamui kot tuneshi isoitak and Ainu rak kur isoitak
[Ref. No. 2]
The epic of a younger sister *kamui* of an owl *kamui*

61
Name of reciter: Karepia Hirame
Kotan kor kamui kot tureshi isoitak [Ref. No. 2]
The epic of a younger sister of an owl *kamui*

62
Name of reciter: Etenoa Hiraga
Kotan kor kamui kot tureshi isoitak [Ref. No. 2]
The epic of a younger sister of an owl *kamui*

63
Name of reciter: Etenoa Hiraga
Huri chikap kamui yaieyuka [Ref. No. 2]
The epic of a *huri* bird *kamui*

64
Name of reciter: Etenoa Hiraga
Huri chikap isoitak [Ref. No. 2]
The epic of a *huri* bird

65
Name of reciter: Etenoa Hiraga
Huri chikap isoitak [Ref. No. 2]
The epic of a *huri* bird

66
Name of reciter: Karepia Hirame
Urir kamui isoitak [Ref. No. 2]
The epic of a sea cormorant *kamui*

67
Name of reciter: Etenoa Hiraga
Shrkap isoitak [Ref. No. 2]
The epic of a swordfish

68
Name of reciter: Kunimatsu Nitani
Shikap kamui yaieyukar [Ref. No. 2]
The epic of a swordfish

69
Name of reciter: Etenoa Hiraga
Onne chip kamui isoitak [Ref. No. 2]
The epic of an old boat *kamui*

70
Name of reciter: Karepia Hirame
Atui orun chip kamui isoitak [Ref. No. 2]
The epic of a ship *kamui*

71
Name of reciter: Karepia Hirame
Onne chip kamui (Nimam katkemat) isoitak [Ref. No. 2]
The epic of an old ship *kamui* (ship women)

72
Name of reciter: Karepia Hirame
Name of *kamui* is not known [Ref. No. 2]

73
Name of reciter: Karepia Hirame
Chise kor kamui isoitak [Ref. No 2]
The epic of a house *kamui*

74
Name of reciter: Kanunmore Hiramura
Hashinau kor kamui isoitak [Ref. No. 2]
The epic of a hunting *kamui*

75
Name of reciter: Kunimatsu Nitani
Hashinau uk kamui isoitak [Ref. No. 2]
The epic of a hunting *kamui*

76
Name of reciter: Etenoa Hiraga
Kanna kamui isoitak [Ref. No. 2]
The epic of a thunder *kamui*

77
Name of reciter: Kunimatsu Nitani
Kanna kamui isoitak [Ref. No .2]
The epic of a thunder *kamui*

78
Name of reciter: Etenoa Hiraga
Kechan kor kamui isoitak [Ref. No. 2]
The epic of a *kechan kor kamui*

79
Name of reciter: Karepia Hirame
Kanto kor kamui yaieyukar [Ref. No. 2]
The epic of a sky *kamui*

80
Name of reciter: Karepia Hirame
Sirampa kamui isoitak [Ref. No. 2]
The epic of a forest *kamui*

81
Name of reciter: Etenoa Hiraga
Pet or ush mat, kamui katkemat isoitak [Ref. No. 2]
The epic of a water *kamui*

82
Name of reciter: Kunimatsu Nitani
Name of the *kamui* is not known [Ref. No. 2]

83
Name of reciter: Kunimatsu Nitani
Name of the *kamui* is not known [Ref. No. 2]

84
Name of reciter: Karepia Hirame
Upashkuma kamui yukar [Ref. No. 2]
The epic of a story *kamui*

85
Name of reciter: Karepia Hirame
Upashikuma kamui yukar [Ref. No. 2]
The epic of a story *kamui*

86
Name of reciter: Etenoa Hiraga
Okikurmi kamui kot tureshi yaieyukar [Ref. No. 2]
The epic of a younger sister of Okikurmi

87
Name of reciter: Karepia Hirame
Ainu hekachi yaieyukar [Ref. No. 2]
The epic of an Ainu boy

88
Name of reciter: Etenoa Hiraga
Samam ni kotuk wa ampe isoitak [Ref. No. 2]
The epic of an Ainu boy

89
Name of reciter: Kanunmore Hiramura
Wen kamui e ikka hekachi yaieyukar [Ref. No. 2]
The epic of a bad *kamui*

90
Name of reciter: Shimukani Shikada
Ainu menoko yaieyukar [Ref. No. 2]
The epic of an Ainu woman

91
Name of reciter: Karepia Hirame
Ainu menoko yaieyukar [Ref. No. 2]
The epic of an Ainu woman

92
Name of reciter: Karepia Hirame
Ainu menoko yaieyukar [Ref. No. 2]
The epic of an Ainu woman

93
Name of reciter: Karepia Hirame
Shine huchi (Tokapchi) esokisoki shirepakashnu
waoitak kote shinotcha [Ref. No. 2]
The epic of an old woman (Tokachi)

94
Name of reciter: Etenoa Hiraga
Matamki tono yaieyukar [Ref. No. 2]
The epic of a Japanese *mataki*

95
Name of reciter: Shimukani Shikada
Ihumke [Ref. No. 2]
The epic of a cradle song

96
Name of reciter: Shimukani Shikada
Ihumke [Ref. No .2]
The epic of a cradle song

97
Name of reciter: Karepia Hirame
Iyonnotka (Iyonruika) chish or itak [Ref. No. 2]
The epic of a lullaby

98
Name of reciter: Etenoa Hiraga
Menash un mat isoitak [Ref. No. 2]
The epic of a Menashi woman

99
Name of reciter: Karepia Hirame
Shipichar kotan repa utar yaieyukar [Ref. No. 2]
The epic of a Shipichar chief

100
Name of reciter: Etenoa Hiraga
Shipichar un kur iroitak [Ref. No. 2]
The epic of a chief of Shipichar

101
Name of reciter: Karepia Hirame
Shipichar un kur yaieyukar [Ref. No. 2]
The epic of a Shipichar

102
Name of reciter: Etenoa Hiraga
Shini nishpa isoitak (wentarap kamui yukar)[Ref. No]
The epic of a rich Ainu

103
Name of reciter: Etenoa Hiraga
Name of the *kamui* is not known [Ref. No. 2]

104
Karepia Hirame
Shinutapka un mat isoitak [Ref. No. 2]
The epic of a women at Shinutapka

105
Name of reciter: Etenoa Hiraga
Otashut un mat isoitak [Ref. No. 2]
The epic of a woman at Shinutapka

106
Name of reciter: Shimukani Shikada
Otashut un mat isoitak [Ref. No. 2]
The epic of an Otashut woman

107
Name of reciter: Etenoa Hiraga
Ainu rak kur isoitak [Ref. No. 2]
The epic of Ainu *rak kur*

108
Name of reciter: Tumonte Hiraga
Aeoina kamui isoitak [Ref. No. 2]
The epic of Aeoina *kamui*

109
Name of reciter: Etenoa Hiraga
Aeoina kamui yaieyukar [Ref. No. 2]
The epic of Aeoina *kamui*

110
Name of reciter: Etenoa Hiraga
Aeoina kamui yaieyukar [Ref. No. 2]
The epic of Aeoina *kamui*

111
Name of reciter: Etenoa Hiraga
Pon Okikurmi isoitak (Wentarap kamui yukar) [Ref. No. 2]
The epic of Pon Okikurmi

112
Name of reciter: Etenoa Hiraga
Aeoina kamui yaieyukar [Ref. No. 2]
The epic of Aeoina *kamui*

113
Name of reciter: Etenoa Hiraga
Aeoina kamui yaieyukar [Ref. No. 2]
The epic of Aeina *kamui*

114
Name of reciter: Karepia Hirame
Aeoina kamui yaieyukar [Ref. No. 2]
The epic of Aeoina *kamui*

115
Name of reciter: Karepia Hirame
Aeoina kamui yaieyukar [Ref. No. 2]
The epic of Aeoina *kamui*

116
Name of reciter: Etenoa Hiraga
Aeoina kamui yaieyukar [Ref. No. 2]
The epic of Aeoina *kamui*

117
Name of reciter: Kunimatsu Nitani?
[Ref. No. 2]

118
Name of reciter: Karepia Hirame
Okikurmi kamui yaki kashpaotte [Ref. No. 2]
The epic of Okikurmi *kamui*

119
Name of reciter: Kunimatsu Nitani
Pon Ainu rak kur yaieyukar [Ref. No. 2]
The epic of Pon Ainu *rak kur*

120
Name of reciter: Etenoa Hiraga
Aeoina kamui (Pon Okikurmi) yaieyukar [Ref. No. 2]
The epic of Aeoina *kamui*

121
Name of reciter: Etenoa Hiraga
Ainu rak kur (Pon Okikurmi) isoitak [Ref. No. 2]
The epic of Ainu *rak kur*

122
Name of reciter: Etenoa Hiraga
Ainu rak kur yaieyukar [Ref. No. 2]
The epic of Ainu *rak kur*

123
Name of reciter: Karepia Hirame
Ainu rak kur yaieyukaar [Ref. No. 2]
The epic of Ainu *rak kur*

124
Name of reciter: Tumonte Hiraga
Ainu rak kur yaieyukar [Ref. No. 2]
The epic of Ainu *rak kur*

125
Name of reciter: Yukie Chiri
Kamuichikap kamui yaieyukar [Ref. No. 5]
The epic of an owl *kamui*

126
Name of reciter: Yukie Chiri
Chironnup yaieyukar [Ref. No. 5]
The epic of a fox

127
Name of reciter: Yukie Chiri
Chironnup yaieyukar [Ref. No. 5]
The epic of a fox

128
Name of reciter: Yukie Chiri
Isope yaieyukar [Ref. No .5]
The epic of a rabbit

129
Name of reciter: Yukie Chiri
Nitatiorunpe yaieyukar [Ref. No. 5]
The epic of an evil in a valley

130
Name of reciter: Yukie Chiri
Pon Horkeukamui Yaieyukar [Ref. No. 5]
The epic of a small wolf

131
Name of reciter: Yukie Chiri
Kamuichikap kamui yaieyukar [Ref. No. 5]
The epic of an owl *kamui*

132
Name of reciter: Yukie Chiri
Repun kamui yaieyukar [Ref. No. 5]
The epic of a sea *kamui*

133
Name of reciter: Yukie Chiri
Terkepi yaieyukar [Ref. No. 5]
The epic of a frog

134
Name of reciter: Yukie Chiri
Pon Okikirmui yaieyukar [Ref. No. 5]
The epic of Pon Okikirmui

135
Name of reciter: Yukie Chiri
Pon Okikirmui yaieyukar [Ref. No. 5]
The epic of Pon Okikirmui

136
Name of reciter: Yukie Chiri
Esaman Yaieyukar [Ref. No. 5]
The epic of a river otter

137
Name of reciter: Yukie Chiri
Pipa yaieyukar [Ref. No. 5]
The epic of a *pipa* shell

138
Name of the reciter is not known
Tusunapanu [Ref. No. 1]
The epic of a shark

139
Name of reciter: Utomuriuku
Tusunapanu [Ref. No. 1]
The epic of a shark·

140
Name of reciter: Wakarupa
Tusunapanu [Ref. No. 1]
The epic of a shark

141
Name of the reciter is not known
Tusunapanu [Ref. No. 6]
The epic of a whale

142
Name of the reciter is not known
The epic of Kotan Utunnai [Ref. No .4]

143
Name of reciter: Matsu Kannari
Pon Oina [Ref. No. 1]
The epic of Pon Oina *kamui*

144
Name of reciter: Matsu Kannari
Poro Oina [Ref. No. 1]
The epic of Poro Oina *kamui*

145
Name of reciter: Sankirotte
Poro Oina [Ref. No. 1]
The epic of Poro Oina *kamui*

146
Name of reciter: Sankirotte
Kamui Oina [Ref. No. 1]
The epic of Oina *kamui*

147
Name of reciter: Takuuno
Kamui Oina [Ref. No. 1]
The epic of Oina *kamui*

148
Name of reciter: Takuuno
Kamui Oina [Ref. No. 1]
The epic of Oina *kamui*

149
Name of reciter: Etenoa Hiraga
Kamui Oina [Ref. No. 1]
The epic of Ainu *Kamui*

150
Name of reciter: Matsu Kannari
Pon Samorunkur [Ref. No. 1]
The epic of Pon Samorunkur

151
Name of reciter: Matsu Kannari
Kamui karsapa Kamui kartuman [Ref. No. 1]
The epic of *kamui karasapa* and *kartuman*

152
Name of reciter: Matsu Kannari
Kemka karip [Ref. No. 1]
The epic of a ring of blood

153
Name of reciter: Matsu Kannari
Nishmakunmat [Ref. No .1]
The epic of a Nishmakun woman

154
Name of reciter: Matsu Kannari
Iyochiunmat kamui reshu mat [Ref. No. 1]
The epic of an Iyochiun woman

155
Name of reciter: Matsu Kannari
Uchiu ninkari [Ref. No. 1]
The epic of an earring which has no joint part

156
Name of reciter: Matsu Kannari
A keusutu iwenresu [Ref. No .1]
The epic of a bad uncle

157
Name of reciter: Wakarupa
Shupne shirka [Ref. No. 1]
The epic of Shupne shirka

158
Name of reciter: Kotanpira Hiramura
Shupne shirka [Ref. No. 1]
The epic of Shupne shirka

159
Name of reciter: Wakarupa
Kutune shirka [Ref. No. 1]
The epic of a sword

160
Name of reciter: Matsu Kannari
Kutune shirka [Ref. No. 1]
The epic of a sword

161
Name of reciter: Etenoa Hiraga
Kutune shirka [Ref. No. 1]
The epic of a sword

162
Name of reciter: Yayashi Hiraga
Kutune shirka [Ref. No. 1]
The epic of a sword

163
Name of reciter: Motozo Nabesawa
Kutune shirka [Ref. No. 1]
The epic of a sword

164
Name of reciter: Matsu Kannari
Tunupe kant kant [Ref. No. 3]
The epic of a Siberian ermine

165
Name of reciter: Matsu Kannari
Ho rim rim [Ref. No. 3]
The epic of a Siberian ermine

166
Name of reciter: Matsu Kannari
Kara rant [Ref. No .3]
The epic of a piece of wood from a ship

167
Name of reciter: Matsu Kannari
Penkina Pankina [Ref. No. 3]
The epic of a *mamushi*

168
Name of reciter: Matsu Kannari
Zusai zori zusai matsu [Ref. No. 3]
The epic of a swordfish

169
Name of reciter: Matsu Kannari
Howa howa howa [Ref. No. 3]
The epic of a carrion crow

170
Name of reciter: Matsu Kannari
Fure kakko kakko [Ref. No. 3]
The epic of a red cuckoo

171
Name of reciter: Matsu Kannari
Harip harip [Ref. No. 3]
The epic of a river otter

172
Name of reciter: Matsu Kannari
Pankutekari [Ref. No. 3]
The epic of a gooney bird

173
Name of reciter: Matsu Kannari
Oisona [Ref. No. 3]
The epic of Oina *kamui*

174
Name of reciter: Matsu Kannari
Towafum [Ref. No. 3]
The epic of Oina *kamui*

175
Name of reciter: Matsu Kannari
Hachinantakusa [Ref. No. 3]
The epic of a sister of Wariunekuru

176
Name of reciter: Matsu Kannari
Oisona [Ref. No. 3]
The epic of Oina *kamui*

177
Name of reciter: Matsu Kannari
Fukayatenterao [Ref. No. 3]
The epic of wariunekuru

178
Name of reciter: Matsu Kannari
Ship [Ref. No. 3]
The epic of wariunekuru

179
Name of reciter: Matsu Kannari
Kaoru [Ref. No. 3]
The epic of Horishiri Mountain

180
Name of reciter: Matsu Kannari
Sorepa sorepa [Ref. No. 3]
The epic of Matsumae *tono*

181
Name of reciter: Matsu Kannari
Han kawa kawa [Ref. No. 3]
The epic of a carrion crow

182
Name of reciter: Matsu Kannari
Sowae sowe [Ref. No. 3]
The epic of a small *kemuriri kamui*

Glossary

Iron (*tetsu*) terminology

Introduction

The terms used particularly in excavation site reports are very confusing and debatable due to the fact that these are descriptions of materials which found as primary data at excavation sites. After careful examination and archaeometallurgical analysis, a different term may be applied to material which has already been described. However, from the archaeological point of view, terms are required in order to discuss the technological process of iron-working activity. Therefore, before any decision about fixing any specific terminology in order to define the characteristics of the site for iron production, I use more general terminology for archaeological finds such as artifacts and structures at sites.

For this reason, the order of this glossary is arranged according to archaeological understanding — the way in which artifacts and structures at archaeological sites are found and sorted out for interpretation.

It is also very confusing and debatable that the terms used in English do not seem to express well the terms used in Japanese iron technology, since the terms and definitions used in Japan are based on historical Japanese iron technology and on the archaeological interpretation of iron technology in Japanese archaeology. These are different from both Western and Chinese terms. I try to explain the way in which these terms are used in Japan and translate them into English.

A. Archaeological site: materials and features

Archaeological sites are identified by archaeologists together with metallurgists, based on comprehensive studies of the materials from the site — leading to the interpretation of iron-production activities, including the technological aspects.

1 Site types
Although there must be slight differences between the terms used to refer to production, industry and working, based on the different scale of production in economic or geographical reasons, these words tend to be used for any place which relates to the production of iron. Such a place is termed a *tetsu iseki*. This includes the meaning of iron-working site and a production site or forging site. A blacksmith's workshop is specifically referred to as a *kaji kobo*.

tetsu seisan iseki : iron-production site
tetsu seisan iseki : iron-industrial site
tetsu iseki : iron-working site
kaji kob : blacksmith's workshop

2 Raw materials (genryo)
tetsu : iron: anything which becomes iron (Fe), and anything made of iron which becomes iron again.

tekkoseki : iron ore
pieces of iron rock which can be smelted into iron. Iron-ore rocks consist of the following different mineralogical materials.

seki tekko : hematite ($Fe_2 O_3$)
ji tekko : magnetite ($Fe_3 O_4$)
ka tekko : limonite ($Fe_2O_3n H_2O$)
ganrintetsu : phosphorus-containing iron ore; ion ore containing phosphorus.

gandotetsu : copper-containing iron ore; iron ore containing copper

satetsu : iron sand
Although iron sand is not treated as different from rock ore in the Western metallurgical framework, on account of the lack of use of iron sand, it is important to consider iron sand separately and treat it differently from rock ore within this study. This is because not only the size of the iron material is different but also the process of its natural formation. Technological processes and iron as a product have been greatly affected by such differences. Iron sand resulting from natural formation is not the same as iron rock ore mashed by artificial power into fine ore grains. To understand Japanese iron technology, it is crucial to realise this difference.

The following are different kinds of iron sand found in Japan:
masa-satetsu
This iron sand can <u>only</u> produce *kera* in a *tatara* smelting furnace. No other iron sand can produce *kera* except *masa-satetsu*. It is very pure and does not contain much titanium or phosphorus. It is found only in Shimane-ken.

akame-satetsu
This iron sand produces *zuku* in a *tatara* smelting furnace. It includes a high proportion of titanium compared with *masa-satetsu*. It is a very fine sand. Its name is derived from its colour (*aka* = 'red'). It is mainly found in Okayama-ken and other areas.

hama-satetsu
Iron sand which is obtained from beach sands on the seashore.

yama-satetsu
Iron sand which is obtained from mountains.

kawa-satetsu
Iron sand which is obtained from rivers.

nenryou : Fue
mokutan or *sumi* : charcoal

3 Installations: features

ro or *hidoko* : hearth
A hearth can be identified from burned soil on the ground surface or from a hole in the surface, which I term a hole-in-the-ground hearth. 'Hearth' also means the remains of refining and forging activity at sites.

ro : furnace
There are many terms for furnace, according to the type of smelting — such as the blast furnace, bloomery furnace, shaft furnace and so on.
I use the term furnace for any type of feature found at a site which is the remains of possible smelting and refining activity.

ko-ro or *yoko-ro* : blast furnace
European context. It was introduced to Japan in the 19th century for the production of cast iron cannons. A blast furnace is used for continuous operation over weeks or months.

seitetsu-ro : bloomery furnace
A European historical term. A bloomery furnace is used in discontinuous operation; it is broken up when the iron 'bloom' is taken out of the furnace. It functions by reducing iron oxides to iron in the solid state.

seiren-ro : refining furnace
A furnace which is used for any kind of refining process.

tatara-ro or *eitai tatara* : *tatara* furnace
A furnace is used to produce *kera* and *zuku* from iron sand. It is located inside a roofed structure. This furnace was perfected and used from the early 17th century onwards.

hakogata-ro : rectangular box-type furnace
A Japanese ancient type of furnace which appears from around the 6th century onwards. The shape of the box is associated with tuyeres in a line on both sides so that the furnace can get lots of air easily. It is believed among metallurgists that this must be the prototype of the *tatara-r o* [see hypothetically reconstructed illustration (Tosa 1986), below]

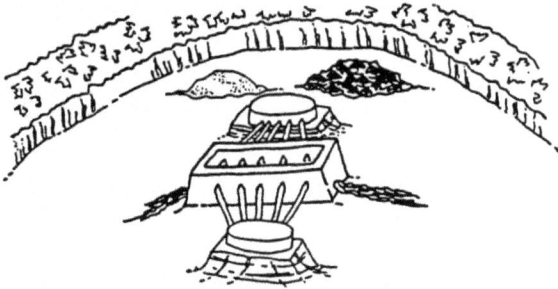

hanchikashiki tategata-ro : semi-underground shaft furnace
Ancient type of Japanese furnace in the Tohoku area [see hypothetically reconstructed illustration (Tosa 1986), bellow].

4   Attachments

haguchi : tuyere
Cylinders which are located between the furnace and bellows. The air blows through them into the furnace from bellows for accelerating burning. They are normally made of clay or sometimes stones.

5   Tools (*kogu-rui*)

igata : mould
A shape into which liquid iron is poured for producing cast iron objects such as iron pots. It is normally made of clay.

rutsubo : crucible
A container which is normally made of clay, to hold liquid iron when the iron is heated and melted within it to produce cast iron.

hishaku : casting ladle
A container with a long handle for use in pouring liquid iron into a mould.

kaji kogu : smith's tools
Tools which are used during the process of forging, such as the hammer (*kanazuchi*), rasp (*kanayasuri*), chisel (*kananomi*), tongs, grinding stones, and anvil.

6   Products (*seisanbutsu*)
[see Flow diagram 4-1 pp. 49-50]

tetsu : iron; Fe
This is produced by the smelting of iron ore or iron sand.

tekkai : bloom
A lump of iron produced by reduction to a solid phase without melting during the smelting of the ore.

hagane : steel
Iron which contains a significant amount of carbon. According to the proportion of carbon which iron products contain, 1.7% is defined as the dividing line between *hagane* and *chutetsu* in Japanese metallurgy (Nishizawa et al. 1979). Metallurgical discussions in Japan are based on this definition.

jigane : iron material
Iron objects are made from this iron material.

wa hagane, wa tetsu or wako : Japanese steel
Steel which is produced in Japan by Japanese methods, using Japanese raw material such as iron sand.

tama hagane
The best Japanese iron which can be used for Japanese sword-making. This is the top part of the *kera*, which contains little carbon.

nanko : soft steel
Any iron which contains less than 1.7% of carbon.

ren-tetsu : wrought iron
Any iron which contains nearly 0% of carbon.

zuku or *sentetsu* : [no English equivalents]
In the Japanese-English dictionary (Kenkyu Sha), this term is translated into English as 'pig iron', although some European metallurgist disagree with this translation. In my interpretation, studies of metallurgy in Europe have developed and have understood details of the process of production, since this term was used in the past and introduced to Japan as an example of the western terminology of iron production. On the other hand, in Japan as a recipient country, the term remains as it was introduced and may still retain its old meaning. However, *zuku* produced by the *tatara* method has no equivalent. Thus, I use *zuku* or *sentetsu*, which contains more than 1.7% of carbon.

kera
Kera is produced by the *tatara* smelting method. It is equivalent to a large bloom of iron. *Kera* is a large lump of iron which contains different proportions of carbon in different parts of the lump. Although the whole production process of *kera* is not fully understood, it might be said that the different proportions of carbon in different parts of the kera were produced in the different parts of furnace associated with different temperatures and different speeds of formation. This produces different types of iron. The *kera* is sorted into three types of iron by breaking it into small pieces. The upper surface of the *kera* is very pure iron with little or no carbon, called *tama-hagane*; the middle of the *kera* is low-carbon steel wrought iron called *kera*; and the base of the *kera* is *zuku* or *sentetsu* with a high carbon content.

chutetsu : cast iron
A molten state of iron direct from the blast furnace which contains more than 1.7% of carbon. According to the proportion of carbon which iron products contain, 1.7% is defined as the dividing line between steel and *chutetsu* in Japanese metallurgy (Nishizawa et al. 1979). Metallurgical discussions in Japan are based on this definition.

tetsu sozai : iron raw material
Material which produces iron

tettei : iron ingot
Raw iron in the shape of a slab. This does not have any implications as regards the production process; it is defined by its shape.

tetsubo : iron bar
Raw iron in the shape of a bar. This does not have any implications as regards the production process; it is defined by its shape.

tetsu-seihin : iron products
Any goods made of iron. There are two categories: *tanzohin* made by the forging process, and *chuzohin* made by the casting process.

niji genryo or : secondary iron products
This can be a raw material for iron products, but it is produced by a secondary source of iron material, not by the smelting process.

furu-tetsu-seihin : scrap iron
These are iron products which have been used or can be used, and will be transformed into other iron products by recycling.

chuzohin : casting products
Goods which are made of cast iron, such as an iron pot.

hochotetsu or namatetsu
Raw iron in the shape of a kitchen knife.

tetsu-nabe : iron pot
Pots made of *chutetsu*.

7 By-products

tessai : slag
A general term for by-products from any kind of furnace.

seitetsu-sai : smelting slag
A kind of slag which is a by-product of the smelting process and formed in a smelting furnace.

seiren-sai : refining slag
A kind of slag which is a by-product of the refining process and formed inside the refining furnace or refining hearth.

kaji-sai : forging/ smithing slag
A kind of slag which is a by-product of the forging/smithing process and formed in the forging/smithing hearth.

ryushitsu-sai : tap slag
A kind of slag produced by run-off from the furnace can be identified at sites from the shape of the slag, which looks as if it cooled down in the air immediately after running directly out from furnace.

ronai-sai : slag inside the furnace
A kind of slag which is formed inside any kind of furnace and found attached to pieces of the furnace wall.

wangata-sai : bottom slag, or slag shaped like the bottom of a bowl
A kind of slag which is shaped like the bottom of a bowl. This shape of slag is known from at Japanese iron-working sites.

tanzo-hakuhen, *tanda-sai* : hammer scale, micro-scale, or iron oxidised scale
Small piece of iron which are produced by hammering soft iron during the process of forging.

B. Reconstruction process

1 Techniques

tetsu gijutsu : iron technology
In a broad sense, all technology relating to iron production and producing iron products.

seitetsu : smelting process
Any process by which raw iron is produced from iron ore or iron sand.

sanka : oxidise/oxidisation

kangen : reduction

zosaizai : additives

fujunbutsu : impurities

kaizaibutsu : inclusions

chokusetsu-ho : direct method
Iron ore or iron sand is put into a smelting furnace with charcoal, and a lump of iron such as a *kera* or bloom is obtained. In the *kera oshi* method, the steel part was extracted from the lump of iron, and then iron objects were made by forging steel.

kansetsu-ho : indirect method
Iron raw material and charcoal are put into a blast furnace together, and the iron raw material is smelted. *Sentetsu*, which contains graphite and cementite, is produced by this process. Subsequently, the *sentetsu* is refined in a refining furnace, which is different from the smelting furnace, and a mass of steel in which carbon is controlled is produced by this process. Steel can also be produced from the lump of *sentetsu* by the forging process. Steel can be produced from *sentetsu* through this process.

zuku-oshi-ho : a tatara method for producing *zuku*
One of the *tatara* smelting methods which produces *zuku* by reduction of *akame* iron sand with charcoal in a *tatara* furnace (traditionally this is called a *motogama*). Molten iron from the hole of the *tatara* furnace is cooled either in air or directly into a pond (traditionally this is called *kanaike*) in order to produce a lump of *zuku*. It was practised in the Chugoku district (in the present Hiroshima and Okayama-ken) where *akame* iron sand was obtained. One process normally takes four nights in a set (traditionally this set is called *hitoyo*, 'one night').

kera-oshi-ho : *a tatara* method for producing *kera*
One of the *tatara* smelting methods which produces Japanese steel by a direct method. It was established in the late 18th century and it is normally called *eidai tatara*. Only *masa* iron sand is used. It is obtained in the Izumo and Hoki districts (in the present Shimane-ken). This method produces mainly *kera* and does not produce *zuku*.

seiren or okaji : refining process
In the Japanese case, any process to produce finer quality iron, meaning iron containing low carbon content for making *hagane* or *rentetsu* from *zuku* or *sentetsu* and *chutetsu*.

sha or *shokoho* in Japanese, and *chao* in Chinese : fining process
This term is only used in textual discussions in Japan on account of the lack of material evidence. Any process for making steel from the liquid state of iron by stirring with a bar in a container type of furnace in China. European metallurgists call it the 'fining process'.

shintan : carburisation
A method which controls the proportion of the carbon content of iron and increases it in order to make steel.

dattan : de-carburisation
A method which reduce the proportion of the carbon content in iron in order to make steel.

kaji or kokaji : smithing/forging processes
Any process in which iron objects or products are formed by the activity of craftspeople such as *tanren* or *tanzou* (hammering and pounding on iron objects)

katanakaji : Japanese sword smithing
The whole process of techniques which produce a Japanese sword.

2 Analysis in metallurgy

Analytical methods used for investigating slag in Japan are all based on JIS (Japanese Industrial Standard).

kagaku sosei : chemical composition analysis
soshiki kansatsu : metallographic examination
satetsu ryushi : iron sand particle
bisai soshiki : micro-structure

The following components can be found under EPMA for metallographic examination:

in iron
cementite: Fe_3C component of iron
pearlite: component of iron
Ferrite: Fe component of iron
ledeburite: component of iron
wustite: (FeO)

in slag
ilmenite: $FeTiO_3$ component of slag; it is also a component of iron sand as Titanium (TiO_2).
fayalite: Fe_2SiO_4 component of slag
wustite: FeO component of slag
ulvospinel: Fe_2TiO_4 component of slag. It is also a component of iron sand.
glass (silicate): SiO_2 component of slag, iron rock, furnace wall, and iron sand.

References

Adami, N., 1991. (translated by Kosaka, H.) *Ainu minzoku bunken mokuroku — obunhen—* Sapporo: Sapporo-do Booksellers.

Aida, K., 1978. Bakumatsu ni okeru ezochi no seitetsu tatara. *Hokkaido no bunka* 39.

Akanuma, H., 1989. Tetsu nabe no zaishitsu. In *Yomigaeru chusei*, (ed.) Kikuchi, T. and Fukuda, T., Tokyo: Heibonsha.

Akanuma, H. and Sasaki, M., 1993. Kinzokugakuteki kaiseki kara mita Kyushu hokubu chiiki ni okeru chusei shutsudo tekki no seiho to ryutsu. *Kobunka dangyo* 30. Kyushu: Kyushu kobunka kenkyukai.

Amano, T., (forthcoming) Yukanboshi C2 iseki no yakin. In *Yukanboshi hakkutsu hokokusho.*

Amano, T., 1983. Satsumon shakai ni okeru kinzokki no fukkuryo to shoyu keitai. *Kokogaku Kenkyu* 30.1.

Amano, T., 1989. Satsumon ki ni motarasareta tetsu no ryo to koreni kansuru sho mondai — Ainu ki tono hikaku ni oite. *Tatara kenkyukai* 30.

Amari, T., 1877. Chishima jyunko gaiki. *Chishima Etorofu shu.*

Anzai, M. et al., 1990. Jinruishi no kanosei. *Gendai shiso* 18.12:44-67.

Arimoto, H., 1916. Ezo to Nogyo. *Kyodo kenkyu* 4.6:355-359.

Asai, T., 1970. Ainu go no bunpo — Ainu go Ishikari hogen no gairyaku. In *Ainu minzokushi.*, by T. Asai Tokyo: Daichihoki.

Asai, T., 1979. Emishi go. In *Emishi*, (ed.) Obayashi, T. Tokyo: Shakai shisosha.

Asai, T. Kono, M., Niui, Y., Haniwara, K., Fujimoto, H., and Yoshizaki, M., 1972. *Symposium Ainu — sono kigen to bunka keisei.* Sapporo: Hokudai tosho kankokai.

Aston, W.G., 1972. *Nihongi — Chronicles of Japan from the Earliest Times to AD.. 697.* Tokyo: Tuttle.

Ban, Gu, (BC 1). *Han Shu* (modern ed. 1962). Shanghai: Chuka shokyoku shuppan.

Barrett, J.G., 1987. Contextual archaeology. *Antiquity* 61:468-73.

Batchelor, J., 1889. *Ainu-English-Japanese dictionary and grammar.* Tokyo: Iwanami.

Biratori-cho, 1974. *Biratori choshi.* Hokkaido: Biratori-cho.

Bird, I., 1880. *Unbeaten tracks in Japan.* London: John Murray.

Bird, I., 1973. (translated by Takanashi, K.), *Nihon okuchi kiko* . Tokyo: Heibonsha.

Buchwald, V. and Mosdal, G., 1985. *Meteoric iron and wroght iron in Greenland* . Meddeleleser om Gronland.

Busk, G., 1868. Description of an Aino Skull. *Transactions of the Ethnological Society of London.* Vol. 6:109-111.

Chamberlain, B.H., 1887. The language, mythology and geographical nomenclature of Japan, viewed in the light of Aino studies. *Memoirs of the Literature College, Imperial University of Japan*, No. 1. Tokyo.

Childe, G., 1956. *Piecing together the past.* London: Routledge and Kegan Paul.

Chiri, Mashiho, 1954. Yukara no hitobito to sono seikatsu — Hokkaido no senshi jidaijin no seikatsu ni kansuru bunkashiteki kosatsu. In *Chiri Mashiho chosakushu* , Vol. 3. Tokyo: Heibonsha.

Chiri, Mashiho, 1955. *Kamui yukaru — Ainu jojishi nyumon* . Sapporo: Aporo shuppan.

Chiri, Mashiho, 1973. Ainu go chimeikai. In *Chiri Mashiho chosakushu* , Vol. 3. Tokyo: Heibonsha.

Chiri, Mashiho, 1974. Batchelor hakase no jisho. In *Chiri Mashiho chosakushu* , Vol. 4. Tokyo: Heibonsha.

Chiri, Yukie, [1922] 1978. *Kamui Yukara.* Tokyo: Iwanami shoten.

Crawford, G. and Yoshizaki, M., 1987. Ainu Ancestors and Prehistoric Asian Agriculture. *Jornal of Archaeological Science* 14:201-213.

Dickins, and Sir Stanley Lane-Poole, 1984. *Life of Sir Harry Parkes.* London: MacMillan and Co.

Dodo Y., 1991. Hokkaido no kojinruigaku. In *Ainu minzoku bunkaza senmon shokuinto kenshukai kogi shiryo.*

Dolukhanov, P.M., 1989. Cultural and ethnic processes in prehistory as seen through the evidence of archaeology and related disciplines. In *Archaeological Approaches to Cultural identity*, (ed.) Shennan, S. London: Unwin Hyman.

Emori, S., 1979. Yukara no rekishiteki haikei ni kansuru ichi kosatsu. *Hokkaido kinseishi no kenkyu.* Sapporo: Hokkaido shuppan kikan center.

Fan, Ye, (AD 398-445). *Hou Han Shu.* (modern ed. 1962.). Shanghai: Chuka shokyoku shuppan.

Fawcett, C., 1986. The politics of assimilation in Japanese Archaeology. *Archaeological Review from Cambridge* 5.1: 43-57.

Fujimoto, H., 1983. *Ainu gaku eno ayumi.* Sapporo: Hokkaido shuppan kikaku centre.

Fukasawa, Y., (forthcoming). Pipaushi iseki ni okeru kaji iko. In *Pipaushi iseki.* Hokkaido: Biratori-cho Kyoiku-iinkai.

Fukasawa, Y., 1989. Ainu bunka to kaji gijutsu. In *Iruekashi iseki hakkutsu hokokusho*, Hokkaido: Biratori-cho, pp. 243-252.

Fukasawa, Y., 1992. Emishi and Ainu. In the Conference Proceedings, *International Symposium on Japanese Archaeology in Protohistoric and Early Historic Period: Yamato and its relations to surrounding populations.* Bonn: University of Bonn.

Fukasawa, Y., 1993. Emishi to Ainu. In *Senshigaku to kanren kagaku.* pp. 293-303.

Fukasawa, Y., 1993. Yukara which are recounted by Suteno Orita in the Shizunai district Hokkaido. In *Shizunai chiho no densho* 3. Hokkaido: Shizunai-cho Kyoiku-iinkai.

Fukasawa, Y., 1995 Ethnohistory toshiteno Ainu kokogaku. *Hokkaido Kokogaku* 31:271-290.

Furukawa, K., 1788. *Toyuzakki* (modern ed. 1964. Ofuji, T.). Tokyo: Heibonsha.

Gray, D. 1954. Metal-working in Homer. *Journal of Hellenic Studies* 74:1-15.

Hadano, M., 1981. Tokachi heiya ni okeru Ainu shuraku no ricchi to jinko no hensen. *Hoppo bunka kenkyu* 14:73-198.

Haddon, A.C., 1927. (translated by Genep, A. Van) *Les races Humaines et leur Répartition Géographique.* Paris.

Haddon, A.C., 1929. (revised ed.) *The Races of Man and Their Distribution.* Cambridge: The University Press.

Haginaka, M., 1982. Yukara to ona. *Kosho bungei kenkyu* 5.

Haniwara, K., 1993. Gendai nihonjin no seiritsu. In *Gendaijin ha dokokara kitaka*, (ed.) Baba, O. Tokyo: Nikkei science.

Hara, Z., 1988. *Tetsu to ningen.* Tokyo: Shin nippon shuppansha.

Hasebe, K., 1917. Sekki jidai jumin ron gakan. *Jinruigaku zasshi* Vol. 32.11.

Hattori, S., 1964. *Ainu go hogen jiten.* Tokyo: Iwanami shoten.

Hayama, T., 1992. Tatara seitetsugyo no hatten. In *Nihon no kinsei* 4, (ed.) Hayama, T. Tokyo: Chuo koron sha.

Hayashi, Minao, 1976. *Kandai no bunbutsu.* Kyoto: Kyoto daigaku jinbun kagaku kenkyujo.

Hayashi, Yoshishige, 1969. *Ainu no noko bunka.* Tokyo: Keiyusha.

Higgs, E., 1971. *Paleoeconomy.* Cambridge: Cambridge University Press.

Hodder, I., 1987. *The Archaeology of contextual meanings.* Cambridge: Cambridge University Press.

Hodder, I., 1990. (2nd edition). *Reading the Past.* Cambridge: Cambridge University Press.

Hodder, I., (ed.), 1982. *Symbolic and Structural Archaeology.* Cambridge: Cambridge University Press.

Hokkaido-cho (ed.)., 1989. *The New Chronology of Hokkaido History*. Sapporo: Hokkaido shuppan kikaku centre.

Hokkaido-cho (ed.), 1969. *Hokkaido historiography*, Vol. 7. Hokkaido.

Hokkaido Kyoiku-iinkai., 1981. *Uilter gengo shuzoku shiryo 2*.

Hokkaido Kyoiku-iinkai., 1990. *Kitagawa gentaro hitsuroku Uilter no kotoba* (4).

Howells, W.W., 1986. "Physical Anthropology of the Prehistoric Japanese". In *Windows on the Japanese Past*. (ed.) Pearson, R. Ann Arbor: Center for Japanese, University of Michigan.

Huan, Kuan., (BC 81) *Yan tie lun* . (see below).

Huan, Kuan., 1970.. (translated by Sato, T.) *En tetsu ron*. Tokyo: Heibonsha.

Iida, K., 1982, a. *Nihonjin to tetsu*. Tokyo: Yuhikaku.

Iida, K., 1982, b. *Seitetsushi kenkyu no shiteki gaikan Kodai nihon no tetsu to shakai*. Tokyo: Heibonsha.

Inoue, K. and Yamada, I., 1982. "Tohoku chiho ni okeru nara heian jidai no pamisu".

Inoue, M., 1976. *Ritsu Ryo — Nihon shiso taikei*, Vol. 3. Tokyo: Iwanami shoten.

Ishizuki, K., 1983. Ine to Tetsu. In *Ezochi no tetsu*. Tokyo: Shogakkan.

Ishizuki, K., 1986. Hokkaido nanbu ni okeru 8 seiki zengo no funbo to sono keito. *Ainu bunka no genryu* . Sapporo: Miyama shobo.

Ito, K., 1989. Tessai to tekkirui no kinzokugakuteki chosa. *Iruekashi iseki hakkutsu hokokusho*. Hokkaido: Biratori-cho.

John, R. N., 1878. The Ainos: Aborigines of Yeso. *The Journal of the Anthropological Institute of Geat Britain and Ireland* 2:248-254.

John, S., 1969. *Ezo under the Tokugawa Bakufu 1799-1821:/An aspect of Japanese frontier History* . Ph.D., Dissertation. University of London.

Jonson, J., Yearos, J. and Ross-Stallings, N., 1994. Ethnohistory, archaeology, and Chickasaw. *Ethnohistory* 41.3:431-446.

Kageyama, T., 1984. *Chugoku kodai no shokogyo to senbai*. Tokyo: Tokyo daigaku shuppankai.

Kaiho, M., 1989. Kokudaka no nai daimyo. In *Yomigaeru chusei*, (ed.) Kikuchi, T. and Fukuda, T. Tokyo: Heibonsha.

Kaiho, M., 1991. Matsumaehan to kokudakasei. *Chihoshi kenkyu* 232:73-81.

Kaiho, M., 1993. Ezo (chusei ezo) no jittai ni tuite. *Hokkaido kokogaku* 29:1-8.

Kawabata, S., 1969. *Nihon fukushokushi jiten*. Tokyo: Tokyodo shuppan.

Kawase, M., 1990. Chugoku chiho ni okeru tatara seitetsu no tenkai. In *Tatara kara kindai seitetsu e* Okada, K. (ed.), Tokyo: Heibonsha.

Kawauchi, Y., 1992. *Min dai joshinshi no kenkyu*. Kyoto: Dohosha.

Kayano, S., 1974. *Uepekere shutaisei*. Tokyo: Arudo.

Kida, T., 1980. Emishi no kenkyu. *Kida Teikichi chosakushu*. Vol. 9. Tokyo: Heibonsha.

Kikuchi, T., 1979. Satsumon bunka no tekki ni tsuite. *Dorumen* 22. Tokyo.

Kikuchi, T., 1980. Satsumon bunka no shumatsu nendai. *Kodai tangyo*.

Kikuchi, T., and Fukuda, T. (ed.) *Yomigaeru chusei*. Tokyo: Heibonsha.

Kindaichi, K., 1923. *Ainu Seiten*. Tokyo: Iwanami shoten.

Kindaichi, K., 1925. *Ainu no kenkyu*. Tokyo: Naigai shobo.

Kindaichi, K., 1931. *Ainu jojishi Yukara no kenkyu*. Tokyo: Toyobunko.

Kindaichi, K., 1942. *Ainu jojishi Yukara gaisetu*. Tokyo: Seijisha.

Kindaichi, K., 1962. Oshu ezo shuzokuko.*Goto bijutsukan getsurei bijutsu koza* 7.

Kindaichi, K., 1960. *Kindaichi Kyosuke senshu*. Tokyo: Sanseido.

Kindaishi, K., 1959-1964. *Ainu jojishi Yukara shu*. Tokyo: Sanseido.

Kitagamae, Y., 1983. *1643 nen Ainu shakai tanboki Fu-risu sentai kokai kiroku*. Tokyo: Yuzankaku.

Kodama, S., 1971. *Meijizen Nihon jinrui gaku senshi gaku shi*. Tokyo: Nihon Gakujutsu Shinkokai.

Koganei, Y., 1904. *Nihon sekki jidai no jumin*. Tokyo: Shunyodo.

Koida, T., 1987. *Ainu funbo tokutsu jiken*. Sapporo: Miyama shobo.

Kokuritsu Minzokugaku Hakubutsukan, 1987. Pilsudski tokushu. *Minpaku kenkyu hokoku* 5.

Koshida, K., 1984. Hokkaido no tetsunabe ni tuite. *Busshitsu bunka* 42.

Koshida, K., 1988. Hokkaido ni okeru chu kinsei kokogaku no genjo to kadai. *Busshitsu buka* 50.

Koshida, K., 1989. Tetsunabe. In *Yomigaeru chusei*, (ed.) Kikuchi, T. and Fukuda, T. Tokyo: Heibonsha.

Koshida, K., 1990. Satsumon Ainu ki ni okeru Hokkaido no tetsu, tekki seisan. In *Tetsu wo toshite kita no bunka wo kangaeru*. Morioka: Iwate kenritsu hakubutsukan.

Kubodera, I., 1977. *Ainu jojishi shinyo seiden no kenkyu*. Tokyo: Iwanami shoten.

Kubota, K., 1986 a. *Seitetsu iseki*. Tokyo: New Science sha.

Kubota, K., 1986 b. *Tetsu no minzokushi*. Tokyo: Yuzankaku.

Kudo, M., 1992. *Kodai no Emishi*. Tokyo: Kawade shobo shinsha.

Kumagaya, T., 1988. Akitaken no kodai seitetsu ro. *Akitaken Maizo Bunkazai Kenkyu Kiyo* 3.

Kumagaya, T., 1990. Akitaken ni okeru kodai chusei no tetsu, tekki seisan. *Tetsu wo toshite kita no bunka wo kangaeru*. Morioka: Iwate kenritsu hakubutsukan.

Kuroda, K., 1942. *Nihon shokumin shiso shi*. Tokyo: Kobundo shobo.

La Perose, 1797. *Vocabulaire des habitans de l'ile Tchoka formé à la baie de Langue Voyage de La perose autor du monde*. Paris.

Lemonier, P., 1983. L'Etude des systèmes techniques, une urgence en technologie cluturelle. *Techniques et Culture* 1.

Leroi-Gourhan, A. et A., 1992. Les Ainos du Japon: 13000 ans d'histoire. *Archeologia* 279: 54-63. Mai. Paris.

Leroi-Gourhan, A., 1964. *Le Geste et la Parole, technique et langage*. Paris: Albin Michel.

Leroi-Gourhan, A., 1973. (translated by Araki, T.). *Miburi to kotoba*. Tokyo Shinchosha.

Leupe, P.A.(ed.), 1858. *Reiz van Marten gerritsz Vries in 1643 near het norden en oosten van Japan, volgens het jornaal gehoden door C. J. Coen, op het schip Castricum*. Amsterdam: Frederik Muller.

Li. H., 1984. A short history of the iron making development in Jürchin society under the Ming Dynasty. *Minzu Yanqui* 5:67-73.

MacCord, H., 1960. Cultural Sequences in Hokkaido, Japan. *Proceedings of the United States National Museum* 112.3443:481-503.

Machida, H., 1986. Harukanaru Hakutosan. *Kagaku*. (November) Tokyo: Iwanami.

Machida, H., Moriwaki, H., and Zhao, D., 1990. The Recent Major Eruption of Changbai Volcano and Its Environmental Effects. *Geographical Reports of Tokyo Metropolitan University* 25.

Mamiya, R., 1808. (1970 re-print). *Kita ezo zusetu*. Tokyo: Meicho Kankokai.

Maruyama, M.,1973. *Matsuura Takeshiro no Ishikari Nisshi*. Sapporo: Todosha.

Matsumae, N., 1863. *Ezo to kikan hochu.*

Matsuura, T., 1850. *Ezogo.* (see Narita 1986).

Matsuura, T., 1857. *Ishikari nisshi* (modern ed. 1973 by Maruyama, M.) Sapporo: Todosha.

Matsuura, T., 1858. *Bogo tozai ezo sansen chiri torishirabe nisshi.*

Matsuura, T., 1855. *Ezogo binran Shiribeshi oroshi.* (see Narita 1991).

Matsuzaki, M., 1990. Kaminokuni katsuyamadate ato no tetsu. In *Tetsu wo toshite kita no bunka wo kangaeru.* Morioka: Iwate kenritsu hakubutsukan.

Mineyama, I., 1980. *Setanai chashi ato iseki hakkutsu chosa hokokusho.* Hiyama-cho Kyoiku-iinkai.

Miura, K., 1991. Honshu no Satsumon bunka. *Kokogaku Journal* 341.

Miura, M., 1989. Kita no koeki shoten. In *Yomigaeru chusei,* (ed.) Kikuchi, T. and Fukuda, T. Tokyo: Heibonsha.

Miya, H., 1982. Tokachibuto Furukawa iseki shutsudono fuigo no haguchi. *Urahoro-cho kyodo hakubutsukan hokoku* 20.

Mogami, T., 1786. *Ezo soshi.* (modern ed. 1965 by Yoshida, T.). Tokyo: Jijitsushin.

Montandon, G., 1931. Ologenese culture et culture Aino. *Extrait du 15e Congress de L'Institute International d' Anthropologe Paris* 730-736 .

Morris, I., 1986. The use and abuse of Homer. *Classic Antiquity* 5.1:81-129.

Murasaki, K., 1978. Sakhalin Ainu. *Asian & African Grammatical Manual* 11z. Tokyo: Tokyo gaikokugo daigaku, Asia Africa gengo bunka kenkyujo.

Naito, S., 1992. Nazo no gengo Ainu go to Europe kei gengo. *Kyoto Daigaku Shinbun,* 16 July.

Nara, N., 1928. Sosei nogu. *Nogyo sekai.* 23.1:189-192.

Narita, S., 1986. *Modern edition of Ezogo, by Matsuura Takeshiro.* Private publication.

Narita, S., 1977. *Modern edition of Matsumaeno ko.* Private publication.

Narita, S., 1977. *Modern edition of Moshihokusa, by Uehara Kumajiro.* Private publication.

Narita, S., 1985. Edo jidai no Ainu go. Ainu no kotoba to bunka. *Gengo.*

Narita, S., 1985. *Ezogo shuroku .* Tokyo: Tosho kankokai.

Narita, S., 1985. *Modern edition of Ezogo shuroku.* Private publication.

Narita, S., 1988. *Modern edition of Ezo tsuushikan, by Yoda Jiro.* Private publication.

Narita, S., 1991. *Kinsei no Ezogo shu:Ezogo binran Shiribeshi oroshi, by Matsuura Takashiro.* Private publication.

Nishijima, S., 1983. *Chugoku kodai no shakai to keizai.* Tokyo: Tokyo daigaku shuppankai.

Nishimoto, T., 1989. Kuma okuri no kigen ni tsuite. *Kokogaku to minzokushi.*

Nishizawa, Y. and Sakuma, K., 1979. *Kinzoku soshiki shashinshu.* Tokyo: Nihon kinzoku gakkai.

Nitobe, I., 1911. Shokumin naru go. *Hogaku kyokai zasshi* 29.2.

Notoya, E., 1864. *Ezogo shuroku* (see Narita 1985).

Obaysashi, T., 1991. *Hoppo no minzoku to bunka.* Tokyo: Yamakawa.

Ogi, S., 1990. Tohoku chiho ni okeru tetsuzan shihai to tatara seitetsu. In *Tatara kara kindai seitetsu e,* (ed.) Okada, K. Tokyo: Heibonsha.

Okada, K (ed.), 1990. *Tatara kara kindai seitetsu e.* Tokyo: Heibonsha.

Okada, Y., 1990. Aomoriken ni okeru kodai chusei no tetsu, tekki seisan. In *Tetsu wo toshite kita no bunka wo kangaeru.* Morioka: Iwate kenritsu hakubutsukan.

Ono, T., 1978. *Giho to sakuhin:Toko hen.* Tokyo: Seiun shoin.

Onuma, T. and Sato, T., 1976. Esashi-cho Assabugawa kako iseki no saishu shiryo. *Hiyama Kokogakkaishi* 5.

Osawa, M., 1982. Suehiro iseki shutsudo tessai no bunseki chosa. *Suehiro iseki niokeru kokogakuteki chosa* Chitoseshi.

Osawa, M., 1983. Hokkaido Horonaipo iseki shutsudo no tessai no chosa. *Hokkaido kokogaku* 19.

Osawa, M., 1985. Kaminokuni Katsuyamadate shuttudo kaji kankei ibutsu no kinzokugakuteki chosa. *Kaminokuni Katsuyamadate chosa hokokusho.*

Osawa, M., 1985. Satsumae, Shizuura D iseki shuttudo no tessai, tetsukki itajo garasu hahen no kinzokugakuteki chosa. *Satsumae iseki.*

Otsuka, K., 1988. *Sogen to jykai no tami.* Tokyo: Shinjyuku shobo.

Philippi, D.L., 1979. *Songs of Gods, Songs of Humans:the epic tradition of the Ainu.* Princeton and Tokyo University Press.

Piaskowski, J., 1989. Phosphorus in Iron Ore and Slag, and in Bloomery Iron. *Archeomaterials* 3.1: 47-59.

Pon Fuchi, 1992. *Ureshipa Moshiri e no michi.* Tokyo: Shinsensha.

Refsing, K., 1986. *The Ainu Language:The morphology and syntax of the Shizunai dialect.* Copenhagen: Aarhus University Press.

Rehder, J.E., 1989. Ancient carburization of iron to steel. *Archeomaterials* 3.1:27-37.

Rostoker, W., Bronson, B. and Dvorak, J. R., 1989. Smelting to steel by the Japanese tatara process. *Archeomaterials* 3.1:11-25.

Sakurai, K., 1979. Kokogaku karamita emishi. In *Emishi,* (ed.) Obayashi, T. Tokyo: Shakai shisosha.

Sasaki, K., 1990. Iwate ken no seitetsu iseki:1. *Iwate kenritsu hakubutsukan kenkyu hokoku* 8.

Sasaki, M., 1989. Kita no tetsu no bunka: Kinzokugaku no tachibakara. In *Yomigaeru chusei,* (ed.) Kikuchi, T. and Fukuda, T. Tokyo: Heibonsha.

Sato, G., 1786. Ezo chi no gi koremade kenbun shioki soro moshi age soro kakitsuke. (see Hokkaido historiography Vol.7).

Sato, K., 1975. Atsukkeshi dojin Daisuke no tanto. *Token bijyutsu* 3.

Segawa, T., 1989. Satsumon jidai ni okeru shokuryo bungyo kokan. *Kokogaku Kenkyu* 36.2:72-97.

Shanks, M. and C. Tilley, 1987. *Social theory and archaeology.* Cambridge: Polity press.

Shennan, S.J., 1989. Introduction. In *Archaeological approaches to cultural Identity,* (ed.) Shennan, S. J. London: Unwin Hyman.

Shepherd, R., 1993. *Ancient mining.* Institution of Mining and Metallurgy. London: Elsevier Applied Science.

Sherratt, E.S., 1990. Reading the texts: archaeology and the Homeric question. *Antiquity* 64: 807-24.

Siebold, H., 1879. Japanische Kjökkenmöddinger Zeitschrift für. *Etnologie* 11:231-234 Braunschweing.

Siebold, P.F., 1854. *Nippon Archiv zur beschreibung von Japan und dessen Neben:und Schutzländern Jezo mit den südlichen Kurilen, Sachalin, Korea und den Liukiu-Inseln.* Leiden (Translated by Kato, K. 1979).

Sima Qian ca., BC 97. *Shi ji* (modern ed. 1959) Shanghai: Chuka shokyoku shuppan.

Snodgrass, A., 1989. The coming of the Iron Age in Greece: Europe's earliest bronze/iron transition. In *The Bronze Age-Iron Age transition in Europe,* (ed.) M.L. Sorensen & R. Thomas. Oxford: British Archaeological Reports. International series 483:22-35.

Stuart, H., 1991. Shakushain no ran to minzoku jiketsu. In *proceedings of Shizunai Symposium, Shakushain 3 2 1.* Shizunai:Shizunaicho, pp. 25-44.

Takahashi Takashi, 1986. *Emishi.* Tokyo: Chuo koronsha.

www.ingramcontent.com/pod-product-compliance
Lightning Source LLC
Chambersburg PA
CBHW061002030426
42334CB00033B/3326